THE CHEROKEE PERSPECTIVE:
WRITTEN BY
EASTERN CHEROKEES

D1526780

Edited by
Laurence French and Jim Hornbuckle

Published by the Appalachian Consortium Press, a division of the Appalachian Consortium, Inc., Boone, North Carolina 28607.

The member institutions of the Appalachian Consortium are:

Appalachian State University
Blue Ridge Parkway
East Tennessee State University
Ferrum College
First Tennessee-Virginia Development District
Lees-McRae College
Mars Hill College
U. S. Forest Service
University of North Carolina-Asheville
Warren Wilson College
Western Carolina University
Western North Carolina Historical Association

Affiliate Members:

The Council on Appalachian Women, Inc.
North Carolina Division of Archives and History

Library of Congress Catalog Card Number: 81-65842

Dedicated to the Cherokee People:
Past, Present and Future

ACKNOWLEDGMENTS:

We wish to express our deepest appreciation to all those who worked with us in the development of this book. We are especially grateful to Rupert Costo and Jeannette Henry of the American Indian Historical Society; Gerald Eller, Borden Mace, Susan Huffman, and Martha McKinney of the Appalachian Consortium; and to Sharlotte Neely, Burt Purrington and Zohara Boyd for their editorial work.

FOREWORD

The Cherokee Perspective is not intended to be a review of historical literature about the Qualla Boundary, nor is it meant to be a sociological study full of bar graphs and statistics. Compiled by Laurence French and Jim Hornbuckle, the book is actually the product of many writers, each of whom deals with a different aspect of Cherokee life. These authors have not *researched* their material; they have *lived* it. Because it was written in this way, the book may have lost something in academic methodology and unity, but it has also gained much in immediacy and impact. The editors have tried to preserve the book's vitality by not meddling with the writers' words too much. If the interviews are ungrammatical, then that is the way the people involved speak. The incoherence of certain dance descriptions, recipes, and folk tales is also deliberate. The old people who are the keepers of these traditions wish to share only part of their knowledge; the rest, they say, must remain within the tribe.

This book is not intended to be a scholarly work. It is a living testament for future scholars to analyze.

Zohara Boyd
Assistant Professor of English
Appalachian State University

FOREWORD

When the Appalachian Consortium Press asked me to do editorial work on a manuscript for a book called *The Cherokee Perspective*, I was pleased to help out because I realized how valuable such an endeavor could be. Besides the value of the book's immediate impact, I was excited about the undertaking, because I saw the book as a means of creating primary source material. Besides my fieldwork, I have conducted ethnohistorical research on the Eastern Cherokees, and I realized the value of such a book to that kind of inquiry.

Most of my ethnohistorical work has been at the Federal Records Center in East Point, Georgia, where all Eastern Cherokee Agency files of the Bureau of Indian Affairs are now housed. Sometimes, I have pored over box after box of dusty documents looking for that letter, diary, or report which would put flesh and blood on an era of Cherokee history, only to have to content myself with school attendance records or purchase orders. After awhile, the feeling is that of being on a treasure hunt. I can remember the joy upon finding out that Henry M. Owl, an enrolled Eastern Cherokee, had written an M.A. thesis in history at the University of North Carolina in 1929. It was full of Owl's opinions, criticisms, feelings, and goals for the Cherokee. It put flesh and blood on the 1920's for me. It was even better than interviewing someone now about that era. The feeling was of interviewing an informant frozen in time for nearly half a century. *The Cherokee Perspective* will have that effect on future generations of Cherokees and Cherokee researchers.

Such an undertaking cannot be totally objective in its outlook, and its value anyway probably lies in the opinions and biases of its writers, the Cherokees. When I read Henry Owl's account of the Cherokees in the 1920's, I did not assume that his point of view was universal. But combined with other sources of information, Owl was invaluable. The editors, researcher Laurence French and Cherokee Jim Hornbuckle, have opinions not necessarily shared by others, but that is as it should be. I do not, for example, share all their opinions. The book's writers also have their own varied opinions. When one puts together the views of each of the writers along with other data, one does get a mosaic of opinions, which is "objective," on which to base an "objective" study.

The Cherokee Perspective has many strong points. One of these is that it includes an article on Snowbird, a traditional community not studied until recently, written by a Snowbird man. When I did my own research on Snowbird, I found it quite difficult to find any firsthand data on the community. Yet, by many criteria it is perhaps the most traditional of Eastern Cherokee communities.

The book appropriately begins with a chapter on Cherokee history and culture which is an important basis for appreciating the folklore and poems that follow as well as a basis for understanding the contemporary problems that are explored. Sometimes the editors include daring accounts, such as that of Indians in local jails, and sometimes the accounts are simply moving, such as those on the preservation of Cherokee crafts and dances. The mini-biographies at the end cover traditional and not-so-traditional people, men and women, old and young.

Firsthand data is critical for the Eastern Cherokees. Probably no other group has been written about so extensively and yet has often been so horribly misunderstood. The Cherokees have a mystique which attracts everyone from boy scouts seeking Indian lore to little old ladies with Cherokee blood. Some Indians themselves have suggested that if everyone who thinks he has Cherokee blood really does, then the Cherokees are ancestors to most of the world's population. Firsthand data helps cut through mystique to reality.

An accurate assessment of the Cherokees is crucial to understanding North American Indian history and culture. The Cherokees are often labeled the most changed of all Native American groups, and yet the core of traditional cultural traits which persists is amazing. Most histories tell only part of the Cherokee story, and the gaps between the data are often larger and more significant than the data. Many histories concentrate on the "progress" of the Cherokees toward Americanization and ignore the factions that have been relatively more traditional. Firsthand data is a significant step toward sorting out the puzzle.

The Cherokee Perspective covers the gamut from fiction to non-fiction and from past to present. It is a valuable collection of the feelings and opinions of more than two dozen contemporary Eastern Cherokees. They tell us something now about Cherokeeness, and they tell the future something, too.

Sharlotte Neely
Associate Professor of Anthropology
Northern Kentucky University

INTRODUCTION

The Cherokees have always been concerned with education and with means of improving educational facilities for the tribe. Following the turbulence of the 1960's and early 1970's, especially that involving the American Indian Movement, concerned Cherokees began to plan their own protest movement. But, unlike the rebellious means used by the American Indian Movement, the Cherokees decided, instead, to work with the existing structure, attempting to get more Cherokees involved in tribal matters and into important positions in the schools, tribal council and BIA management.

As a means toward these ends, Cherokee students at the Qualla Boundary started a student organization in 1973 with the intent and purpose of improving the educational prospects among Native Americans attending non-Indian colleges and universities. Most agreed that cultural shock, strain and conflict played a crucial role in past educational failures among Cherokee students in their higher educational pursuits. Consequently, a priority objective of the group was to ascertain the reasons for these failures and to provide workable solutions to the problems.

At a well-attended community meeting, held at the Cherokee Boys Club, a master plan was drafted incorporating cultural workshops, special tutorial programs, college/high school Indian student liaison programs and adult Indian educational programs. Soon these participants, including Cherokees ranging from elementary school age to senior citizens, became interested and deeply involved in their cultural heritage, both past and present. At the same time they were concerned with what they considered to be the existing "white-wash" of their cultural heritage. They realized that most of the writing on their culture was done by non-Indians, and while most of these individuals were highly trained and well-meaning, the students felt certain of these Cherokee portrayals lacked authenticity, or at least suggested an ethnocentric white bias.

A major objective of the concerned Cherokees was to research their own culture, and with this mandate, they set out to accomplish this task. They went up into the coves and talked with the traditional elders, corroborating all information once it was obtained and transcribed. They were most fortunate that the American Indian Historical Society took an interest in their cause, lending invaluable encouragement and support. The Society made provisions for the publication of a special Qualla issue of the *Wee Wish Tree*, which served as a model for this larger work.

To encourage more Cherokees to join the effort, special college courses were offered at the Cherokee High School under the supervision of Dr. Laurence French, Project Coordinator and Faculty Advisor to the Cherokee Student Organization. Many of the articles in the book are a direct result of these courses. Clearly, the rewards of this project were much greater than originally anticipated, and today all those who participated have come to feel a great sense of pride regarding this endeavor. A final note is that many now have their degrees and are teaching in the reservation schools or are working in the areas of law, health and social welfare.

*Laurence French
and Jim Hornbuckle, Editors*

TABLE OF CONTENTS

PART ONE

PART TWO

PART ONE

CHAPTER I
The Cherokees—Then And Now

AN HISTORICAL GLANCE:

Laurence French and Jim Hornbuckle

Introduction

The Cherokees represented the largest southeastern tribe at the time of white contact, with an estimated population of about 20,000.[1] The Spanish explorer DeSoto apparently was the first European to enter Cherokee territory, doing so in the spring of 1540 when his group ventured into what is now Highlands, North Carolina, a mountainous region where southeastern North Carolina, northwestern South Carolina and northeastern Georgia meet. The Indians there called themselves "Ani-Yun-Wiya," meaning the "Real People" or the "Principal People." Others referred to them as "Cherokee" (*Tsalagi*), meaning "Cave People." The Europeans spelled this word "Chalaque" in 1557, "Cheraqui" in 1699 and "Cherokee" in 1708. This last term has survived to the present. It has no meaning in the Cherokees' own language.

Language

Linguistically, the Cherokees are related to numerous other tribes, including both the Iroquois and Tuscarora Indians. The Iroquois were and still are the largest northeastern confederacy of tribes, while the Tuscarora were eastern North Carolina cousins to the Cherokees. Today, the Tuscarora probably make up the largest component of a non-tribal confederation, the Lumbee Indians. Speculation has it that thousands of years ago the ancestors of both the Iroquois and Cherokees comprised the same parent tribe, which ranged from the Saint Lawrence River to the Florida Everglades. Over time, the two groups divided their territory, with the Iroquois remaining in the north and the Cherokees in the south. A further division among the Proto-Cherokees supposedly occurred when a coastal group split from the larger tribe, creating the Tuscarora Indians. This popular scenario has recently been challenged by information generated from current archeological research by the University of North Carolina, most notably at the Warren Wilson College site in western North Carolina. This site represents the oldest continuous "dig" in the eastern United States, having been active for over a decade now, and suggests that the Cherokees may have lived in this area for at least four thousand years or more, longer than originally believed. This has led to new speculation concerning the Iroquois/Cherokee relationship. Now, there is speculation

3

that this larger confederation originated in the southeast with the Iroquois breaking away about a thousand years ago and moving north, rather than the reverse.

Physical Appearance

Lieutenant Henry Timberlake remarked in the early 1700's that Cherokees were of middle stature with light brown or olive complexions. He considered them to be both handsome and proud. He went on to say that they had erect posture and were well built with small hands and feet. The females dressed in midlength buckskin skirts, waistcoats, leggings and moccasins. They wore their hair long, braided or coiled on top of their heads. Men wore buckskin loin cloths, shirts and moccasins during warm weather, adding leggings during the winter. They shaved their head and face except for a patch on the back of their head. Here they wore one feather which indicated their clan affiliation. Children went unclad, weather permitting, until puberty, at which time they followed the prescribed dress pattern for their sex group.

Traditional Cherokee Culture and Belief System

The Cherokees at the time of white contact claimed some 40,000 square miles of territory encompassing areas in eight southern states — Georgia, Alabama, South Carolina, North Carolina, Tennessee, Kentucky, Virginia and West Virginia. The Powhatan, Monacan, Miami, Shawnee, Tuscarora, Catawba, Cherawa (Sara), Creeks and Chickasaw were among the Cherokees' immediate Indian neighbors during aboriginal times. Other Indian tribes living at various times in what is now the state of North Carolina were the Hatteras, Chowan, Weapemeok, Woccon, Cape Fear Indians, Coosa, Occaneechee, Keyauwee, Eno and Saxapahaw. The Cherokees considered themselves to be the "principal people" mainly because they represented the largest southeastern Indian tribe at the time of white contact.[2]

This self-image played an important role in their aboriginal belief system. Although the early Cherokees did not worship personages, they nonetheless did have a common, shared belief system, one that parallels Christianity. They viewed earth as a great island floating in a sea of water. Above the earth island was the "sky vault" made of solid rock. The earth island, according to this belief, was secured to the sky vault by four cords, each attached to one of the four corners of the earth island. On this island, the Cherokees were the principal people. The similarities between early Christian beliefs and those of the aboriginal Cherokees are interesting. It was only in the early 1500's that the Christian concept of heaven and earth met with serious opposition. Prior to the "Enlightment" and the period of exploration, the Catholic Church assumed that the earth was flat and surrounded by water. Accordingly, heaven was thought to be immediately above earth, giving the impression that this was a concrete structure. And, lastly, Christians felt they were the principal people on earth. Hence, by comparing the aboriginal Cherokee belief system with that of the European Christian beliefs of that time, we see certain commonalities.

Clearly, the greatest difference between the two beliefs concerns objects of worship. European Christians believed in Christ, while the Cherokees believed in Nature. They, like other Indian groups, learned to respect the natural phenomena that played such an important role in their survival. Creatures of all sizes including the bee, buzzard, wolf, bear, deer, crow and owl, as well as plants, fish and even the terrain—the rivers, valleys and mountains—all played an important role in the Cherokee belief system and social structures. (This will become clearer as we discuss the tribal organization and family structure of the early Cherokees.) Nature and its inhabitants were credited with making the earth. These creatures were supernatural, much like the white man's God. The main difference is that nature, not man, emerges as the most powerful entity.[3] This philosophy more closely represents the Oriental view of man than that posited by western cultures and is typical of small-scale societies everywhere. Tales abound concerning supernatural creatures such as giant yellow jackets and great buzzards. These tales were significant to the aboriginal Cherokees because they explained those difficult questions which every social group must address: the beginning of time, the origin of man and the meaning of life. The Cherokee system apparently worked well for the tribes during aboriginal times, and the changes that took place in their belief system were mainly due to pressures generated by white contact and conflict.

Tribal Organization

The early Cherokees did not have a centralized, state-level political structure as such. Their political organization most closely approximated that of a chiefdom, i.e., a kin-based, segmented, non-egalitarian, small-scale society. Most Native American groups are usually referred to, however, as tribes. From the records of early explorers, notably Adair and Timberlake, it is estimated that between 16,000 and 20,000 Cherokees, living in 60 or more villages, occupied this vast territory of some 40,000 square miles. While there was no permanent tribal-wide social structure, tribal leaders did emerge on occasion during a crisis or situation that warranted such leadership. For the most part, the Cherokees exercised local automony with the various villages. The larger link between the villages was the clan structure, consisting of seven matrilineal clans. Since the 60 or so Cherokee villages were

5

distributed over this vast territory, five natural regions emerged over time: the "Overhill," "Lower," "Middle," "Valley" and "Out" towns. In turn, many of these geographical sections spoke their own dialect of the Cherokee language. This language variation attests to the self-sufficiency of the Cherokee village structure. Like most southeastern Indian groups, the Cherokees maintained stable farm villages and did not move from one campsite to the next. The permanency of their villages was also reflected in the construction of their homes. Cherokees never lived in teepees or similar portable structures like nomadic groups of the Plains or Northern Forest. Early white explorers found the Cherokees living in permanent villages of log and clay dwellings. The villages themselves were located on level land near rivers and other waterways and were usually close to forest areas. Each of the villages housed between 300 and 600 people with separate, private homes available for about every ten persons. This means that the smaller villages consisted of 30 log homes, while the larger ones were double that size. The villages closely resembled those of medieval Europe with the homes clustered together in the village proper surrounded by fields, gardens, pastures and often by a pole fence designed to protect the village perimeter. In fact, it is this basic village structure that many white frontier communities were based upon. Farming was very important to the Cherokees' survival, and the permanency of their villages suggests a sophisticated knowledge of cultivation, since the former generally would not have been possible without the latter. Fishing and hunting supplemented their agricultural subsistence.[4]

Each village had a town house, which was used for public meetings. The importance of this structure was stressed by both its size and design. It was the largest village structure and was often elevated on a mound so as to emphasize its significance. It consisted of seven sides, one for each of the Cherokee clans. The town house represented the heart of the village, and to signify this, a symbolic flame was kept burning in the house throughout the year. The town house also served as the village religious center and the most important social institution within the aboriginal Cherokee society. It provided the binding force necessary for this otherwise highly decentralized people to stay together as a tribe. All important matters were discussed publicly within the town house. No one was omitted, and all adults, both males and females, could participate. Decisions were based upon consensus, and once agreement was reached, all concurred, even the dissenters.[5] People grouped themselves according to clan affiliation, and not by sex, age or viewpoint. They sat in their respective sections with the arbiters seated in the center, close to the flame of vitality. Each village had two chiefs who represented white and red factions typical of southeastern Indians, and the

6

nature of the discussion determined which chief presided over the town meeting. The "white chief" regulated domestic affairs, which were especially important from spring planting until the fall harvest, while the "red chief," or warrior chief, was more important during the winter season, which was the time for war. Females played an important role in both domestic and war councils, with evidence indicating that on occasion they even served as "white chiefs." The fact that most village chiefs were males does not, however, imply that the females played subordinate roles to men. Females seem to have had an equal voice in all village councils, in addition to playing a very crucial role in the social regulation and survival of the Cherokees as a cultural group. Hence, a basically equal sexual division of authority existed among the early Cherokees. The males played the dominant role in external affairs such as wars, hunting and intervillage competition, while the females regulated intravillage domestic affairs as well as intervillage clan matters. The females may have even had the upper hand, since males had little say regarding clan regulations and sanctions, while females played an important role even on the war council where an assemblage of "war women," or "pretty women," offered counsel concerning strategy, time of attack, fate of captives and other important matters. European females were, of course, quite subordinate to their male counterparts during this same period and remained so for nearly four centuries after their initial settlement in America.[6]

The clan structure held the Cherokees together as a people. It provided their identity and regulated marriages and mobility as well. The Cherokees had a matrilineal/matrilocal system, meaning that the female played a dominant role within the family structure. The Cherokees traced their lineage through the female. When a Cherokee couple married, they moved to the home of the bride.

Early Cherokees identified themselves according to their clan affiliation. The seven clans were the "Wolf Clan," the "Deer Clan," the "Bird Clan," the "Red Paint Clan," the "Blue Paint Clan," the "Wild Potato Clan" and the "Long Hair or Twister Clan." An unmarried male would refer to his mother, in particular, and her clan, in general, for his family identification. Once married, he would then also refer to his mother-in-law and her clan for his identity. Females merely associated with their own clan and with the clan of their immediate female superior (mother, etc.). Evidence indicates that most of the 60 villages had all seven clans represented. Those few that did not have all seven clans represented became known as "neutral villages."

The village and clan structure together provided a strong unifying force which allowed this highly decentralized, widely dispersed people to remain as one tribe. Each of the four main

7

districts, excluding the out towns on the periphery, had at least one strong village which acted more or less as its informal capital. During times of strife, the chiefs of these district capitals would meet and devise a plan of action. If necessary, one of these district chiefs might temporarily emerge as the tribal leader, stepping down as soon as the crisis passed. Similarly, each clan had a "mother village" where the ultimate matriarch resided. Clans, regardless of district affiliation, consulted with their respective "mother villages" concerning family norms, regulations and sanctions. Thus, while there were over 60 autonomous villages, each with its own town house and chiefs (red and white), the larger tribal organization consisted of district "capitals" (at least four) and seven "mother villages" (one for each clan). Both males and females were enfranchised, with both sexes sharing in the authority and responsibility of village life.[7]

The Family Structure and Village Life

The early Cherokee family can best be explained within the larger context of the seasonal cycle, the clan and the village. Moreover, this approach focuses attention on the important role nature played in Cherokee life. Unlike our twelve-month, four-season year, the Cherokee year was divided into two seasons, summer and winter. The summer extended from planting time up until harvest time, while winter was that time following harvest until spring planting. This was a natural, functional year based upon their agricultural way of life. Each season was punctuated by distinctive events and festivals much as the Christian year is.

All Cherokees worked hard during the summer season, planting, fishing and hunting. The women did most of the farming, while fishing and hunting were left to the men. A common form of intervillage entertainment during the summer season was the "stick ball" game, from which modern-day lacrosse developed. Here, a ball made of stuffed animal skin was placed in the center of a field, with opposing teams attempting to bring the ball across their respective goal line located at opposite ends of the field. Small wooden sticks with netted ends were used by the players to scoop up, carry and throw the ball. Apparently, it was a "no-holds-barred" game with serious injuries and even death sometimes resulting. These games reached unbelievable levels of emotion and excitement, with numerous spectators of both sexes and of all ages loudly cheering on their teams. This represented one of the few activities in which such overt public license was tolerated. Clearly, this activity seemed to relieve the strain and tension generated by the arduous summer season.

Winter season was the time for hunting, intertribal wars and the avenging of unsettled altercations, while six major festivals highlighted the summer season. The early Cherokees celebrated the "First New Moon of Spring," the "New Green Corn Festival," the "Green Corn Festival," the first appearance of the "October New Moon," the "Establishment of Friendship and Brotherhood" and the "Bouncing Bush Festival." The "First New Moon of Spring" celebrated the spring planting, while the "New Green Corn" and the "Green Corn" festivals rejoiced in the crops' progress. The first appearance of the "October New Moon" looked forward to the anticipated harvest, while the "Establishment of Friendship and Brotherhood" and the "Bouncing Bush" festivals celebrated the cooperative harvesting effort put forth by all villages. These last two festivals allowed each Cherokee to begin a new year free of sins, crimes or hardships. They also signified the New Year for the village itself. Old clothing, furniture and the like were ceremonially burned in a large communal bonfire followed by the extinguishing of the "sacred fire" in the town house. Next, homes, the town house and the village square were all swept clean, the exterior of the town house was whitened with clay, and a new fire was lit for the new year. All personal, tribal, village and clan transgressions were forgiven, and refugees could return home from neutral villages, while everyone purified himself by drinking the "black drink" (which induced vomiting) and bathing in the nearest stream. These activities lasted about a week. Every seventh year, a seventh major festival, the Uku Dance, was held to reinstate the principal white chief. Three other significant festive events occurred during the Cherokee year: the "Victory Dance," the "Animal Dance" and the "Ball Play Dance." These events commemorated the war party, the hunt and stick ball competition respectively.

The "Victory Dance" emphasized the importance associated with the warrior role among Cherokee men. The young Cherokee male was conditioned for the warrior role, this clearly being the most important facet of the male's overall status. But unlike the movie version of the Indian massacre, war, at least among the Cherokees, represented a highly regulated event. Wars were based on vengeance and directed toward other tribes. Many of these encounters involved altercations with other tribes that violated the Cherokees' vast territorial boundaries. Retaliation was considered successful when the number of enemy killed equaled the losses of one's own tribe. Wholesale massacres were unknown and certainly were not condoned, according to Cherokee custom. Nonetheless, many early white observers who witnessed the frenzy and enthusiasm of the Cherokee war party felt that the Cherokees may have deliberately sought out excuses for war. After a battle, the warriors returned with their captives. Captives were killed only if it was necessary to balance the vengeance tally. Actually, Cherokee warriors were quite subdued following a battle, in compliance with their custom requiring a

9

prescribed purification period. However, their enthusiasm was merely kept latent during this time, and the "Victory Dance" marked the official end to the purification period and the beginning of the war party celebration. Again, the intensity of this celebration shocked white observers, who described it more as an orgy than a dance. Apparently, both male warriors and females participated in the frenzied activity.

The "Animal Dance," on the other hand, was designed to bring good fortune to the hunters. Here special dances were performed for particular animals. Adorned in animal skins and wooden animals masks, the hunters pleaded with Nature to help them in their hunt. They addressed the particular animal desired—racoon, beaver, buffalo, bear or deer—pleading with it to allow itself to be killed, hence aiding in the survival of the Cherokees. This festival indicated their reliance on nature for survival. The humbleness of the dance also reflected the subordinate role the Cherokees felt man played in the larger universe.

The "Ball Play Dance" occurred prior to the intratribal stick ball games and included the use of conjurers and taboos.[8]

It is within the context of this dual season, focusing on these festivals and events, that the Cherokees carried on their domestic lives. The early Cherokees maintained extended families, meaning that the grandmother, her husband, her married daughters and their husbands and children probably all shared the same house. At any rate, an average of ten persons lived in each family dwelling. These homes were constructed on vertically set logs, roofed with bark and insulated with clay. There was one entrance, and an opening in the roof served as a smoke exit for the fire pit, which was centrally located in the house. These homes were usually without windows. Privacy was not a paramount issue, given the Cherokees' communal way of life. Apparently, this arrangement worked well, since it survived for over a thousand years prior to the advent of the white man.

The village farm, itself, was a communal effort, with all men and women joining in the initial groundbreaking and planting. Then, the fields were left to the women, while the men hunted, fished, repaired homes and fences, dug out canoes, made blowguns and bows and arrows, mended nets and performed other chores. The rearing of the children was totally dominated by the females, who seemed to possess tremendous authority in these matters. They also fired clay cooking utensils, wove sashes and baskets, tanned and prepared animal skins for clothing and collected herbs and wild vegetables, which also played an important role among the early Cherokees. The women used them for spicing or augmenting meals, while medicine men used them for medical cures as well as for both white and black magic. In the fall, the entire village cooperated in the communal harvest. Thus, the early Cherokee village was a balance between a specific division of labor based upon sex and communal cooperation and sharing.

The major external check on taboos, custom violations and the administering of sanctions was the intratribal clan structure. The Cherokee ethos or value system helped to sustain their harmonious domestic lifestyle. This society had no policemen, courts or written laws. It was regulated by custom, dictated and enforced through consensus and not through formal law. Gearing (1962) summarized the Cherokee ethos as "Old equals good equals honor." This represented a complicated psychological and social process which served to perpetuate both harmony and the status quo. Deference, ritual purification and avoidance were the three most crucial values associated with the Cherokee ethos, which stressed cooperation rather than competition. Thomas (1958) labeled the Cherokee ethos "The Harmony Ethic," thereby setting it apart from the white "Protestant Ethic." The Cherokees' early belief system must indeed have been a strong and powerful one since attributes of it have survived up until the present. Of the three basic values, ritual purification seems to be the only one that has been largely lost; and this occurred mainly because of the demise of wars, stick ball and the hunt, coupled with the Cherokees' conversion to Christianity. Perhaps the similarities between Christianity and the aboriginal Cherokee ethos are the reason deference and avoidance have survived. After all, it is within the Christian perspective that these deep-seated values continue to have meaning for the Cherokees.[9]

Deference, then as today, was expressed in terms of respect, especially when complying with a friend or relative's wishes and not in terms of formal obligation such as exists in our society (civil, juvenile and criminal law as well as numerous lesser legal obligations).

Avoidance represented the actual implementation of the deference value. Here, elaborate networks of avoidance provided the needed regulatory sanctions, thereby minimizing the need for and use of formal controls such as police power, courts and corporal punishment. Ostracism was the most common control mechanism, while death was reserved only for the most serious transgressions. Ostracism as a control sanction also included disapproval and ridicule, while death fell into the realm of vengeance. Both types of control were administered by the clan. Serious transgressions included murder, violation of mourning taboos and the abusing of women and children. In these instances, vengeance became a clan responsibility. The clans involved (victim's and offender's) acted as "corporate individuals" in resolving these matters. Often they sought a reasonable compromise regarding the obligatory avenging of the transgression. Clan obligations and not emotions prevailed, creating an environment of rational justice. If the two clans could not reach a satisfactory compromise, then the issue was brought before the village council for advice, again leaving the ultimate solution to the respective clans involved. If the verdict was death, the offender would be notified, yet allowed to remain free until the execution date. Individual shame sufficed in most instances as a device for detainment. But those few who did not savor the idea of death often attempted to escape to a neutral town, one that was not represented by the avenging clan. If successful, they would be compelled to remain there until after the new year purification ritual whereby their transgression would be forgiven, and they could then return to their home village without fear of clan reprisal.

The early Cherokees had two types of capital punishment: honorable and dishonorable. Honorable death involved being killed in a stick ball game. Here the offender's death was prearranged by the two clans involved in the altercation. Members of the avenging clan would then gang up on the offender and kill him during the contest. This was the most honorable type of death, bringing the least shame to the offender and his clan. Dishonorable death, however, was designed to humiliate the offender or his clan. To illustrate, the offender might be bound hand and foot, carried up a mountain and thrown off a cliff.

At the other end of the Harmony Ethic continuum is the Cherokees' unique perception of the individual. Once Cherokees were properly identified and labeled according to their clan and village affiliation, they were allowed considerable latitude in their own personal behavior. This not only shocked whites who came into contact with them but amused their neighboring tribes as well. Not adequately understanding the Cherokee ethos, many of these outsiders considered the Cherokees to be juvenile and promiscuous, mainly because they seemed to lack personal constraint even once they reached adulthood. This personal behavior was associated with certain traits, many of which have survived to the present. They are as follows:

1. The avoidance of overt hostilities regarding interpersonal matters and an emphasis on nonaggressiveness.
2. The use of a neutral third person, or intermediary, for resolving personal altercations.
3. A high value placed on independence.
4. A resentment of authority.
5. A hesitancy to command others.
6. Caution in interactions with other persons.
7. A reluctance to refuse favors and an emphasis on generosity.
8. A reluctance to voice opinions publicly.
9. Avoidance of eye and body contact (handshakes, back slapping, etc.) when conversing with others.

10. Emphasis placed on group cooperation and not on individual competition.

During aboriginal times, summer stick ball competition and winter war parties provided temporary escape from the dictates of the Harmony Ethic, allowing both males and females an outlet for pent-up frustrations. The new year purification ritual and its week-long celebration culminated in a total emotional purge of any tensions acquired during the year. This system seemed to work well for the early Cherokees. But white insistence on eliminating these ritualistic tension outlets, while not replacing them with any viable alternatives, has greatly increased the frustration level of many contemporary Cherokees, making them susceptible to the same personal and social problems that other people in our society have.

The early Cherokees' personal freedom is best expressed in terms of the family process. Young Cherokee children were socialized to play the appropriate sex role. The female stages of development included infancy, childhood, womanhood and, for a few mature women, the higher statuses of "clan matriarchs" or "pretty women" (those providing counsel to the red chief). Males followed a similar process, developing from infancy to childhood and then adulthood and the higher statuses of chief (red or white) and "beloved man" (distinguished warrior) for a few mature men. Children learned their respective adult roles from immediate family members, although these people were not necessarily their biological families. Boys and girls learned their respective roles through apprenticeships, usually during adolescence. Pottery, basketry, blowgun making, fishing, hunting, farming, building construction, cooking and tanning all required periods of internship and were learned in the context of the larger extended family.

Once the children reached puberty and acquired the necessary skills for their sexes and age groups, they were eligible for marriage. Again, contrary to the popular Indian stereotype, brides were not bought, given away or bargained for. Dowries were unknown among the Cherokees. In fact, the Cherokees generally practiced free mate selection centuries before it became a popular European and American practice. The decision was ultimately left up to the prospective bride. Her hand was asked for, and only she could consent. Once married, males had to move into the home and village of the bride's mother. The only constraints on the free choice of marriage partners were rules of exogamy prohibiting one from marrying within one's own or one's father's clan. Corresponding rules of endogamy encouraged one to marry into either of one's grandfather's clans. Marriages were regulated by the women in the village. The clan, that is, the female members, punished both male and female marital offenders when they violated sacred clan taboos, the most serious

13

transgressions being those involving neglect of wife and children and violations of widow's and widower's mourning customs. Even when a husband neglected his wife and children, other males played insignificant roles in these matters. Records indicate that violators of family taboos, including men, were often publicly beaten by female members of the abused person's clan.

Otherwise, there was considerable freedom within marriage. Most Cherokee families were, and still are, small, consisting of three to four children. Moreover, the wife had considerable license regarding family size. Not having today's knowledge of birth control or abortion, a mother was allowed to perform infanticide if she wanted to rid herself of an unwanted child. A male's doing the same thing constituted murder.

Divorce was a rather simple process. The female merely placed her husband's belongings outside the dwelling if she chose to divorce him, while the husband simply moved out if he chose to initiate divorce. Since brothers-in-law and other male relatives did not get involved in these matters, the male peer group was seldom disrupted by a marital breakup. Children were cared for by the wife's clan and seldom posed a problem. If a mother wanted to relieve herself of older dependent children, she merely gave them to someone within her clan who would love and care for them. Amazingly, this system allowed maximum personal license among adults with minimum trauma for the children. More responsibility, however, was expected concerning widows and widowers. The widows were expected to marry their dead husband's brother, the levirate, while the widowers were expected to marry their deceased wife's sister, the sororate. It is not known how rigidly this custom was enforced since the divorce process was so easy. Another common practice was for males to marry outside their own village, signifying considerable intervillage mobility, at least within each of the four major tribal districts.

CONTACT, CONFLICT AND CHANGE:

Laurence French and Jim Hornbuckle

Initial White Contact and Influence

Sporadic white contact occurred for over a century after DeSoto's initial venture into Cherokee territory. Much of this contact was initiated by the Cherokees themselves, who traveled as far away as Spanish Florida in war parties. The spoils of these attacks provided both horses and firearms for the Cherokees. The first major white influence leading to more or less continuous Cherokee/white interaction occurred in 1673 with James Needham and Gabriel Arthur. Eleven years later (1684), eight village chiefs signed the first Cherokee peace treaty. The treaty was signed in hieroglyphics since the Cherokee syllabary was not created until 1821.

White trappers and traders interacted with the Cherokees for the next century, some dealing in the flourishing Indian slave trade. Cherokees and other Indian groups were encouraged by white slave traders to sell their captives to them. Although Governor Sayle of South Carolina outlawed Indian slavery in 1671, Lauber (1970) indicates that the traffic in Indian slaves continued. Demands for Indian slaves were great and were encouraged by the Spaniards, French and English. The Westo, Esaw, Congaree and Savannah tribes all preyed upon the Cherokees, selling their captives to the English. Many Indian slaves ended up in New England, Canada, the West Indies and even Europe. The Indian slave trade lasted about a century (1680's to 1780's), and by 1780, all the Indian nations within English colonial territory in the South were either extinct or had retreated westward into Cherokee and Creek territory for protection. The Indian slave trade, along with the Old World diseases, accounted for the demise of the dozens of Indian tribes neighboring the Cherokee Nation in what is now North and South Carolina. Nash (1974) found that in 1708 the population of the Carolinas consisted of 5,300 whites, 2,900 African slaves and 1,400 Indian slaves. History indicates that neither Blacks nor Indians took slavery lightly, as many rebellions occurred during this time. Whites, however, used Blacks to quash Indian slave uprisings and vice versa, instituting a divide and rule policy. Diseases, like the Cherokees' disastrous smallpox epidemic of 1738, completed the decimation of southeastern Indian tribes.[10]

Toward the end of the devastating Indian slave trade (1775), Colonel Richard Henderson and eight associates were successful in obtaining a large tract of Cherokee territory, encompassing what is now central and western Kentucky and parts of North Carolina and Tennessee, from a few susceptible village chiefs.

15

This purchase, incidentally, was for a private corporation, The Transylvania Land Company. The chiefs' payment for this land was two thousand pounds and a log cabin filled with trading goods. This sale shocked the Cherokees into action; and in 1806, in an effort to discourage this from happening again, the Cherokees made it a capital offense to sell Cherokee land to outsiders.

Whites used more than deceit and slavery as weapons against the Cherokees; they used war as well. In 1759, South Carolina mounted a large, armed expedition of 1,700 soldiers led by Governor Lyttleton against the Cherokees. Two years later, in 1761, 1,800 British regulars and 700 provincial militiamen again attacked the Cherokees, burning villages and crops. These encounters served to establish the new eastern boundary of the Cherokee territory and forced the Cherokees to acknowledge the English as their permanent neighbor. Later it was the Americans in this position, and in 1776 the Cherokees suffered four devastating attacks by American troops. Hence, the Indian slave trade, diminishing territory, Old World diseases and increased altercations with whites forced the Cherokees to reevaluate their traditional ways and to develop a system that would stand up to these new challenges.

The Emerging Nation

At first, the most significant "mother town," Kituwah, in the Middle District, and the Overhill District capital, Chota, served as transitory tribal centers, while village chiefs developed a comprehensive plan of tribal unity. By 1792, the chiefs organized the "Grand Cherokee National Council." This steering committee was mandated to resolve the issues of national leadership and centralized government and to develop a viable political philosophy sufficient to deal with their new white neighbors. Little Turkey, a "beloved man" from Ustanali village, emerged as the first Principal Chief of the Cherokees. This early attempt at tribal political organization took on many of the aspects of the old village system. Rule was still by consensus and not by formal law, and representation and power were distributed according to village and clan affiliation. At the apex of this hierarchy was the Principal Chief, also known as the Chief Speaker or "Most Beloved Man of the Entire Nation." Next, there were four regional chiefs, one from each of the four district capitals. The remainder of the National Council was comprised of village chiefs.

This system worked until the death of Little Turkey in 1807, at which time rapid changes occurred. Formal laws replaced consensus, and the Cherokee political organization took on more and more qualities of the white man's system. In 1808, the tribal police force (Regulating Companies), introduced in 1797 to curb horse theft, was upgraded into a more permanent national police force now named "The Light Horse Guard."

Clearly, the year 1808 marked the official beginning to the Cherokee republic known later as the "Cherokee Nation." The Principal Chief and Vice Chief were now selected by the National Council made up of village chiefs, with these leaders and the council empowered to enact and enforce tribal laws. By 1810, the clan structure was weakened considerably, vesting more power and authority in the National Council. This was deemed a necessary step since folk and formal control competition would only have complicated matters. Also, the traditional clan blood vengeance and the new rule of law proved to be incompatible, resulting in the former being outlawed. Unfortunately, this transfer from a folk to a formally structured society greatly undermined the progressive and powerful role Cherokee females once played. The transition was not a smooth one; and in 1809, there was a movement to divide the tribe into two groups—the "Upper Cherokees," composed of traditionalists, and the "Lower Cherokees," composed of more acculturation-minded Cherokees. President Thomas Jefferson discouraged the split, enticing the Cherokees to continue their pursuit of a unified democratic nation.

Mindful of Colonel Richard Henderson's deceitful land purchase, the Cherokees enacted one of the first tribal laws dealing with diminishing territorial claims. Skeptical of the white man's promises and treaties, the National Council made it a capital offense in 1806 for Cherokees to sell tribal land to non-Cherokees. In an effort to show the strength of the new government, a spectacular case was made of Doublehead, a village chief and outspoken opponent of Chief Little Turkey. Apparently, Doublehead had signed away some Cherokee land to the United States, represented by agents of President Jefferson. Two up-and-coming Cherokees, "The Ridge" and Alexander Saunders, were designated as Chief Doublehead's assassins. The death of such a visible and vocal village chief was probably designed to accomplish the following:

1. To emphasize the superiority of the new National Council over the old autonomous village system,
2. To make Cherokees aware of the critical land situation and
3. To send a message to the United States officials that the Cherokees were aware of their deceitful tactics.

The Cherokee leaders were quite perceptive on this last issue. While President Jefferson was apparently encouraging the Cherokees to pursue their objective of an autonomous nation, he was also setting the stage for its demise. The 1802 Georgia Compact proved to be the vehicle for not only the Cherokee Removal,

17

but for the removal of the other four "Civilized Tribes" (Choctaws, Creeks, Chicasaws and Seminoles) as well. This arrangement between the State of Georgia and the United States provided the federal government with all western lands claimed by Georgia beyond the original colonial boundaries in exchange for Jefferson's promise to remove all Indians from the state's borders. These borders refer to those which Georgia, South Carolina, Virginia, North Carolina, Kentucky, Alabama and Tennessee agreed upon when they ratified the United States Constitution (1788-1800). These potential state borders dissected the Cherokee territory, leaving no land at all for the Cherokees or any other Indian groups. President Jefferson's deal involved removing all Indians west of the Mississippi River. The 1785 Hopewell and the 1791 Holston Treaties, which preceded the 1802 Compact, followed a similar pattern, again being designed to further weaken the Cherokees. To complicate matters, the United States ignored the Cherokees' claim to sovereignty, placing them under the jurisdiction of the respective states claiming Cherokee territory.[11]

Despite these efforts to undermine Cherokee progress, the nation emerged anyway. In 1792, Ustanali replaced Chota as the tribal capital, and it was also in the late 1700's that New Echota, near modern-day Calhoun, Georgia, became the national capital. Black Fox succeeded Little Turkey as Principal Chief, served for only a short time and was replaced by Path Killer, who ruled during the most crucial period of national development (1808-1827). The next Principal Chief became the most famous of all Cherokee leaders—John Ross. Ross ruled for four decades, serving as chief during the height of the Cherokee Nation, during Forced Removal and during the development of the new western nation (Oklahoma).

In 1817, the first steps were taken in establishing the Cherokee "republic." That May, the Cherokees established a national bicameral legislature, consisting of an upper house (Standing Committee) where the members were to be selected by and from members of the lower house (National Council). The Standing Committee, later renamed the Naitonal Committee, consisted of 13 members elected by the National Council for two-year terms. The National Council members were, in turn, elected from their own districts. The old four regional districts were now doubled, creating eight districts overall, each with four elected members to the National Council and its own district judges and marshal. Two national districts also had a circuit judge and a Light Horse Company (national police). Path Killer was Principal Chief of the new nation, Charles Hicks was both Vice Chief and National Treasurer, John Ross was President of the National Committee (upper house) and "The Ridge" (Major Ridge) was

Speaker of the National Council (lower house). In 1823, the nation created a Supreme Court, hearing 21 cases its first term. Then, in 1827, only 46 years after the United States Constitution was adopted and ratified, the Cherokee Nation adopted its own constitution. The preamble emphasized the preservation of democratic principles, individual freedom, and respect for God.

> *We, the representatives of the people of the Cherokee Nation in convention assembled, in order to establish justice, ensure tranquility, promote our common welfare, and secure ourselves and our posterity the blessing of liberty, acknowledging with humility and gratitude the goodness of the sovereign Ruler of the Universe, in offering us an opportunity so favorable to the design, and imploring His aid and direction in its accomplishment, do ordain and establish this Constitution for the Government of the Cherokee Nation.*

All male Cherokees 18 years or older were enfranchised, while those 25 or older could run for the National Council. The Principal and Vice Chiefs were elected by the National Council for four-year terms. The Principal Chief had veto power which in turn could be overriden by a two-thirds vote of the council. The National Treasurer was selected by a similar process but for only a two-year term. The three Supreme Court justices were elected for four-year terms as was the National Marshal. District judges and sheriffs were elected in local elections and served two-year terms. United States President John Quincy Adams publicly welcomed the Cherokee Constitution. However, a core of conservative Cherokees, under the leadership of White Path (an elected councilman), attempted a revolt intended to repudiate the constitution, abandon Christianity and revert back to the old village tribal system. The revolt was short lived, but the discovery of gold on Cherokee territory in 1829 only served to increase white/Cherokee tensions and White Path's effort to destroy the newly founded nation.

The Cherokee political revolution was supported by an equally impressive cultural revolution. In 1740, the Moravian Society of United Brethren established the first successfully organized Cherokee mission. In 1758, the Presbyterians established their mission, adding a mission school in 1803 under the direction of the Reverend Gideon Blackburn. Reverend Blackburn's Hiwassee School had some two dozen students, encouraging him to start a second school in 1806 at Richard's Field. But, in 1810, poor health forced Reverend Blackburn to close his schools. The nation later established its own school system which taught both Cherokee and English. Sequoyah's syllabary aided in the written preserva-

19

tion of the Cherokee language taught in the traditional school environment. In 1828, seven years after Sequoyah developed his Cherokee alphabet, the Cherokee national newspaper, *The Phoenix*, was created. It was estimated that by 1830 half of the Cherokees' 16,000 population could both read and write Sequoyah's alphabet, while a smaller group could read and write English as well. The Cherokee Nation was so successful that by 1825 the nation was operating "in the black." There were successful farmers, herdsmen and merchants, with Cherokee trade reaching as far southwest as New Orleans. White eastern liberals were astonished at the Cherokees' high level of social, political, religious and technological development in such a short period of time with a minimum of outside help. The Cherokees, without a doubt, proved that American Indians could reach a level of cultural development equal to that of the white. While this impressed many, it upset others.[12]

The Cherokees' rapid culture change was the result of a conscious effort on the part of certain Cherokees to "accommodate" to white Americans as part of a larger effort to cope with the white onslaught. While other Indian tribes tried warfare, intertribal political alliances and cultural revitalization movements, the Cherokees, or one faction of them, tried accommodation. When they "fought" the white man, it was through the courts, not on the battlefield. They hoped to convince the white man, through their Christianity, political system and American lifestyle, that they were not "savages" but "civilized" neighbors, undeserving of removal. The faction pressing for accommodation included many Cherokees with white relatives or who had themselves intermarried with whites, thus being more exposed to American society. In the inaccessible mountains, resided traditional Cherokees who resisted accommodation. In the end, accommodation failed.

Forced Removal

The Cherokee removal was part of a larger plan to force all Indian groups west of the Mississippi River. Five tribes (Cherokee, Creek, Choctaw, Chickasaw and Seminole), those referred to as the "Civilized Tribes," especially impeded white development in the Southeast. The smaller tribes were all but destroyed during the century of Indian slavery and Old World diseases. Intertribal wars were promoted by the whites for the purpose of furthering this destruction. The five civilized tribes were more difficult to destroy. Instead of succumbing to white plans of self-genocide, these Indian groups adopted the white man's form of government and culture to their way of life. The most successful group was the Cherokees. This irritated those whites who wanted to rid their state of these "savages."

Removal had its beginning in 1802 with President Jefferson's Georgia Compact. The Cherokees, however, resisted all attempts at removal, except for a small group voluntarily moving to what is now Arkansas. This group represented a small core of conservative Cherokees who adamantly opposed the development of the nation. Instead of changing its traditional ways, this group moved West in 1817, only to be moved again in 1828 to what was then known as "Indian Territory" (Oklahoma). Perhaps the most important event leading to the forced removal of 16,000 Cherokees was the election of Andrew Jackson as President of the United States in 1828. Immediately following Jackson's inauguration, Georgia enacted a law annexing all Cherokee territory falling within its proposed borders, doing so over strong objections from the Cherokee Nation. Georgia not only ignored the Cherokees' plea but openly encouraged overt aggressive acts directed against the Cherokees by Georgia residents. Both Georgia and President Jackson refused to protect the Cherokees from this harassment.

Jackson's actions were challenged by the United States Supreme Court in *Worchester vs the State of Georgia*. When the Court denied all claims of the United States and of individual states regarding sovereignty over the Cherokee Nation and declared the Cherokees a dependent, domestic nation, Jackson defied the Court, while Georgia intensified its harassment of the Cherokees, confiscating their schools, council house and printing plant and encouraging white raids upon Cherokee plantations and towns. These white raiders were known as "pony clubs." The State of Georgia went so far as to divide the Cherokee Nation into "land lots" and "gold lots," the former consisting of 160 acres and the latter 40 acres each. These lots were then distributed among Georgia citizens through public lottery with each citizen receiving a ticket. This occurred in June 1830, two years after Jackson was inaugurated and five years prior to any formal Cherokee Removal Treaty. All this time, Principal Chief Ross pursued legal recourse as a solution to this problem, doing so while the President of the United States and the State of Georgia resorted to more barbaric methods. This certainly provided an unusual twist to the common assumption that the Indians were subhuman savages, while whites were civilized and orderly. The Cherokee Forced Removal, one of the most shameful events in American history, refuted this common image.[13]

The chain of events leading to the "Trail of Tears" officially began with the 1835 "New Echota," or "Removal," Treaty. The Reverend Schermerhorn was commissioned by President Jackson to obtain a treaty from the Cherokees. Deceit had to be used since all parties knew that Chief Ross and the vast majority of Cherokees were openly opposed to forced removal. The plan was to incapacitate Ross while Schermerhorn enticed Major Ridge and other council members to sign the treaty. Chief Ross was called to Washington, D. C., while Schermerhorn got Major Ridge and 19 others to sign the Treaty of New Echota, which, in effect, agreed to removal, meaning that the Cherokee Nation could now be moved in its entirety west of the Mississippi River to "Indian Territory," land set aside for the five civilized tribes and other Indian groups.

Jackson knew that Ross would continue to object to the Treaty, and he had the Cherokee Chief arrested and jailed on several occasions. Jackson was a frontiersman and "Indian fighter." In fact, both John Ross and "The Ridge" served under him in the 1813-1814 Creek War. Both Cherokees rose to the rank of major, which explains the change in "The Ridge's" name. What Jackson did not understand was that it was not Ross alone who resisted being displaced from his traditional home. Hence, while Schermerhorn and the "Treaty Party," as those who signed the treaty became known, conspired, Vice Chief Lowery obtained 15,904 Cherokee signatures protesting the treaty.

Nonetheless, the United States Congress ratified the treaty in May of 1836 by a margin of one vote. The treaty was legal and binding according to the United States, and the Cherokees were given two years to remove themselves west to Indian Territory. The specifics of the treaty stated that all Cherokee land east of the Mississippi River was ceded to the United States in exchange for seven million acres in Indian Territory and $5,000,000. In implementing the treaty, Jackson had the Cherokees disarmed (July 30-September 1, 1836). The Cherokees did not resist because most believed that the United States would come to its senses and change its mind. After all, the whites never bothered to honor any of the other treaties, and history had shown the Cherokees to be the most "treatied" Indian group in the country. Only the families of the "Treaty Party" and their small following moved voluntarily and in comfort. As the time ran out for the others, frantic efforts were made to get the United States to repeal the treaty. In February of 1838, Chief Ross presented another petition, this time with 15,665 signatures or nearly the total Eastern Cherokee population. Congress declined by a vote of 36 to 10. President Martin Van Buren refused to intervene, and in April General Winfield Scott took command of the 9,500 member occupation force and started building stockades in which the Cherokees were to be incarcerated until forcefully removed. Then in May, exactly two years after the Removal Treaty became official, General Scott began the roundup. Cherokees were arrested in their homes, in the fields, everywhere, and were allowed time to pick up only a few provisions before being herded into the makeshift stockades to wait months on end for removal.

A Georgia volunteer who later rose to the rank of colonel in the Confederate Army wrote, "I fought through the Civil War and have seen men shot to pieces and slaughtered by the thousands, but the Cherokee Removal was the cruelest work I ever knew."[14] Impatient white mobs followed the troops, looting the abandoned homes, plantations and villages. Within a month, over 10,000 Cherokees were confined within the stockades, ill fed and ill treated. Some Cherokees successfully avoided detention, hiding out in the Appalachian Mountains. But once the Cherokees realized that the whites were going to rid themselves of the Cherokees at any cost, Ross convinced the United States that he could lead his people west without military assistance. This last group left in October with approximately 16,000 Cherokees in a 600-wagon caravan.

Ross became the "Superintendent of Cherokee Removal and Subsistence," even over the strong objections of former President Jackson. The "Trail of Tears," as the removal is commonly called, cost thousands of lives. Hundreds died in the stockades; over 1,600 died along the trail itself, while hundreds more died shortly after reaching their destination from the hardships associated with removal. Overall, over 4,000 died as a direct result of removal, quite a high proportion of the 16,000 Cherokees who actively resisted being forcefully expelled from their nation.[15]

Emergence of the Eastern Band

The Appalachian Cherokees, notably the villages of Alarka, Aquorra, Stekoih and Cheeoih, consisted of conservative Cherokees who neither participated in nor endorsed the Cherokee Nation. They clung to the traditional ways, placing great emphasis on the old village and clan system. Other disenchanted conservative "full bloods" joined their ranks until the time of removal. The 1835 Cherokee Census bears this out, indicating that of the four major Cherokee concentrations (old tribal districts), the North Carolina Cherokees (Appalachian) had both the fewest Black slaves and the fewest whites living among them, although they represented the second largest population concentration.[16] The North Carolina Cherokees were allowed to avoid removal due to special arrangements made on their behalf by their white legal counsel, William Thomas. To avoid removal, the Appalachian Cherokees had to separate themselves from the Cherokee Nation and to accept North Carolina's sovereignty over their villages. Some Cherokees living outside the boundaries of the Cherokee Nation in North Carolina had already accomplished this status prior to the removal era. Many felt this action would serve to preserve their way of life; therefore, they delegated Will Thomas with a special power of attorney, allowing him to represent them in these legal matters.

Thomas had lived among the Cherokees since childhood, working for a white businessman and politician. Since his early teens, he had managed the man's trading post located on the white/Indian border. Soon, Thomas had his own trading posts, dealing mostly with the Appalachian Cherokees. The Regional Chief of this area, Younaguska, liked "Little Will" and made him his adopted son and an honorary member of the tribe. By the time Thomas was 31 years old, he had considerable power and authority among the Appalachian Cherokees. It was then that he represented his adopted family, the Appalachian Cherokees, during the negotiations concerning the 1835 New Echota or "Removal" Treaty. In 1836, he successfully secured a written agreement which entitled the North Carolina Cherokees to a proportionate share of the $5 million cash settlement as well as excluding them from being removed. A sizeable contingent of North Carolina Cherokees elected to remain behind, doing so legally and not as fugitives. Other Cherokees did manage to evade removal by hiding in the mountains. They could not have represented a sizeable group, however, since the total Appalachian Cherokee population only accounted for about 1,000 Indians, including those legally entitled to remain plus any fugitives.

The tale of Tsali probably best explains the real sentiment of the Appalachian Cherokees. Tsali has become a folk hero and an inspiration as a resistant against the removal of which he was to become a victim. Tsali, an influential local Cherokee leader who served as both a village chief and later as a member of the National Council, apparently was attempting to avoid the roundup by slipping into Appalachian Cherokee territory, only to be detected while camping along the Little Tennessee River by a detachment of General Scott's soldiers. In the ensuing altercation, some soldiers were killed and others wounded, while Tsali and his band sought refuge in the rugged Appalachian Mountains. In order to discourage this type of behavior, General Scott decided to make an example of Tsali. Younaguska, fearing that federal troops would have a difficult time distinguishing between his people (those legally mandated to remain east) and the wanted refugees, consented to aid in the search for Tsali and any other refugees hiding out in his territory. General Scott was receptive to this plan, sending Euchella and an armed contingent of Cherokees under the direction of Colonel Foster and his troops to find and punish Tsali. Euchella's group caught Tsali and, under federal pressure, executed him and all male members of the group with the exception of Tsali's youngest son. The females were placed in the Fort Scott stockade and later removed with the rest of the Cherokee Nation. As a reward for his services, Euchella and his men and their families were allowed to remain east along with

Younaguska's Cherokees. In some respects, Tsali thus became the savior of the Eastern Band through his sacrifice.[17]

In all, about a third of the North Carolina Cherokees elected to remain east, and of those, only a small proportion legally complied with the conditions set forth in the 1835 Treaty, that of registering individual land tracts (deeds) and filing for state citizenship. Apparently, these Cherokees only wanted to retain their old lifestyle and had little interest in adopting the legal and social structure of North Carolina.

Again, Thomas represented his adopted people in a paramount legal battle, this time before the North Carolina General Assembly. He argued successfully for the authority to have the North Carolina Cherokees incorporated into a state corporation with himself assigned the role of corporate president and trustee. This corporation later became known as "The Eastern Band of Cherokee Indians." Thomas then went to Washington, D. C., where in 1848 he got Congress to authorize an award of $53.33 for each North Carolina Cherokee listed on the original 1835 census. Thomas then was authorized by virtue of his executive position within the Cherokee corporation to use this money to purchase land for the Eastern Band. Better lands had by this time already been grabbed off by white settlers, and the Cherokees were left with more mountainous tracts. Those few Cherokees who bothered to register their land in compliance with the 1835 Treaty owned their land outright, but this only accounted for some 17,000 acres. In comparison, by 1850, 38,000 acres were purchased for the Eastern Band Corporation. However, Thomas deeded all this land to himself and not to the Cherokees, since by this time it was illegal for non-whites to own land in North Carolina. He also borrowed money to purchase this land, a loan Thomas never repaid, even when reimbursed by the United States Government.[18]

When the Cherokees expressed an interest in the Civil War, Thomas, obtaining the rank of colonel in the Confederacy, commanded a regiment which included a battalion of Cherokees, Thomas' Legion. It was after the War that the federal government started to investigate Thomas' accounts and his role as legal guardian of the Cherokee trust fund. During the federal investigation, Thomas, his health failing due to the war, was unable to appear before the investigative bodies. Realizing the danger of any individual being chosen guardian, the Eastern Cherokees invited the United States Government to serve as trustee, and the Cherokees took on reservation status.[18] Thomas' legal actions in behalf of the Eastern Band led to over a century of litigation which was finally resolved in 1973.

THE CONTEMPORARY SCENE:

Laurence French and Jim Hornbuckle

Introduction

The Cherokee Corporation ceased to exist in the eyes of the federal government in 1925, when the Eastern Band transferred all money, land and collective property to the federal government, which was to hold these assets in trust for them. The Eastern Band was now under federal sovereignty. Its federal reservation status was terminated by the 1924 Baker Roll. At this time, many felt that the Eastern Cherokees would receive a final allotment of land and money such as their western counterparts had received at the turn of the century. In anticipation of sharing in the resulting monetary settlement, many non-Indians joined the rolls by simply bribing those conducting the census. These "pseudo-Cherokees" are referred to as "five dollar Indians" even to this day. Fortunately, the Eastern Band was spared termination, and, instead, it came under federal protection and was changed from a state corporation into a federal reservation. The largest land tract is called the "Qualla Boundary." This, plus Snowbird, Tomotla and the 3,200 Acre (Thomas) Tract, comprise the Eastern Band of the Cherokee Indians' reservation.

The social conditions of the Eastern Band did not improve until the Great Depression, with the "Indian New Deal," and road building and other federally-sponsored programs (CCC and WPA). This work provided income to Cherokees who never before had held steady, paying jobs. Processed foods, store-bought clothing and other manufactured products now became the norm instead of the exception. Needless to say, the Cherokees welcomed this newfound prosperity.

These federally-sponsored work programs also helped to open up the otherwise isolated Southern Appalachian region. Ever since the late 1800's, state and federal plans had been prepared for a national park in this area. The reasons for a national park were to share the area's unique beauty with all Americans and to make the area more accessible to its indigenous population (white, Cherokees and Black). The Eastern Cherokees played an important role in the development of the Great Smoky Mountains National Park from the beginning. In 1899, the Eastern Band sold the 33,000-acre Love Speculation specifically for the purpose of an Appalachian park. Then, in 1933, North Carolina and Tennessee both transferred Southern Appalachian acreage to the federal government to be used for the park. It was during this time that Cherokee laborers began building the main access road (U. S. Route 441) through Cherokee territory to the proposed park site. And in order to ensure national regulation of both the proposed park and its main drawing card, the Cherokee Indians, the federal government assigned official reservation status to the Eastern Band in 1934 under the Wheeler-Howard Reorganization Bill. Thus, the stage was set for developing Southern Appalachia. These plans were contingent upon the development of the Tennessee Valley Authority; the Blue Ridge Parkway; the Great Smoky Mountains National Park; the Cherokee reservation; Gatlinburg, Tennessee and other towns as tourist attractions to the park. The Great Smoky Mountains National Park opened in 1938, transforming the Eastern Band from an isolated, obscure Indian group into the most visited Native American group in the United States.

The Qualla Boundary

Today, the Eastern Band is often referred to as the Qualla Boundary, but the millions of seasonal tourists know it mainly as "Cherokee." Altogether, the Eastern Band consists of some 56,500 acres held in federal trust for the Cherokees. Because of the Eastern Band's reservation status, the Cherokees are exempt from paying property taxes. Nevertheless, the tribal government levies its own sales tax, which is used for fire, police, sanitation and human services. The Cherokee schools are federally administered, as are health and other services. The two basic federal agencies serving the Qualla Boundary are the Bureau of Indian Affairs (B.I.A.) and Public Health Service (P.H.S.). These agencies serve the 7,000 Cherokees living on or near the reservation.

Cherokee families of the Eastern Band can be classified as either "affluent," "traditional" or "transitionary." The "affluent" Cherokees, while few in number, represent the phenomenal success of regional development in Southern Appalachia since the Great Depression. These are the families that profited from the tourist development. They live much like their successful white counterparts, owning beautiful homes and expensive automobiles and adhering to the business and social customs of the Protestant Ethic. They value education as a means to success, making certain that their children acquire proper, quality education. For many of these Cherokees, English is their only language. Actually, these Cherokees are not easily distinguishable from other middle class Americans.

The "traditional" Cherokees are those who have tried to preserve the old ways. They represented the vast majority of the Eastern Cherokees at the time of removal and were still a sizeable group until the advent of the Great Depression and the opening of the Great Smoky Mountains National Park. Today, about a third of the Eastern Band could be classified as "traditional," with the largest groups residing in the Snowbird and Big

27

Cove Communities. These Cherokees usually live in isolated coves away from the tourist scene. Children learn Cherokee as their first language, acquiring this and other attributes of their traditional culture within the family setting. Often, multigenerational families and close relatives share one of these small community clusters, dividing up domestic tasks. Fields, livestock and gardens, as well as the important skills necessary for a nearly self-sufficient lifestyle, are shared by the kinfolks. The old and the new coexist in a delicate balance between compulsory education and home apprenticeships, Christianity and traditional mythology, modern medicine and folk medicine, formal legal controls and customary law, federal subsistence and assistance and self-suffi iency and individual autonomy. What is amazing is the ability of these people to resolve these contradictory pressures and still maintain a close semblance of the old ways.

The "transitionary" Cherokees represent a new breed emerging with the tourist industry. They are Cherokees who do not fully belong to either the "affluent" or "traditional" classes. They are caught in a cultural lag. They are Indians, yet many cannot speak their native language and know little about their rich traditional culture. However, these same Cherokees have not sufficiently acquired the skills necessary to compete successfully within the larger dominant society. They are caught in between two cultural worlds. Although many of these people receive certain basic support through federal, state and tribal programs, this often is not enough. These Cherokees are an inadvertent product of the rapid economic and social change that has accompanied Southern Appalachia's new tourist status. A direct relationship seems to exist between the prevalence of social problem and personal maladjustments and the economic success of tourism in the area.

"Transitionary" Cherokees comprise the majority of the Eastern Band. Not all are caught up in the dire consequences of social problems and personality maladjustment. Many are seeking either to learn and preserve the old traditional ways or to acquire the skills necessary to compete in the larger white world. Another popular route for "transitionary" Cherokees is to combine the best of both worlds, to be bicultural, learning their native language and their rich heritage while also acquiring higher education so as to compete in the larger, dominant society.[19]

Most of the reservation is situated in rugged, highly vegetated mountainous terrain. In all, there are nine communities — Cherokee (Yellow Hill), Painttown, Soco, Big "Y", Big Cove, Birdtown, the 3,200-Acre Tract, Tomotla and Snowbird. All but Tomotla and Snowbird are located on the Qualla Boundary. Snowbird is 60 miles away, and Tomotla 80. Although the old clan system no longer plays an active role within the Eastern Cherokee tradition, some feel that certain of these communities were initially designed as "mother villages" in order to preserve the clan structure within the isolated Appalachian district after the bulk of the nation was removed west of the Mississippi River.

Cherokee is the business, administrative and tourist center of the Eastern Band. The two main access roads, U.S. Routes 19 and 441, pass through Cherokee, with the latter leading directly to the Blue Ridge Parkway, the Great Smoky Mountains National Park, and into Tennessee. Route 19 follows on through to Bryson City on its westward course and to Maggie Valley eastward, both local tourist attractions. On these two routes, lies the heaviest concentration of tourist attractions, including restaurants, gift shops and theme parks. These structures are colorful, often depicting Plains Indian teepees, Northwest Coast totem poles and Southwest thunderbirds. Cherokee men dressed in "war bonnets" stand outside these places of business as added attractions.

Both tribal and federal agencies are located in the Cherokee Community. These agencies plus the Qualla Co-op Gift Shop, the elementary school, the Indian Health Service Hospital, pharmacy, outpatient clinic, U.S. Post Office, banks and the Cherokee Historical Association office, as well as their new $1.5 million museum, are all situated in a congested section of Route 441, just where it makes a right angle off Route 19 heading toward the national park. Across the Oconaluftee River, another road known as the "backside" or Acquoni Road runs parallel to this section of Route 441. Located on this road are two of the three boundary industries, The Cherokees and White Shield of Carolina, as well as the vast Cherokee Boys Club facility, the Rescue Squad, most tribal services, the Qualla Civic Center, the Mutual Help Housing facility, the Children's Home Chapel, a cluster of gift shops and the new $7.5 million high school. Several bridges link these two parallel roads.

By taking the second bridge from the center of town and continuing along this road across Highway 441, one will end up in the large parking lot belonging to the Cherokee Historical Association and used for its enterprises—the Oconaluftee Indian Village and the outdoor drama *Unto These Hills*. Also located on Route 441, closer to the national park entrance, is "The Boundary Tree," a tribal enterprise consisting of a motel, service station, and restaurant complex. Continuing on Route 19 where it and 441 separate, one arrives at the new Holiday Inn facility. From this brief travelogue, one can imagine just how congested the Cherokee community can be during the peak of the tourist season. Yet, in spite of all these tourist and governmental structures, the community claims 828 permanent residents whose homes are nestled in little coves and clearings away from the main tourist strip.

The eight other communities are mainly residential, yet none of them, with the exception of Snowbird and Tomotla, totally escapes the outreaches of the tourist industry. Painttown closely challenges Cherokee with its commercial development. It has Frontierland, which is one of the Cherokee's major tourist attractions. The community is located on that part of Route 19 which goes east toward Soco and eventually out of the reservation and into Maggie Valley. Painttown has 774 permanent residents, who, again, mostly live off the main tourist route. Down the road is Soco Community, which is one of the largest on the boundary in size. Although some commercial enterprises continue to dot Route 19, most of Soco's residents live a considerable distance from the tourist trade. These 746 Cherokees live on Old Soco Road, Washington Creek Road, Blue Wing Road, Long Branch Road, Macedonia Road and Old Mission Road. The clusters of homes are often quite far apart, separated by dense woods, ridges and branches (brooks). Soco and Maggie Valley are, in turn, separated by a rugged ridge, and the transition from the reservation into the white settlement is quite spectacular. Many of Soco's residents are "traditional" Cherokees, and it is not unusual to see small, unpainted, yet sturdy cabins off in clearings. Many small wooden churches, mostly Baptist, are scattered throughout the community. There is no industry in Soco, but it does have a major tourist attraction, Santa's Land, which is close to the Painttown line on Route 19.

Big "Y" is the smallest boundary community with only 371 residents. These people live along Wright's Creek, Swimmer Branch and Big Witch Roads, separated from the tourist trade by a rugged mountainous terrain. There are no commercial attractions or industry in this community. It contains the tribal timber reserve, but no logging is allowed on it. Soco and Big "Y" are adjacent communities and form a single township or voting precinct known as the "Wolftown Township."

Physically, Big Cove is the largest community within the Eastern Band. It is one of the strongholds of the "traditional" Cherokees. Big Cove is a spectacular area with high rugged ridges surrounding it and only one access road. Those living in the most remote parts of this community must travel 14 miles to Cherokee, much of the distance over a meandering mountain road. Many of these Cherokees choose to remain isolated from the rest of Cherokee, especially from the tourist element. Many of its 709 residents share in a collective kinship subsistence organization, relying as little as possible on outside resources. Ironically, the deep mountain cove was once destined to become a tourist lake; but, fortunately, the Cherokees rebelled against this idea. This resistance by the Cherokees greatly altered the original National Park Service plans. The Blue Ridge Parkway, for example, was rerouted to terminate in the valley at Big Cove. The original plans were for the combined Sky Line Drive/Blue Ridge Parkway to pass through Virginia and North Carolina and into Tennessee. While this action saved Cherokee from being cut in half, it did not really hinder the tourist trade. Now the Blue Ridge Parkway and the Great Smoky Mountains National Park merge in Big Cove. Because of the situation, some campgrounds are located at the entrance of the Big Cove Community. Since these facilities are for tourists traveling in their own self-contained campers, fewer of the glittering attractions associated with the other tourist districts are found here. Moreover, the tourists and Big Cove residents seldom interact, unlike the other tourist situations on the reservation.

Birdtown Community is the most heavily populated community with 1,057 Cherokees living there. It is located in a wide valley providing an environment suitable for homes sites. Off the main tourist route, its roads, Adams Creek, Goose Creek and Old Route 4, provide access for the local residents. Yet, even this Indian "suburban" community is feeling the tremendous pressure of the tourist industry and its effort to expand and absorb even more of Cherokee's restricted land area. Motels, crafts shops, restaurants and campgrounds have recently found their way into Birdtown. Several Baptist churches and a few general stores serve the particular needs of the Indian population.

The seventh community, Snowbird, is located some 60 miles away from the Qualla Boundary. It is located in Graham County, west of Jackson and Swain Counties, which encompass the Qualla Boundary. Since this tightly knit community of 463 Cherokees does not participate in the tourist trade, it comes the closest, along with Big Cove, to representing how things were for the Eastern Cherokees during their first century of isolation (1835-1935). The traditional ways are still quite strong among these Cherokees. Interestingly, young Snowbird Cherokees are compelled to attend the local public school (Graham County Schools). Yet, in spite of this exposure to the very conservative white mountain community value system, most of these Cherokees survive with their own native cultural heritage intact.

Not far from Snowbird is a small contingent of Cherokees residing in the adjacent western county, Cherokee County, in the Tomotla community. While living closer to Snowbird than to the Qualla Boundary, these 149 Cherokees have little in common with either group. Most are referred to as "White Indians," as are many on the Qualla Boundary, meaning it is difficult to distinguish them both physically and culturally from their white neighbors.

Another sizeable trust area is the 3,200 Acre Tract, technically part of Birdtown, located close to the Qualla Boundary in Swain County. It is, however, separated from the boundary by "deeded" land. The 162 residents live in homes scattered along the ridges making up this tract. These Cherokees either go to the boundary or to adjacent white communities for their everyday needs. Nonetheless, they have access to the Birdtown Community regarding any tribal privileges such as voting. All told, over 5,000 registered Eastern Cherokees officially reside on the reservation. Another 2,000 live near the reservation, some on their own deeded property, and the total tribal enrollment may top 8,000.

Tribal Government

The Qualla Boundary, the 3,200-Acre Tract, Snowbird and Tomotla are divided into six voting precincts: Yellowhill, Big Cove, Birdtown, Wolftown, Painttown and Cheroah. Yellowhill is the precinct name for Cherokee Community, Wolftown is a single precinct for Soco and Big "Y" Communities and Cheroah is the precinct for Snowbird Community and the Cherokee County settlement of Tomotla. Birdtown includes the 3,200-Acre Tract. Each precinct or "township" elects two representatives to the Tribal Council every two years. This is done through general elections in which all enrolled residents of these townships who are 18 years old or older can vote. Elections are determined by a mere plurality, and many elections have been won by a single vote.

To qualify for council, a Cherokee must be an enrolled resident of his or her precinct, 21 years old or older and at least 1/16 Eastern Cherokee (blood degree). The 12 elected councilmen then select their own officers: a chairman, a vice chairman, both Indian and English clerks, an interpreter, a marshal, a messenger, a janitor and an officer manager. All six precincts also participate in the election of the Principal Chief and Vice Chiefs who serve four-year terms. Again, a mere plurality of the votes is all that is required to be elected.

To be eligible to run for either Principal or Vice Chief, a Cherokee must be an enrolled member of the Eastern Band, 35 years old or older and at least 1/2 Eastern Cherokee (blood degree). Once elected, the Principal Chief selects his executive advisor whose appointment must be ratified by the Tribal Council. Thus, Cherokee tribal government consists of a 12-member Tribal Council and a three-member Executive Committee, an organizational structure that corresponds closely to the original system first established in the 1820's. The Tribal Council is similar to the old National Council, or lower house, while the Executive Committee corresponds closely to the old National Committee, or upper house. The major differences is the size of the two systems. It would not be feasible today to have a large council or committee.

Thus, the current system actually represents a reduced model of the old national system.

Tribal government handles the day-to-day operations of the reservation, doing so through boards and committees. Enrolled members can approach individual board or committee members or introduce resolutions at the regular Tribal Council meetings, which are open to the public. Interestingly, the Cherokee form of government during both aboriginal and present times has long used American-style democratic practices. Today, close parallels can be found between the New England "town meeting" form of local government and that of the Cherokee Tribal Council meetings. It should be noted, however, that the federal government, through the Secretary of the Interior and the Bureau of Indian Affairs, has the ultimate voice regarding major tribal resolutions. While the Tribal Council has the authority to receive and pass resolutions, these must be approved by both the Principal Chief and the Bureau of Indian Affairs' Superintendent and then forwarded to the Secretary of the Interior for approval. The Executive Committee and Tribal Council, on the other hand, have virtually total control over the administration of federal and state grant programs as well as the regulation of tribal enterprises.

Tribal Government Model of the Eastern Band of Cherokee Indians

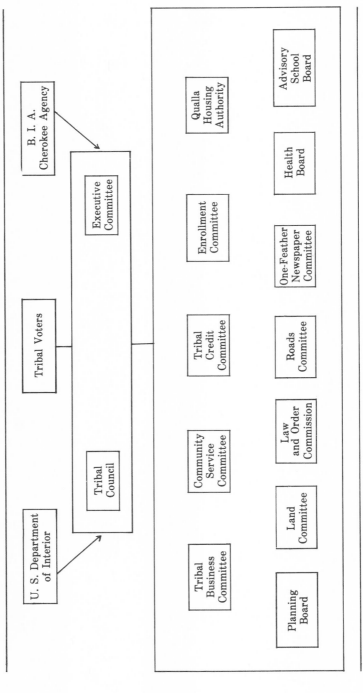

The Role of Tourism

Today, the Eastern Cherokees are the most visited American Indian group in the United States, and this is due mainly to their tourist image. Tourism has proved to be a mixed blessing to the Cherokees. While it has brought a new level of prosperity to the tribe, it has also been the source of increased social problems. But given a choice today, few Cherokees would elect to go back to the old pre-Depression days when poverty, hardship and isolation were the Cherokees' lot. Today, many are optimistic that somewhere within their complex contemporary lifestyles lie the solutions to the Cherokees' problems. Perhaps this is so. At any rate, a new breed of Cherokee, born during the tourist realm, has emerged, determined to work toward maintaining this new level of prosperity while at the same time alleviating the sources of mental and social problems among his people. If this happens, then the Appalachian Plan, conceived in the last century, finally will have fulfilled its original purpose of opening up this once remote area so that both the indigenous population (whites, Blacks and Cherokees) and outsiders can share in its natural beauty while at the same time raising the standard of living of those once isolated within these mountain communities.

Tourism has created a situation similar to the old aboriginal days, that of a dualistic year. Again, the year is divided into two distinctive seasons, summer and winter. That is one of the problems with tourism; the employment is seasonal and the pay poor. Today, the summer is the tourist season, and during the six months from April to October, millions of tourists converge on Cherokee. Recently, the seasonal total reached eleven million people. Then, as if thrown back into time, the reservation is again suddenly transformed into a remote, often desolate, setting during the winter season. This cyclic impact of tourism has had adverse psychological, cultural, social and economic effects on the Cherokees, the nature of which will be discussed later in this section. First, let us look at the "tourist situation."

There are actually two tourist circuits in Cherokee, one designed for the average "blue collar" tourist seeking escapism and another which caters to the more sophisticated tastes of the tourist elite (middle and upper classes). The main tourist strip appeals to the majority of the visitors—the average tourists. Here, families shop, talk and eat in a festive atmosphere, buy trinkets and have their pictures taken with "chiefs." For these people, Cherokee is a fun place that gives them a chance to get away from it all.

In certain respects, Cherokee has been a tourist attraction ever since the first white contact when traders and trappers found the Cherokees to be an enjoyable, yet curious, group. Today, tourists still feel excitement in being among the Indians. People's fantasies often run wild, some seeing the Cherokees as proud and noble Native Americans, others viewing them as barbaric savages. Few tourists make any distinction between Cherokees and other Indian groups, since their knowledge of Native Americans is frequently based upon media stereotypes. The public's fascination with Indian culture, as portrayed by the media, makes Cherokee a popular tourist attraction and the Cherokees the most visited American Indian group in this country. The proprietors of the tourist attractions take full advantage of this fact. Millions of tourists leave Cherokee believing that they have, in fact, visited an authentic Indian village, one that is representative of our nation's nearly 800,000 Native Americans. To make matters worse, about one-third of all Cherokee tourist enterprises are white-owned or leased, and these comprise the largest money-making operations.

The other tourist attraction offers an alternative to the street tourist scene. Through the establishment of the Cherokee Historical Association, a non-profit organization, an attempt has been made to provide a cultural tourist environment, one that distinguishes between the authentic Cherokee culture and the media Indian image presented in the streets. The Cherokee Historical Association was formed to preserve the original Cherokee culture through the creation of three tourist offerings: the drama *Unto These Hills*, the Oconaluftee Indian Village and the new $1.5 million Cherokee Museum. The idea for the drama originated with Foght's Appalachian Plan, and the stage script was later written by Kermit Hunter, a graduate student at the University of North Carolina.

Unto These Hills is an emotional portrayal of the history of the Cherokees, from initial white contact in 1540 up until the Removal and the establishment of the Eastern Band of Cherokee Indians. A similar production, *The Trail of Tears*, was later developed for tourists visiting the Western Cherokees in Tahlequah, Oklahoma. The Oconaluftee Indian Village is located next to the Mountainside Theatre, which produces *Unto These Hills*. Here the Cherokee Historical Association has created a replica of an early eighteenth century Cherokee community. The village opened in 1952 and, like the drama, has proved to be a success among the tourists visiting the Qualla Boundary. The most recent (June, 1976) addition to the Cherokee Historical Association's tourist enterprises is the $1.5 million museum located on the main tourist route (441) in the Cherokee community.

One of the most interesting phenomena associated with Cherokee tourism is that of "chiefing." Here, phenotypical Indian males dress up in colorful Plains Indian garb, including the full-feathered bonnet of a war chief. Some Cherokees refer to these pseudo-chiefs as "grasshopper chiefs" or "postcard chiefs." The former label reflects the fact that these chiefs come out in the spring and disappear in the winter much like a grasshopper. This is a full-time seasonal employment for about two dozen Cherokee males, while dozens of others do it on a part-time basis. It is hard work since the "chief" often has other obligations to the shop sponsoring him, such as janitorial services, and he is apt to work 12-hour days, seven days a week.

Apparently, "chiefing" was one of the "Indian attractions" mentioned in Dr. Foght's Appalachian Plan. The first "chiefs" appeared with the parkway and the Great Smoky Mountains National Park right after World War II. It is alleged that Tom Jumper was the first "chief." Today, "Chief Henry" claims to be the most photographed Indian chief in the world. Not all "chiefs" are as successful as "Chief Henry," yet chiefing does provide a livelihood for men who otherwise might not be employed during the tourist season. The "chiefs" make most of their money from tips paid by tourists who photograph and pose with them. The usual tip is 25 cents, although substantially larger tips are not uncommon. Most "chiefs" stand beside a fake teepee located in front of the shop sponsoring them, waving to tourists, enticing the travelers to visit them and the shop. Signs indicate that tips are required when photographing the "chiefs," and some have even devised unique acts such as group dances where the hat is passed after the performance. Other shops employ Cherokee girls dressed as "Indian princesses." While some Cherokees feel that "chiefing" is a degrading profession, others justify it because it brings money into the community. One thing is certain and that is the fact that thousands of tourists leave Cherokee glad that they had the opportunity to talk with a friendly "chief," many coming back year after year repeating this process.

Overall, tourism seems to be both disruptive and beneficial to the Qualla Cherokees. Its contradictory nature provides a challenge for future generations of Cherokees. Hopefully, they will be able to resolve this dilemma within the present framework of cultural, social, economic and personal interaction.

Cherokee Progress

Once separated from the larger Cherokee Nation following Removal, the Eastern Cherokees attempted to reinstate the old village cooperative system known as the Gadugi. Earlier, it was stated that the entire village cooperated in the aboriginal agricultural endeavor. This system of cooperative agriculture was merely an attempt to preserve that system. Part of the reason for this was the need to consolidate land and other limited resources facing the isolated mountain Cherokees. Eventually, white expansion and development offered an alternative to the Cherokees' limited cooperative farming endeavors. Cherokee males now were hired out as day laborers. Eventually, the Gadugi collapsed when the State of North Carolina began taxing them as corporations. This led to the decline of the once prosperous Cherokee community farms. Later, the federal Indian agency attempted to develop community farm organizations as a substitute for the Gadugi system. The federal program could not, however, replace the old Gadugi system; and, as a result, the Cherokee economy declined during the first three decades of this century.[20]

Federal dependency started with the takeover of the educational system in the late 1800's, continued with the community farm organization project and culminated in the Eastern Band's reservation status in 1925. The public works program of the Great Depression finally pulled Cherokee out if its economic slump. This progress was shortlived, however, with the war economy eliminating many of the public works programs and with the new park program severely restricting logging operations. Ironically, as the tourist industry opened up Southern Appalachia, bringing thousands of outsiders into Cherokee on a seasonal basis, the average Cherokee initially benefited little from this. Consequently, the Eastern Band suffered another economic depression during the recession of the mid and late 1950's. This situation was exacerbated by the closing of the Indian boarding schools under the new federal termination program. The fear of termination and the elimination of some federal programs forced the Eastern Band to initiate its own economic measures.

In 1952, the tribe imposed its own sales tax in order to provide police, fire, sanitation and recreational facilities for the Cherokees. The tax, originally three percent, was raised to four percent in 1970. Now, three-fourths of the tax supports Cherokee tribal community services, while the remaining one-fourth goes to the Cherokee Tribal Council fund for administrative purposes. The tribal levy, plus lease revenues for white-run tourist businesses and for logging stumpage, provides the major tribal monies. Tribal enterprises such as the Boundary Tree motel, gas station and restaurant and federal and state sponsored human services programs (grant-operated) also contribute to Cherokee's current economic and social environment. The reinstatement of federal programs greatly aided the Cherokees in the mid-1960's. Today, educational and health needs are furnished largely by federal agencies.

Light industry was brought to the reservation during the mid and late 1950's and early 1960's. In 1956, a tourist-related industry, Saddlecraft, established itself in Cherokee, producing moccasins and other craft items to be sold in the local market during the tourist season. It has since changed its name to The Cherokees and now has a nationwide distribution of its goods.

Later, in 1959, White Shield Industry was established and, in 1963, Vassar Corporation joined the Cherokee industrial complex. While these industries proved to be a blessing during the depressed 1950's and early 1960's, many Cherokees today feel the low pay and the companies' opposition to unionization make them less attractive employers.

The mid and late 1960's witnessed a tourist boom in Cherokee; and, to accompany this, new attractions suddenly appeared, including Frontierland, Santa's Land and the Holiday Inn, as well as numerous new motels, restaurants, shops and campgrounds. Today, there are more than 200 separate tourist attractions located on the Qualla Boundary. As the tourist industry expanded, so did the tourist trade; and, by 1972, eight million people visited Cherokee during its tourist season. Remote Cherokee settlements such as Snowbird, Tomotla and the 3,200-Acre Tract are without any tourism or industry, causing permanent hardships for their unemployed. It is estimated that the overall employment distribution for the tribe is as follows:

Manufacturing of nondurable
   tourist-related goods 25%
Professional and related services 21%
Other industries 15%
Manufacturing of durable goods 10%
Personal services 10%
Construction 9%
Wholesale and retail trade 6%
Agriculture and forestry 2%
Transportation, communication
   and utilities 2%

The six-month tourist season provides 90 percent of the reservation's income. This has created a situation in which some Cherokees live quite well during the summer, but are unemployed and socially depressed during the winter off-season. For some Indians, the tourist business is quite lucrative, leading, as mentioned earlier, to a number of affluent Cherokees. Increased tourism has also affected the traditional Cherokees who would prefer to remain apart from tourism and outside influences. As more land is ceded to the tourist industry, it is becoming increasingly difficult for traditional Cherokees to remain isolated. At the present time, only one percent of the total reservation (56,000 acres) is used for the purpose of agriculture. Even the family garden has been abandoned by most Cherokee families. Not one Cherokee family makes it livelihood solely from farming.

This is the cost of progress. Some feel that the only answer to the dilemma is better educational opportunities for the Cherokees, while others suggest abandoning tourism and other white customs and returning to the old ways. Any realistic program will most certainly have to incorporate both the dominant contemporary societal values as well as the Cherokees' rich cultural heritage. This blueprint for the future is not only possible, it has already begun. Recent federal programs have provided quality homes for many Cherokees and have improved transportation by surfacing hundreds of miles of reservation access roads. Such measures, together with the Cherokees' renewed interest in their own culture, provide an atmosphere of progress.[21]

REFERENCES AND NOTES FOR CHAPTER ONE

1. Since no accurate census was possible at the time of the white contact, 20,000 is a liberal estimate of the Cherokees at that time, while conservative estimates range between 16,000 and 18,000. Also see Glen Fleischmann, *The Cherokee Removal, 1838* (New York: Franklin Watts, Inc., 1971); James Mooney, *Myths of the Cherokee and Sacred Formulas of the Cherokees* (Nashville: Charles Elder Reprints, 1972); Douglas Rights, *The American Indian of North Carolina* (Durham: Duke University Press, 1947); and John Phillip Reid, *A Better Kind of Hatchet* (University Park: Pennsylvania State University Press, 1976), p. 2.

2. See Douglas C. Rights, *The American Indian of North Carolina* (Durham: Duke University Press, 1947) and James Mooney, *Myths of the Cherokee and Sacred Formulas of the Cherokees* (Nashville: Charles Elder Reprints, 1972).

3. Also see Duane King and Laura Hill, "The Mythico-Religious Origin of the Cherokees," *Appalachian Journal, Special Cherokee Issue* 2, no. 4 (Summer 1975): 259-264.

4. Most early documentation on the aboriginal Cherokee lifestyle came from the diaries, letters and memoirs of James Adair, Wiliam Fyffe and Henry Timberlake. Also see Grace Steele Woodward, *The Cherokees* (Norman: University of Oklahoma, 1963).

5. See Fred Gearing, *Priests and Warriors* (American Anthropological Association, vol. 64, no. 5, part 2, October 1962) and James Mooney, *Myths of the Cherokee and Sacred Formulas of the Cherokees* (Nashville: Charles Elder Reprints, 1972).

6. See John Reid, *A Law of Blood* (New York: New York University Press, 1970) and Fred Gearing, *Priests and Warriors* (American Anthropological Association, vol. 64, no. 5, part 2, October 1962).

7. See John Reid, "A Family Writ Large," *A Law of Blood* (New York: New York University Press, 1970).

8. See Grace Steele Woodward, *The Cherokees* (Norman: University of Oklahoma Press, 1963), pp. 48-50.

9. See Fred Gearing, *Priests and Warriors* (American Anthropological Association, vol. 64, no. 5, part 2, October 1962); James Mooney, *Myths of the Cherokees and Sacred Formulas of the Cherokees* (Nashville: Charles Elder Reprints, 1972); and Robert K. Thomas, "Eastern Cherokee Acculturation," (Master's Thesis, University of North Carolina, 1958).

10. See Gary B. Nash, *Red, White and Black: The Peoples of Early America* (Englewood Cliffs, NJ: Prentice Hall, 1974) and Almon W. Lauber, *Indian Slavery in Colonial Times* (Williamstown, MA: Corner House Press, 1970). Nash noted that in 1708 the Carolina colony consisted of 5,300 whites, 2,900 African slaves and 1,400 Indian slaves. Moreover, most male Indian slaves were sent out of their colony of capture because of the fear of escape or insurrection (p. 112). Lauber went on to claim that Cherokees were made slaves to their white captors until the 1760's.

11. See Glen Fleischmann, *The Cherokee Removal, 1838* (New York: Franklin Watts, Inc., 1971); Grace Steele Woodward, *The Cherokees* (Norman: University of Oklahoma Press, 1963); Henry Thomas Malone, *Cherokees of the Old South* (Athens: University of Georgia Press, 1956); Edward Dale and Gaston Little, *Cherokee Cavaliers* (Norman: University of Oklahoma Press, 1939); John Reid, *A Law of Blood* (New York: New York University Press, 1970); James Mooney *Myths of the Cherokee and Sacred Formulas of the Cherokees* (Nashville: Charles Elder Reprints, 1972); and John P. Brown, *Old Frontiers* (Kingsport, TN: Southern Publishers, Inc., 1938).

12. See Peter Collier, *When Shall They Rest* (New York: Holt, Rinehart & Winston, 1973).

13. See Bernard W. Sheehan, *Seeds of Extinction* (New York: W. W. Norton, 1974); also see Henry Malone, *Cherokees of the Old South* (Athens: University of Georgia Press, 1956).

14. See James Mooney, *Myths of the Cherokee and Sacred Formulas of the Cherokees* (Nashville: Charles Elder Reprints, 1972), p. 130.

15. See John P. Brown, *Old Frontiers* (Kingsport, TN: Southern Publishers, Inc., 1938); Glen Fleischmann, *The Cherokee Removal, 1838* (New York: Franklin Watts, Inc., 1971); and Peter Collier, *When Shall They Rest* (New York: Holt, Rinehart & Winston, 1973).

16. See Douglas C. Rights, *The American Indian of North Carolina* (Durham: Duke University Press, 1947), p. 193.

17. See Denton R. Bedford, *Tsali* (San Francisco: The Indian Historian Press, 1972).

18. See Fred B. Bauer, *Land of the North Carolina Cherokees* (Brevard, NC: George E. Buchanan Press, 1970). The late Fred Bauer was a former Vice-Chief of the Eastern Band of Cherokee Indians.

19. See John Gulick, "The Cherokee Reservation: Its Nature and History," *Cherokees at the Crossroads* (Chapel Hill: University of North Carolina Press, 1960), pp. 1-22; and Harriett Kupferer, *The "Principal People," 1960* (Anthropological Papers, no. 78, *Bureau of Ethnology Bulletin* 196), pp. 215-325.

20. See "The Free Labor Companies," in John Gulick, *Cherokees at the Crossroads* (Chapel Hill: University of North Carolina Press, 1960), pp. 89-90.

21. See "Population and Economy Study," *Comprehensive Plan -Volume I* (Cherokee, NC: Eastern Band of Cherokee Indians, 1974).

CHAPTER II

Comments on the Cherokee Way of Life

EDUCATION
The Cherokee Boarding School:

*Karen French Owl**

The Cherokee Boarding School began in 1881. It was built by Quakers from Indiana—the Society of Friends—and operated by them until June 30, 1892. The Quakers were not permitted to operate the school after 1892 because Chief Nimrod Jarrett Smith vetoed a resolution by the Tribal Council for the continued operation of the school.

The Quakers' control of Cherokee schools ended for basically two reasons: a controversy surrounding the abilities of the local Quaker Superintendent for Education and the end of the "Quaker Policy" on the national level which began a trend away from missionary, non-Indian schools to federally-operated ones.

After Quaker control ended, the federal government took over the school under the direction of the Bureau of Indian Affairs. In 1892, there were 13 teachers at the school, nine females and four males. The teachers' salaries were $30 per month.

The school was operated in a military manner. Students wore uniforms; the girls had different colored dresses to wear for each activity, and the boys had different colored shirts. The students reported for roll call at various times of the day. The daily schedule was as follows:

5:00 - 9:00 a.m.	Breakfast and work detail
9:00 - 11:15 a.m.	Classes
11:15 - 12:00 noon	Lunch
12:30 - 1:30 p.m.	Individual work detail
1:30 - 4:00 p.m.	Afternoon classes
4:00 - 6:00 p.m.	Supper
6:30 - 7:00 p.m.	Recreation
7:00 - 8:00 p.m.	Study hour
8:30 p.m.	Lights out

The students were assigned work stations and reported to their stations at least twice a day, depending upon their work detail. The school had its own bakery, kitchen, dairy and garden; and the students actively competed for the better work assign-

* This information was obtained from Ms. Owl's uncle, Carl Lambert, the Cherokee Historian. It was transcribed from taped oral conversations.

ment in these areas. The students provided most of their own food products and performed much of the maintenance of their school facilities.

Their classes consisted primarily of basics in mathematics, reading and language usage (English only). Students were punished for speaking Cherokee; some had their mouths washed with soap for speaking Cherokee and some were beaten. Boys received instruction in agriculture while girls took home economics.

All students attending the school were not boarding students. Those who lived nearby came to the school during the day and went home each evening. These day students were permitted to wear their own clothing and were not expected to wear the uniforms provided by the school. By the 1930's, community-based day schools were firmly established, and boarding school attendance was beginning to decline. The boarding school had so few students in the early 1950's that it was discontinued in 1954. This was the same year that bus service was provided for the community day schools. Each community school now had students from various parts of the reservation.

When the buildings are gone, all that will remain of the Cherokee Boarding School will be the memories of those students who attended. Former students of the boarding school have mixed feelings about their times at the school. Most of them did not like going to the school, mainly because they did not get to see their homes and families except on the weekends when family members were allowed to take them home. Their freedom to explore the mountains and streams was curtailed. Nonetheless, many former students attribute their successes in life to the boarding school. They state that they would not be where they are today without having attended the boarding school.

Educational Needs of the American Indians: Anonymous Cherokee Educator

It is my opinion, established by my personal education, formal and informal, plus having served as an educator for 18 years, that the educational needs of the American Indian can best be summed up by the following. Of course, this list is not necessarily in order of importance.

> 1. *Develop a program that will change the American Indian's behavior patterns. It is generally accepted that the American Indians are passive in nature. So, they need to develop a more aggressive attitude. I do not mean that they should become more hostile. But they should set higher and more realistic goals/standards and start clawing and scratching to reach them.*

45

2. *We need to develop a system whereby we get qualified Indians into the mainstream of life. We must develop quality programs that put Indians in positions that can affect change. Allow the qualified Indians to determine their own destiny. But we need to develop programs for the American Indians that will ensure that we get qualified Indians making these decisions. As of now, the white man is still dictating the policies that directly or indirectly affect the American Indian's entire life.*

3. *Take the "tom foolery" out of the Indian Preference Act. This is one of the most ill advised moves that the federal government has come up with. Sure, it looks good on paper, but the fact is that this rewards mediocrity. American Indians are being elevated into positions in which the only qualification that they have is their degree of Indian blood. Consequently, the entire program is going down the drain. And I am not at all sure that this is not the overall plan of the bureaucracy. Think about it! The American Indians are making an attempt to come out of their shells, determine their own futures, so to speak. This move is sure to be defeated if the present trend is allowed to continue. We do not have the numbers of qualified American Indians required to handle the intricate details involved in the implementation of programs and the restructuring of future programs to meet the rapidly changing needs of the American Indian.*

4. *A change in the present "Something for Nothing" policy. There must be a great effort made toward changing the American Indian's outlook toward life. Not only should he be motivated to achieve, but how and why to achieve. When one is given the chance to succeed, it has a tendency to "blind" one's perspective to the old cliché of "paying the price." Failure loses its significance when it is "free." The American Indian must be taught the importance of "earning" one's own way. Success has an entirely different meaning to the individual who succeeds by his own initiative.*

5. *The American Indian must be taught to live in the present and for the future, not in the past. Of course, teach him that his cultural heritage is very important, to be proud of it and help preserve it for future generations. But, as badly as I hate to say it, we live in, and are governed by, the laws of a white society. Therefore, if we are to take our rightful place beside the white man in all aspects of society, we must think and act like our counterparts.*

46

6. *Formal education plays a vital role in the future of our American Indian people. I am an advocate of the multitrack educational system. Too often we find that educators teach to only one section of the curve, teaching, for example, college preparatory subjects and foolishly forgetting that a far greater percentage of the students have very little, if any, desire to enter college. The other students "root hog or die." Consequently, we have self-appointed experts teaching those few things the educator feels are important, but not necessarily important to the student. We must develop the vocational aspects of Indian education. Also, the law of supply and demand in the work world should be stressed. Do not teach a student to be a computer programmer unless you also teach him that in order to succeed, in this particular field, he will have to leave the reservation. It is pointless and a waste of time and money to teach an Indian professional fundamentals only to have him return to the reservation to lace drums or go on welfare.*

7. *Education committees are another form of "trickery" the bureaucrats have dreamed up to add to their long lists of charades. The American Indian Education Committees are in no way, shape or form equal to their white counterparts. These committees exist in name only and their only function is as consultants. The Indian is allowed to recommend; but the final choice, in matters of importance, remains in the hands of the white man.*

8. *The Bureau of Indian Affairs has a rule that Indian employees cannot hold tribal office. Here again the bureaucrats, even if it is unintentional, have developed a system to keep the Indian in his place. The most qualified Indians that we have, by their degree of formal and/or informal training, are employed by the federal government. Consequently, our tribal affairs are being conducted by incompetent, uneducated Indians, not by design but by necessity. Now, this is not to say that we do not have any qualified Indian administrators. But I am positive they are the exceptions rather than the rule.*

In summary, I would hasten to add that this is only one man's opinion, and the only way I can qualify my philosophy is from my experiences and the fact that I was born and raised on an Indian reservation. If this does not earn the right to an opinion, nothing will.

I can state freely, without reservation (no pun intended), that the American Indian can only better himself by learning to understand the white man's way of life; learn to stand on his own two feet; develop the feeling that if there is someone ahead of him, he is in the wrong place; reach down, grab his boot tops and start pulling; stop standing around waiting for someone to offer him a better life, free of charge and requiring little or no effort on his part; stop feeling that because his ancestors were mistreated the world owes him a living. In other words, if the American Indian is ever to reach goals/levels in comparison to his white counterparts, he must accept the fact that his counterparts have risen to their status by dedication and hard work, not by feeling sorry for themselves and that no one gave it to them.

I fully realize that a lot of my people would take issue with a lot of what I have said. And it pains me to have to say these things. Nevertheless, I am convinced that this is the situation as it is today.

Cultural Clash in Education:

Laurence French and Jim Hornbuckle

Introduction

The Protestant Ethic exemplifies the official policy of the paternalistic federal and state agencies mandated to regulate their Indian wards. These agencies subscribe to the Protestant Ethic and its values of achievement, motivation, and educational, occupational, financial and material success. They attempt to implant these cultural values through secondary institutions, making certain to maintain a social and often physical distance between them and the group they are regulating. This formal separation between the regulators and the regulated often succeeds in generating an insurmountable communication gap. The lack of primary interaction between the two groups denies either group the opportunity to empathize with the other. And the flow of communication in these situations is usually one-way, initiated by the dominant regulating agencies and directed toward the dependent, subordinate group. This is unfortunate, since these regulating agencies seldom receive or solicit needed information and feedback from those they are regulating. Hence, the reservation system shares many of the shortcomings Goffman (1961) associated with total institutions. A small elite group of regulators determine policy according to their beliefs and cultural perspectives, while maintaining rigid physical and social distance between themselves and those being regulated. The irony is that these systems are nourished by their failure. Prisons, mental hospitals and Indian reservations all have as their clients social members who are considered to be deficient in some respect, according to the dominant normative structure. Therefore, they are perceived as needing special training in order to overcome their shortcomings. Yet once they have been subjected to these institutional environments, their chances of recovery or adjustment become all the more remote. This is because there is a vast difference between what these institutions are mandated to do and what they actually accomplish. Ideally, Indian reservations are designed to prepare Indian wards to adapt to the competitive white world. Actually, the opposite occurs. Instead of teaching independence, reservations foster dependency. The more Indians are subjected to the regulatory agencies, the more they become dependent upon them.

Goffman (1961) feels that white self-interest plays an important role here. Prisons, mental hospitals and Indian reservations provide high status jobs for many members of the dominant majority society, and each of these types of institutions have, in fact, evolved over the years into multi-million dollar enterprises. Like any other large business enterprise, these regulatory institutions believe in progress, growth and, most importantly, survival. If prisons, mental hospitals and Indian reservations performed their jobs and, in fact, adequately prepared their clients to become self-sufficient members of the larger society, then these institutions would diminish in numbers and size in direct proportion to their effectiveness. But, by making their clients dependent upon them, these institutions guarantee their own existence, and even their own expansion, since they produce their own failures. White-dominated Indian reservations, then, like mental hospitals and prisons, become custodial and not treatment institutions.

Crucial to all these dependent institutions is the stripping process whereby the individual is psychologically stripped of his or her homeworld identity. For American Indians this involves being denied their cultural heritage. For Native Americans, the stripping process involves many structured programs, from beating them or washing out their mouths for speaking their native language, to the more subtle, "progressive" programs such as "follow through," in which the young Indian child is overwhelmed with the Protestant Ethic during those susceptible early years in school (kindergarten through third grade). Nevertheless, all of these programs produce a similar result, that of creating confused, dependent, marginal Indians.

These programs fail because once they strip the Indian of his cultural identity, denying him access to his people's ways and hence his own psychological security, the regulating agencies fail to fill this void with a viable substitute. And even if they did adequately prepare the Indian for white middle-class America, there is no guarantee that the dominant society would accept the Indian. Since few are adequately prepared, most are socialized to live an adolescent existence. Federal paternalism creates adolescent wards who are torn between the arbitrary expectations of adult responsibility and those of childhood dependency. One has only to examine the behavior of reservation Indians to see how effective this program of federal paternalism has been. Certainly, these once proud people did not manifest these traits prior to the reservation system.

The nature and extent of white secondary controls have varied over time but nonetheless have had a tremendous impact on the Eastern Band. Secondary controls represent formal institutions mandated to carry out specified functions. Educational, economic, religious, legal and human service institutions are some of the most significant institutions within our larger society. These functions were once performed by the basic primary unit—the family. Urbanization and industrialization have changed this arrangement, replacing the multi-faceted extended family with the small nuclear model. The nuclear family, as a separate unit, could no longer provide for all these needs; therefore, people became dependent on outside, or secondary, agencies for these services. Thus, a basic difference between folk and Western-type societies is the way in which basic community needs are met. Folk societies, such as the early Cherokee model, provide for most of these needs within the context of the extended family situation, while in Western societies separate, secondary institutions have emerged to provide these needs, mainly as a result of the limitations associated with their smaller family units.

Social theorists have long associated distinct cultural ethics with these two types of societies, suggesting that the folk societies are comprised mainly of primary and informal social controls, while urban/industrialized, Western-type societies dichotomize primary (family and peer groups) and secondary (education, economic, religion, legal and service institutions) controls. Durkheim (1901) emphasized the significance of the "collective will" or a primary concensus among folk societies. Sumner (1910) called this process "folkways." This clearly describes the aboriginal controls utilized by the early Cherokees. Secondary controls, in contrast, rely on formal organizations, bureaucracies, rules and regulations, all coordinated within a rigid division of labor designed to facilitate a specific institutional philosophy, policy or function.

There is little doubt that the educational institution is our most powerful secondary control organization. Compulsory education laws require a minimum of ten years in school, exposing the child to these controls at a very young and susceptible age. In fact, the most crucial formative years are spent in school. Most would agree that education certainly is beneficial to both the student and the society, for a high literacy rate is an asset to any cultural group. But, one must keep in mind that the educational process involves more than merely learning academic subjects; the school is one of the most powerful socializing agencies in our society, second only to the family. Herein lies the educational dilemma. Often, the socializing factor outweighs the academic function leading to a counterproductive situation. School systems which place strong emphasis on rigid cultural controls usually generate hostile academic environments that produce failure and bitterness instead of intellectual fulfillment. The early mission and federally-run Indian schools were of this type. Education was not an end in itself, but rather was seen as the primary vehicle for resocialization.

These types of educational institutions were first started in the late 1700's as a service to the entire Cherokee Nation and continued to develop until Removal. Educational efforts were reestablished among the Qualla Cherokees in the late 1800's with the Quakers' endeavor to civilize and educate the Eastern Cherokees. At this time, the "Friends" entered into a ten-year contractual agreement with both the Cherokees and the federal Indian Agency, establishing the physical institutions and academic models that were absorbed by the federal government after the Quakers' contract was terminated in 1892. This model included both a centralized boarding school and community day schools. The school system limped along in the interim decade until it came officially under total federal control in 1901, a situation which has continued to the present. The joint boarding school and day school system continued into the early 1950's when a new consolidated day school system replaced this older model.

Discipline and white enculturation were the methods of the old system. Children were sent to school as early as ages three and four and remained in school until the eighth grade. No high schools were available under the old system, although a few gifted Cherokee students had access to outside high schools and colleges. But, for most students, school was a harrowing experience. Enculturation was pursued with zeal, and children were whipped and had their mouths washed out with soap for speaking Cherokee. Ostensibly, this method was effective, since most elements of the traditional Cherokee culture were extinguished during this period. The bitterness associated with the boarding schools is still felt by many older people. No one knows how this experience may have influenced others such as their children and other close relatives.

The day schools were little more than one-room school houses, located in Snowbird, Big Cove, Birdtown, Cherokee and Soco. A woman who taught in one of these community schools for a quarter of a century said it was not uncommon to have a student/teacher ratio of 70 to one. Even with the consolidated

51

school system in the 1950's, students could still be compelled by court order to attend Indian boarding schools in the west. Students who attended these schools in Oklahoma tell of similar techniques of severe discipline, rigid formality and social and physical distance between students and teachers. They also tell of another interesting situation, that of inter-tribal hostilities. The Bureau of Indian Affairs maintained some of these schools much like reform schools. Indians with behavioral or learning problems were sent to these special boarding schools from a number of reservations, creating a heterogeneous Indian population. As in other total institutions, the rigid formality and distance between the staff and students, coupled with the students' separation from their traditional environment, forced them to rely on the student subculture for the fulfillment of primary emotional and psychological needs. This proved to be traumatic for many. Native Americans, like any other diverse group, are comprised of numerous tribal groups, many of which have little in common. This cultural diversity resulted in the emergence of a subcultural stratification system and a network of prescribed interaction patterns. Therefore, each tribal or geographical group formed its own cohesive group with hostilities directed toward certain other groups. Members were expected to date and associate only with their own acceptable group network, with violations usually resulting in intergroup fights.

Kupferer (1960) had some interesting comments on the Cherokee boarding schools. She found that those who most resented the schools were conservative Cherokees:

> The mention of school elicits such reminiscences as: "They put dresses on me to keep me from running away; think maybe I be ashamed to go through Cherokee in a girl's dress, but I did anyway." This speaker is a young man in his early 30's. Another man about 56, recalls that there was a "little stone house they locked the runaway boys in . . . they kept them from speaking Indian, too." Speaking about forbidding Cherokee speech, another said, "They used to make us work, or whip us, if they caught us speaking Indian. I didn't like that at all. I'm proud to say that I can read and write in my own language." A woman of 65 agrees with his comments, adding, "Seemed like they wanted us to be white." One final anecdote illustrates how vivid these recollections are for some. "Thompson," I said, "tell me about when you were in school." Thompson is a man over 70. "One feller he hold one arm and another— sticks about that thick—(he used his forefinger to illustrate the size) and whup me." "Why?" I asked. "Runnin' away; after that I runned away and never come back. They shouldn't have done that to me." (Kupferer, 1960: 186).

Toward A Working Educational Model

Many scholars have addressed themselves to the restrictive nature of our middle-class educational system. Thomas and Wahrhaftig (1971) emphasized the futility of our educational system based on the Protestant Ethic when it is applied to cultural out-groups, notably the Ozark whites and Cherokees residing in Oklahoma. These authors felt that American subcultures, especially those that do not subscribe to the dictates of the Protestant Ethic, do not benefit from our education process. The system fails because it no longer adequately absorbs marginal members into the dominant middle-class lifestyle. And while numerous others have written on the effects of multicultural learning situations, one thing becomes quite apparent — our formal educational system serves a role other than merely "educating" *per se*. Its most crucial mandate is to "socialize," that is to prepare students in such a fashion that they will be able to function within the existing socio-cultural system. This is where the challenge lies for the creation of a working educational model.

The challenge is to strengthen and preserve the positive attributes of our country's marginal subcultures using the cultural milieu as a vehicle for preparing these people to cope within multiple-cultural environments. Reinstating their cultural pride without adequately preparing them for the challenges of the dominant culture will be as futile an effort as past efforts have been. These efforts restricted access to their traditional culture while only partially availing them access to the dominant culture. And even among those few who have been successfully "assimilated," many often later come to resent this success and begin searching for their lost heritage.

Any viable multi-cultural educational model will place tremendous responsibility on the academic end of this relationship. The most important factor will be overcoming ethnocentrism, or what Max Weber referred to as our "value orientation." Teachers must be sensitive to their students' needs and must be able to empathize with their students. To do this, they must first become aware of the cultural differences existing between the larger dominant society and those of the particular subculture. Burger (1968), in discussing ethnopedagogy, emphasized the role of the teacher as a bicultural agent. This is an important first step. Equally important, the instructional model must be capable of explaining the dominant value system in terms of the subcultural value system. Dreeben (1967) stressed the relationship of learning norms of independence, achievement, universalism and specificity within our educational system. These are all important values within the Protestant Ethic. Again, the challenge is to translate these values in terms of the particular folk culture in which often the group, and not the individual, may be the primary focus of attention. A third step involves the teachers' interest in their students. Rosenthal and Jacobson (1968) mentioned this in their work "Pygmalion in the Classroom." They found a direct relationship exists between teacher expectation and student achievement. It is not enough merely to have Indian or Black teachers teaching minority students. Race or sex of the teacher apparently plays a minor role in regards to actual academic productivity. What really counts is having concerned, competent teachers.

A group of concerned Cherokees have been actively working on the educational problem existing at the Qualla Boundary. They have been working on this for a number of years now, and progress would probably have been minimal if it had not been for the construction of the new $7.5 million Cherokee high school. While such an elaborate facility in itself will not improve the level of instruction, it is hoped that it will inspire new hope in many students who otherwise would leave school prematurely. Especially important is the new adult education center operating at the school. College-level courses are for the first time being offered on the reservation, making it possible for adults to complete up to two years of college. Again, these programs by no means guarantee success. In order to ensure success, however, concerned Cherokees have offered their own input into the educational situation. First, a Native American student organization was formed. The organization's objectives are:

1. To promote a sense of unity among Cherokee students attending college.
2. To encourage other Cherokees, both adults and high school students, to go on to college.
3. To establish a tutorial and counseling program designed to help the Cherokee student adapt to this new cultural and academic setting. Few faculty and administrators realize that the Cherokee "Harmony Ethic" differs considerably from the larger white "Protestant Ethic." For this tutorial and counseling program to be effective, the faculty tutors and counselors will have to first familiarize themselves with these cultural differences.
4. To establish a Cherokee Studies minor or concentration for Cherokee students. This would be multi-disciplinary and would aid these future leaders in preserving their cultural heritage.
5. To actively promote the Cherokee culture.
6. To gain recognition for the Cherokees' academic accomplishments and to use the organization as a vehicle for

obtaining grants, scholarships, etc., as well as exploring potential job prospects and graduate studies.

In addition, the Cherokee Student Organization sponsored a community-wide meeting for Cherokee input into a federal grant awarded to Western Carolina University, a state university located some twenty miles away from the reservation. Their suggestions were as follows:

1. THE DEVELOPMENT OF A SUMMER PREPARATORY PROGRAM FOR CHEROKEE HIGH SCHOOL STUDENTS AND ADULTS ANTICIPATING FURTHERING THEIR EDUCATION:

   Here, it was suggested that special programs be devised and implemented to ascertain the particular needs of Cherokee students while still in high school. The special programs should include such topics as "how to study," "what is expected of the college student," "adjusting to cultural shock," as well as special preparatory courses for those with academic deficiencies. Most felt that these preparatory programs should utilize special classroom environments, ones that draw the student into the curriculum.

2. ACADEMIC YEAR TUTORIAL PROGRAMS FOR ENROLLED REGULAR STUDENTS:

   It was strongly felt that one of the most important goals of any revised program designed to improve the quality of Cherokee education is the availability of concerned, competent tutors and counselors. At the time of the meeting, many felt that without this service Western Carolina University's high Cherokee attrition rate would just continue.

3. THE DEVELOPMENT OF A SPECIAL ADULT EXTENSION PROGRAM AT CHEROKEE:

   This has already been established since the organization's initial meeting, but, again, many are concerned with the quality of this program. It seems that, as in the past, limited communication between high administrative officials was involved in the establishment of the Cherokee extension campus. If these same people have failed in past efforts, what makes them so certain that renewed programs will bring about more productive results? Many Cherokees who are receptive to the educational needs of their people, but who are seldom consulted, feel that for the extension program to truly benefit the Cherokees, items (1), (2), (4), (5) and (6) of this proposal must first be seriously considered.

55

4. ONGOING NATIVE AMERICAN CULTURAL WORK-SHOPS:

This proposal was felt to be a very important one, especially by those members of the tribe who have had exposure to outside academic institutions such as Western Carolina University. It is felt that Western Carolina University faculty, especially those involved in teaching Cherokee students, should participate in these workshops. These cultural workshops certainly should be compulsory for tutors. This type of exchange is needed because students and faculty often come from different cultural backgrounds, unaware of conflicting values that may impede the learning process (ethnocentrism).

5. THE ESTABLISHMENT OF A STUDENT COMPANION-SHIP PROGRAM:

Here, members of the Cherokee Student Organization would work on a one-to-one basis with potential college students, helping orient them to their new academic environment. This program is intended to better prepare the potential student psychologically, culturally and academically for his prospective role as a university student. This interchange could lead to orientation credit for the new student and credit toward the "Cherokee minor" for the assisting Cherokee Student Organization member (see item #7).

6. THE UTILIZATION OF A CHEROKEE ADVISORY GROUP:

This organization should consist of members from the Cherokee Student Organization, tribal council, the Cherokee Advisory School Board, the Bureau of Indian Affairs and others with the purpose of aiding in any and all Western Carolina University matters relevant to channels of communication between the University and the Qualla Boundary, providing valuable input and feedback concerning Cherokees' educational needs.

7. THE CREATION OF A CHEROKEE MINOR AT WESTERN CAROLINA UNIVERSITY:

Strong interest was shown toward the development of Native American courses at Western Carolina University, which would not only benefit Indian and non-Indian students alike but would provide for a Cherokee minor for students from the Qualla Boundary. This would provide an additional incentive for many potential college students, while at the same time providing an invaluable service by helping the Cherokees to preserve their cultural heritage.

Conclusions

This model represents the initial stages of what concerned Cherokees perceived as a workable, multi-cultural program for their people. Clearly, the model's application extends beyond any particular academic institution and pertains to all Native American groups. The model is unique in that it was developed by Native Americans having a "Cherokee perspective" about contemporary Indian education. Moreover, the model aided Western Carolina University in developing its Indian education programs, some of which are now being offered on the Cherokee reservation (Cherokee campus). Many Cherokees and non-Indians feel that this is a promising beginning.

TRADITION AND CHANGE

Traditions Kept by the Snowbird Cherokees
of Graham County:

*Herbert and Yvonne Wachacha**

The Snowbird Indians of Graham County have kept their Indian identity out of pride and determination and while doing so have managed to avoid adopting much of the lifestyle of the larger white society. Keeping the Indian culture alive in the Snowbird Community has been very difficult since there is constant interaction with whites not only in the community but also in education and employment. Yet, the Snowbird Indians have largely been able to retain a pure Cherokee bloodline and to preserve their native language. Today, the Indian population in the community numbers about 350. In the Snowbird area, especially in Snowbird Creek, the Cherokee and white land tracts are interspersed in checkerboard fashion, causing tense interethnic relations. But, with all the pressures put upon the Snowbird Indians to adopt the white society's culture, they are very much Indian and are proud of it.

The people of the Snowbird Indian community strive to help each other when problems arise. The old people of the community are treated with great respect by the younger Cherokees, for they are considered wiser because of their age. While white society considers old people as helpless social dependents, Cherokee elders are the primary transmitters of tribal traditions and beliefs.

Recently, an elderly Indian lady bought a pig but did not have a pen to keep it in. About ten men from the community built a pen for her. While the Indian men worked, their wives prepared a large dinner at the elderly woman's home. When the job was finished, everyone sat down to eat a hearty meal. They joked and laughed and told stories in the Cherokee language. No money was expected for the job they had done. Most of the people feel it is their duty to take care of the older people in the community, for few, if any, are ever sent away to a home for the aged.

When funds for a project are needed, Snowbird people have box suppers and bingo games. People bring food, usually in a shoebox, consisting mainly of the traditional foods such as bean bread, ramps, hominy and many more Cherokee foods. These box suppers are sold to the highest bidder.

---

*Editors' Note: Information contained in this section is supported by Dr. Sharlotte Neely's ethnohistorical research, "Ethnicity in a Native American Community," Ph.D. Dissertation, University of North Carolina, 1976.

The Indians in Snowbird have very few personal relations with their neighboring whites, but live in harmony and respect with one another. Unlike the Qualla Boundary, the Snowbird Indians do not depend on whites nor do whites depend on Snowbird Indians to attract tourists to obtain a source of income. Most whites in the area seem to resent the Indian's nature and never fully understand it, thus creating stereotypical images of the Indians. Whites living in the reservation borderline areas are inclined to be the most prejudiced, feeling that the Snowbird Indians are lazy, drunken, dumb and on the government dole. Therefore, many of the Snowbird Indians do not give their friendship lightly, for the white has to prove himself worthy, but when confidence is gained the friendship is a highly rewarding one.

The two of us live in a completely Anglo community in the Stecoah section of Graham County. People in this section have very strong feelings about interracial marriages, and I, Yvonne, broke an unwritten law by marrying Herbert, an Indian. On one occasion, help was needed in the building of the Stecoah community's church, and Herbert was asked to aid them. For three weekends, in his spare time, he went to work on the building with the other church members. Not once was he invited to attend or join the church. The community seems to ignore my husband in all social organizations, such as Rescue Squad meetings and other meetings about improving the community. If there is a men's softball league, my husband is never informed; this hurts his pride very much, for he feels unaccepted. Most of the reaction in the community to Indians stems from the fact that not many have had personal friendships with a different race, and they see the stereotyped Indian. My husband feels the coldness of the community towards him, so he returns to Snowbird to find social acceptance and his identity as a person.

The Snowbird Indians have had to put on two faces, one for their own people and one for the whites, in order that they might preserve their own culture and identity.

The Cherokee language is spoken fluently by most Snowbird residents over the age of 18. In a Cherokee-speaking family the language is used at all times, even in the presence of non-Cherokee-speaking whites. Cherokees seem to be very proud to know and speak the language. Most children do not learn much English until they enter grade school. All of the Snowbird Indians, except for a few older people, are bilingual, speaking both the Cherokee and English languages. The Cherokee language is very important to the Snowbird Indians, helping them to maintain their own tradition.

Religion plays an important part in the life of a Snowbird Indian, for it is the main social outlet for young and old alike. All of

59

the community, except for a very few, attend church functions regularly.

There are three Indian churches in the Snowbird area; in all three the sermons are preached in the Cherokee language. Once a week, mostly on Tuesday, the Snowbird Indians go to the top of a mountain to pray. Some Sundays the people bring food and serve dinner, and afterward there is singing.

Most of the Snowbird Indian people are very conservative in church. The neighboring white churches make it a rule to point out any wrongdoings of the deacons; the Snowbird Indians hardly voice any bad comments against a person.

Their attitude toward the death of a person in the community is quite different from that of the white society. For three days, the deceased Snowbird Indian is placed in the church, where people from the community sit up with the deceased's family to comfort them in their sorrow. Singing groups come and sing over the body during this period. Refreshments and food brought by the people are not only served to the immediate family but to all the people of the community. When the funeral is over, everyone returns to his home to rest. One Indian preacher suggested that after attending a funeral for three days, the participant was "contaminated" and should stay home as much as possible to "recover."

Once a year, in the summer, a "Trail of Tears Singing" is held outdoors in an open field. The field is cleared off by the men of the community for the singing, mainly because there is not enough space indoors for the number of people attending this function. Singing groups from the surrounding areas and from out of state are invited to sing. The Indian people of Snowbird feel stronger ties with other traditionalist Cherokees, even those of Oklahoma, than with non-traditionalists. The "Trail of Tears Singing" gives the people a chance to socialize with the Indians from Oklahoma. Many Indians from Oklahoma, who are mostly "full bloods," are invited to stay as guests in the homes of Snowbird Cherokees while attending the singing. The singing event is informal with no charge to anyone. Refreshments are sold to help pay travel fare for some of the singing groups.

Since the early 1960's, the Snowbird Indian children were forced to attend white-dominated public schools. Most of the children had spoken the Cherokee language and had never used the English language to the extent of competing in school with children whose native language was English. This caused the Indian children to fall behind in their studies. The change was so great that one man stated that the Cherokee children were either forced to abandon their Indian identity or to drop out of school completely. He also suggested that the Indians in Snowbird would do better if they did not have to experience the cultural shock and assimilation that public schools cause by trying to change the Indian's identity.

The Snowbird Indian children of today have learned to adapt to the white society's school, but not to the point of changing their Indian culture. The Indians who attend public school are treated fairly equally by the other children, mostly because the Indians have proven to be superior in sports, and the school is known for its athletic department.

Snowbird Indian students are not outspoken; hence, many do not get involved in activities other than sports. Most seem to fear failure. The few that do participate in the various clubs are very highly acclaimed by the school. Very few ever take studies seriously enough to go on to college. Some just do not seem to want to change their culture and lifestyle and to be considered by their people as a "smart-ass whitey."

The Snowbird Indians are co-workers with the whites in the various plants and other places of employment in Graham County. A few of the middle-aged people work for a program sponsored by the government designed to help the needy people in the community. Many people of the Snowbird Indian community feel that the government hands out jobs to the Indians living on the Qualla Boundary, but, at Snowbird, we have to live and work just like the white folks. Some feel that the "white Indians" are the ones that get the high paying jobs on the Qualla Boundary, while the full bloods of Snowbird are forgotten.

Even with the close working contact with whites, the Indian-white relations are strained. There is no personal interaction after work hours, and the only reward of the job is the income.

In recent years, many new brick homes have been built by the government for the people of Snowbird. The people make payments on the new homes according to their income and the number of children in the family. This advancement in housing has caused the whites to feel some petty jealousy toward the Snowbird Indians, but the Indians could not care less about others' attitudes.

The Snowbird Indians are not commercialized. On the Qualla Boundary, an artificial Indian culture is portrayed to lure tourists to the area. The Snowbird Indian, however, has maintained a natural Indian culture without influences to change it. Many of the Snowbird Indian women make authentic Cherokee beadwork and baskets, some of which are sold on the Qualla Boundary.

Many of the older men and women, today, practice herbal doctoring and the art of conjuring. The herbal doctors treat sick babies for common ailments. For the adults, the common cold, broken limbs, toothache, sick stomach and many more ailments are treated. Many put religion and conjuring together, believing the Lord endowed certain people with the power to heal the sick afflicted by evil spirits. Plants and herbs were put here by the Great Spirit to help the sick, but only a few have the knowledge to use them. The Snowbird Indians who are known to be herbal doctors and conjurers speak very little English but write and speak the Cherokee language. The alphabet of the Cherokee was not only used in writing, but was used to record traditional prayers and ritualistic ceremonies. Before they die, medicine men reveal their secrets to a special few.

On one occasion, I talked to a Snowbird Indian girl who was having fainting spells in her last months of pregnancy and had gone to an Indian doctor. When I asked her questions about her visit to the Indian doctor, she said she could not tell to whom she went or the procedure that was used to help her. If she did, the cure would not work, and she would become sicker.

In my husband's family any problems that arise are thought to be the result of another family's conjuring against them. In one incident before I married my husband, he went to his going-away party before reporting back to the service and wrecked his car returning home from the party. He was not hurt except for a few cuts and bruises, but he could not return to the Marine base. Two days after the wreck, he and his mother came up to where I lived at the time. She was going to see a conjure man on the Qualla Boundary because she felt someone in the Snowbird area wanted her son to wreck. Unaware of how serious she was, I spoke up and told her maybe the alcohol was the cause of the hex. I don't think I made such a good impression on my future mother-in-law.

When the young people in the Snowbird area become problems, their parents believe someone is conjuring against them. They will go to the most powerful conjurer and pay him for rolling the beads and chanting against the other family. Some even go as far as Oklahoma to hire the best conjurer.

Many ways to fight off evil spirits and hexes are taught to the Indian children at a young age. One way I have been told is to wash your face in a clear, running stream early in the morning, facing the rising sun. This is done in order to protect yourself from enemies.

From the viewpoint of the Snowbird Indian, the magic of the Cherokees is not to be taken lightly. All people in Snowbird are serious about their beliefs, and even the whites are afraid to say anything against it.

The Cherokees and the Great Depression:

Karen French Owl

The era of the Depression had varying effects on individuals, depending upon their jobs, economic status and ambitions. The following paragraphs relate the memories of two Cherokee men who lived through the Great Depression. I will refer to them as Mr. A and Mr. B.

Mr. A is a full-blooded Cherokee Indian and lives on the Qualla Boundary. He works for an agency of the federal government and is an ordained Baptist minister. In 1929, Mr. A was 14 years of age and lived with his family in a remote area of the Boundary. Mr. A remembers his family as being self-sufficient. His family grew its own food and made most of its farm tools. Hunting was their favorite recreation which also provided a supply of meat for their table. Life for Mr. A was affected very little by the Depression, in that most of the food and clothing that his family had was made and produced by them. Items needed from a store, which involved a two-day journey, were bought with trade items that were grown or made by the family. Mr. A remembers that some items were not available at times. He did not know the reasons nor did he care about the absence of certain items. To Mr. A, the Depression was only a word.

Mr. B was a young man during the Great Depression and was living in Oklahoma when it began. He was working in a bakery and remembers people standing in long lines to buy the necessary family items. Many items were scarce, and they cost more than most families could afford. When the bakery closed during the depths of the Depression, Mr. B returned home to the Qualla Boundary. Upon his return, he found that life was somewhat easier at Cherokee. He remembers that almost everyone had enough to eat. Because most inhabitants of the Boundary were accustomed only to essentials, they did not suffer tremendously during the Depression.

Each man has different memories of the Depression era, yet their memories are typical of many Cherokees who lived during that era. Their life-style on the Boundary made their existence during the Great Depression easier than in many other parts of the country.

Interviews with Cherokee Traditionalists:

Karen French Owl and Richard Crowe

R. F. — Cherokee Male

I.: What are the major differences between our culture today and how it was in the old days?

R. F.: Well, during the time when I was growing up we were living in the heart of our culture. The only activities we had that we looked forward to was on weekends when we had our tribal pow wows. I remember dancing all night, having a good time. It's very disturbing to see that this culture has been torn and that our younger people have not had the interest to keep our culture burning

63

*like other tribes and other reservations.
However, I think some of the young people now
are beginning to organize and to bring back
some of the dances, which I think is a start in
bringing some of our culture back like they once
were.*

I.: *Were there problems in those days which no
longer exist?*

R. F.: *No, I wouldn't say that there were. I think we
didn't recognize the problems like we do today.
We had problems with drinking being the cause
of some of our Indian people fighting among
themselves and hurting one another and even
would involve death. But people then would kind
of slow down and it would kind of get to them in
a way where you wouldn't see the drinking or
any of this hostile play being done for quite
some time now. But I can see today that the
same hostile play will develop, and it doesn't
faze our people in this generation at all. It's just
something that happens every day is the attitude that they're taking. Where back in the
early years, I feel people had more respect. If
they drank, you did not see them in public as
much as you do today.*

I.: *Do you think there are problems today that
didn't exist in the old days?*

R. F.: *Well, yes, I would say that my heart really
bleeds for the younger generation that has to
face the problems that we did not face during
my youth. We did not know and did not have
any knowledge of any dope like our younger
generation is involved with today. I don't know
what I would think if we had seen any of this in
our younger days. I think this, too, has a lot to
do with the respect the younger generation has
for their parents. There is a gap between the
parents and children today, which wasn't a gap
and no problem at all between the parents during our youth. We find that the youth are more
aggressive of being on their side of any conversation that may develop, more so than when I
was growing up because we had respect for our
parents. What our parents said we shut our
mouth. We didn't dare make any kind of comment, and we appreciated our parents because I
don't know what I'd have been today if I did not
take that into consideration.*

64

I.: Well, then, you think the family has changed a lot?

R. F.: Oh, it has. It really has. I think, too, that the parents of today's youth that have come up the way I just mentioned where they had respect for their parents tried their level best to bring their children up in that manner. We don't have near the problem with our children because I think we understand what took place and what we want our children to have this day and time as much as a lot of homes we find on the reservation that it tears my heart to know that the children don't have this kind of respect for their parents. I don't think it's to the point that they don't respect their parents; I think the parents just don't want to give in and hear their side of the problems. After awhile, it develops till the children say, "Well, if I can't talk to my parents, who can I talk to?"

I.: How has housing changed?

R. F.: I would say it has changed 100 percent. I remember many times sleeping upstairs in my grandfather's house and it snowing with wind blowing through the cracks and it'd hit you in the face. We would have to dig our way out through snow to cut wood to help our grandfather saw wood with a crosscut saw, and now today they have power saws that can cut ten times as much wood in a few moments as it took us in a whole day. Then, here we have oil heat. When you build a farmhouse, you've got a warm house. The house is insulated. More people are getting good homes. We're just thrilled to death that our people now can truly say that we're coming up from the time of log houses and one or two window houses. We have more light, and our children don't have any excuse now of not having good lights to study for their better money or their education.

I.: What about entertainment from then to now?

R. F.: Well, I still say that we entertained ourselves by finding things to do that we would be involved and always away from the older people. I remember many times that we would build homemade sleds and go up the mountain where there were some of these pine ridges. That was a thrill to slide in pine needles and take us some kerosene oil and a rag, and we'd rub the

65

*kerosene on our sled runners till we got the
speed we wanted. When we got through sliding
we would play tag on trees. That would last all
day long. Like I said early, weekends we would
look forward to going in different homes and
seeing them play. They made their own
homemade games. They used homemade baskets
they called blackjack. Back then people baked
sweetbread out of syrup. That's what they would
bring, and I know that they would bet the sweetbread in the games. About midnight, we would
all get around and eat the sweetbread together.
That was some of the entertainment we had. Today, they have entertainment of movies. I
remember first going to the boarding school. It
was a thrill for me to be counted as a good boy. I
didn't have no demerits. I wasn't punished in no
way, and for my reward I was chosen to go to
the first silent movie that I ever seen in Sylva.
It was a thrill. Then later years come the sound.
Our young generation today have drive-in
theatres and all of this now that they can go and
play various other games. There's games that we
never dreamed of ever seeing that the children
have today. But still altogether our Indian
children here at Cherokee still lack the recreation program that I would like to see them have
that would keep them off the streets and that
they would have a place to come and go for their
own entertainment rather than on the backsides
and up on the mountain roads off drinking and
carousing around.*

I.: *What about the tribal government?*

R. F.: *Now, you're asking about something that I really
love to get into. I feel that there needs to be a
change in our tribal government. By this I mean
a change of our administration. We are sitting
on a gold mine here, and we don't have the initiative to develop the gold mine we are sitting
on. We have followed the same administration
year after year until it's at a standstill. I'd say
that right now the Cherokee Indian government
is 15 years behind time. We should be that far
ahead. I can see things now that need to be
developed. I can easily recommend five, ten, 15
year programs if the tribal government today
would only listen and begin to take some of the
suggestions some of our people are making. I
would say that we have a tribal government, but
it can be bettered. Above all, it grieves my heart*

to know and to realize that our older people, our great-grandparents that stood as the leaders of our tribe, they believed in the leadership of a high God. Today, at our present council, I'm sorry to say that we may have one on the council who can get in touch with God. The rest of them, they don't respect God. All they think about are having good times and drinking, and these are our leaders. What can they say to our younger generation if our younger generation can point their fingers at our leaders and say, "Who are you to tell me what I shouldn't do whenever you are doing the very same thing here." So, if we're going to be leaders, let's be the leaders that God would have us to be. Let's be the leaders that we can truly say we have the leadership of the Holy Spirit. I don't know what I would do if we had a chief and a vice chief, every time the council went into session, that would go in and say, "People, we are here to carry on and transact our people's business, but before we go on, let me be the one to lead you in the word of prayer." I don't know what I'd do if we had this kind of chief that would do this. This, to me, would be what God wants us to do. This is the only way we're going to get out of the slum that we're in. Until we get men in there that fear the Lord and will do what God will have us do by the leadership of the wonderful Holy Spirit to guide our people.

I.: How has the B. I. A. changed?

R. F.: Well, the B. I. A., I'll say whenever I first went to school, I remember them being very, very disciplined to the Indian people. When we were put in boarding school, our parents didn't have no control over the children as they do today. Children went to boarding school they were entirely in the hands of the officials of the B. I. A. If you got a whipping, your parents couldn't come down and jump on the teachers or to discipline areas like they do today. A tale can be told on any of our teachers today, and the parents are ready to go jump on the teachers and would hit the teachers if they could get by. I think at the time we realized or knew that we were in the hands of somebody with authority. They even punished us for talking in our own native language. That's why I can't speak the Cherokee language like I would like to. It's simply that it was scared out of me in boarding school. I don't know how many times they

67

*washed my mouth out with a cake of soap for
talking Indian language. I've told many people
that I'd make today's laundromats sick of the
soapsuds that come out of my mouth. All in all, I
thought it was good. We learned to have this
kind of respect for older people. I think one of
the things I'm thankful for is that I learned to
drill and do some of the training they get in
military training today. I learned how to march;
I learned how to drill while I was in boarding
school, which I didn't have to do when I was in
service. I would say from that point that our
schools were equivalent to the public schools today. You had to study. They didn't pass you just
because you were too old to be in one class. I
think whatever they call it, progressive education, there was no such thing as that. You were
promoted by how much you learned, by how
much knowledge you had. This was good. Seems
like somehow today our education needs to be
reviewed, taken inventory of and become a part
with the public schools. Now I know that you
children have been accounted as a "A" student
in Cherokee High, and I have said many times, I
wouldn't know or not. I wouldn't know until you
stood alongside of a non-Indian, and then if you
made the grade over a non-Indian, I would say,
yes, you are an "A" student.*

I.: *Do you feel that the B. I. A. has too much control over the Cherokee?*

R. F.: *No. I don't think they got any control at all. I
think more and more they're trying to educate
our leaders to the point where they would love
to see our people take over a lot of responsibility that the B. I. A. has now in self-determination
program. It's our leaders that's afraid to grasp
this kind of responsibility. I think they're going
to have to learn and going to have to be trained
what responsibility is. I feel that government is
too slack in this respect. I don't think they are
emphasizing this too much to our tribal leaders,
and giving them that kind of training that they
should be giving them for this kind of responsibility.*

I.: *Do you think if they had the leaders to do it that
they would let them take over?*

R. F.: *I think so.*

I.: *Do you feel that those "chiefs" downtown help
or hurt the Cherokee image?*

68

R. F.: I don't think it makes that much difference. After all, an Indian with feathers is a chief to white people. Really and truly, I don't think it makes that much difference. How many of our people actually know just how the Cherokees dressed? Did the Cherokees wear feathers? We don't know. This is one phase of our culture that we don't know. I wish we did and begin to dress like our forefathers did, especially on Indian days.

I.: Do you think the young people today are better prepared?

R. F.: Much better. If they'd only take the advantage. I would love to see them go on to higher education where one day they could step into the leadership slot. It's time that our younger people began to think in this manner, because the older people are already set in their mind and you cannot change it. So you're going to have to develop this kind of change with our younger people that have this kind of ability to go on and get that education, prepare themselves so that can come. It's going to be a struggle; I'm not going to say that it's going to be an easy task for them. I'm not going to say though that people are going to be easily persuaded. I think that the more young people who get this kind of education will learn more of what is needed for our people here and that I hope they can take this initial stand and be our leaders of tomorrow.

I.: What was family life like in the old days?

R. F.: I think it was closer. Like I said, we knew what respect for our parents meant, and we were tickled to death to be at home with our parents. Many, many people cannot say that they were in a position to be with their parents. The only time we had a chance to be with our parents during the school year was on vacation, and then our parents had to come get us out of school for the occasion. We find that this was a thrill to know that we were coming back home to eat our Indian food that we were so used to. It was a thrill for us. That's something else that has died out. You don't find this Indian food like we did whenever we were young.

I.: Did you speak Cherokee in the home?

R. F.: Yes.

I.: Did you speak both Cherokee and English?

69

R. F.: No, we tried to forget the English. In fact, a lot of our parents would understand Cherokee better. My father could speak enough English to be understood, but he couldn't raise a conversation in English too well.

I.: Was the boarding school the only school you went to?

R. F.: Yes, except I went for a couple of years to a vocational training school in Asheville. That was in the latter part of 1940 and 1941. Then, from there I volunteered for the service.

I.: How far did you go in boarding school?

R. F.: Tenth grade.

I.: When you were growing up, how did you court?

R. F.: I guess we went more to the girls' homes. We didn't take her out as much as they do today. The parents were stricter on the girls than they are today. I never did court your mama by ourselves. We always had to take her brother or her dad with us to the movies. The only time I got to hold her hand in the movies would be when the lights went out.

I.: How has religion changed over the years?

R. F.: Well, I would say that people really lived closer to the Lord. There was more love shown in the older days than it is in the present day. People did respect and fear the Lord. Very, very few times in my days have I seen the older people drinking on the Lord's Day or in public. If they drink, they never came out in the public. Nowadays, it don't make any difference. They don't even have any respect for the dead; they'll come and drink or come in under the influence when there's a death. They'll even come into the church under the influence. That you did not see in the old days. I would say that our people showed what a Christian really was more so than they do today. I wish it wasn't that way. I wish it could be the same today as it was back in the older days. Back then, the preacher preached hell and damnation. People accepted it, they believed it. Today, the word says that people's hearts will harden and it's this way today. People say that they know Jesus pardoned their sins, they say they are Christians, but I don't know. It's hard to prove sometimes whether they really know what the meaning of Christiani-

70

ty is. You can preach to people today, and they look at you like it's a mystery story or something. It's something that you say, do you believe it or not. That's the attitude that people have. I would say that the Christian life today has many, many obstacles, and they're going to face more according to the teaching of God's word. The Bible is being fulfilled more every day. There's just not the complete change in a person today as there was in the older times. Like I say, the main thing lacking in our churches today is the love. It was a thrill for people to visit one another in churches, especially in our union meetings and our associations. Why, people would come all the way from Robbinsville and wouldn't go back until the whole week was over with. They would stay with families. People would invite them. People visited one another more than they do now. Nowadays, you see somebody coming to visit you, the first thing that comes to their mind is what have they come to borrow now? What made him come? They don't realize that maybe he's just coming to visit, to pay his respect. But, we always had an intention of saying something. This is why I say there is bound to be something lacking in our religion from the older religion that our forefathers experienced. Then, everybody had to walk, too. They didn't have modern facilities like we have today. They walked, and maybe this is what kept them closer to the Lord, because their faith was much, much greater than our faith today.

I.: Do you think the world is facing major problems with the development of industry?

R. F.: I wouldn't say the industry, but the world does play a greater part, because people have a lot more things to face than our forefathers.

I.: Was religion taught more in the homes then?

R. F.: Yes, I would say it was a thrill to see them read in their Indian Testaments under the light of an oil lamp. It was a thrill to gather around a big fire in the fireplace and hear them singing the old time praises to God. I would say that this modern generation is falling away from this. They can't even get our children together to have a family altar. I think that up until we go back and follow the footsteps of our forefathers that showed us the way and develop these

71

things, we'll not be as close to God as our older people were. But that don't mean that we can't get close to God. I say that it's within ourselves, that we are robbing our own selves of the blessing that God would pour out to us if we would only do what He wants us to do.

I.: *What do you feel are the major overall differences between the old days and today? What do you think are the best and the worst things that have happened?*

R. F.: *Well, I think, as I said, during the education period of people going to boarding school, the people had more opportunity to go on without too much problem into higher education. A lot of our children graduating from high school today are having difficult times because of some of the studies that they have to have to go on to college that a lot of them are dropping out because of this strain. I think this is bad. It makes our people feel that they're failing and it wasn't their fault. I think that our people are once again coming back to our leaders. This is why we're going to have to educate the community from the grass roots of people. If this is what they want, then their voice is going to have to be heard to make this kind of change. I feel that our people have in their social life better understanding. They are in a position now where they can respect and take advantage of the facilities of better health care. If they've got good health programs that they can utilize, then this will educate them to have a better, healthy life. After all, this is some of the things that our people have been without for years. Now, a lot of our families at one time, worms was counted as one of the worst diseases our children could have, simply because we did not have the health facilities that we have today. We drink water from our springs. We did not know anything about inside bathrooms like we have today in our modern homes. I just think this is a great change from the time of my youth up to the present time.*

I.: *So you think that if the younger generation takes advantage of the opportunities they have that they will be able to change?*

R. F.: *Yes. I know they will.*

72

G. O. — Cherokee Male

I.: *What are the main differences in the culture of today and that of the old days?*

G. O.: *Well, in my days, it was a different world from today. They are living with a modern world. People are living with the advancing of time and they don't have the old-timey way of living. You didn't have the conveniences of living that you have today. You had to do without a lot of things that are convenient to you today.*

I.: *Were there problems in those days which no longer exist?*

G. O.: *Well, yes. Mainly transportation, because we had to walk everywhere we wanted to go, unless you were fortunate enough to have a mule or a horse. The roads are good now, but they were more or less trails in those days.*

I.: *Are there problems today which did not exist in the old days?*

G. O.: *Why, yes. There's all kinds of problems today. Your children are a big problem today, where they didn't exist in the old days. Back in those days you didn't have drugs, and the alcohol wasn't as plentiful as today and cars, and all those things weren't a detriment to life then as they are today.*

I.: *Has the family changed much?*

G. O.: *Yes, families changed a lot. Some don't raise as big families as they used to, and the children of today aren't as obedient as they were in the old days. They were more interested in doing things at home than in taking off down the road to see what the neighbors were doing.*

I.: *Has the housing changed much?*

G. O.: *Yes, the housing has changed. Why, you could see that. In the old days the houses were made with what they had to make houses with. They didn't have modern machines and tools and modern conveniences you have today to build houses with. It was mostly done with manual labor back in those days. You didn't have factories to put out products like they do today.*

I.: *What about entertainment?*

G. O.: *Entertainment has grown. It's more modern than back in those days. Then we only had our own games and our dances. We walked miles to our Indian dances that we don't have today and our ball games. We had very little ball games like today. Baseball, basketball and football we had, but not like it is today. Our main games were our own Indian games and dances.*

I.: *What about the tribal government? How has it changed?*

G. O.: *Well, I think the tribal government today, now this is my own opinion, is more of a tradition than it is a government. Back then we had the old Indian council that really governed the people, their ways of doing things, and they settled differences. But today they more or less, seems to me like, they're just carrying on a tradition, but it's more in a modern way than it was back in those days.*

I.: *Then you feel that the tribal government had more say-so back then?*

G. O.: *Yes, they had all the say-so.*

I.: *What about the Bureau of Indian Affairs? How has it hurt or helped the Cherokees?*

G. O.: *Now, I could say yes, it's helped, because it's given them opportunities that may have come along anyway, but it gave them the opportunity to come and get their education and training.*

I.: *Do you feel that the B. I. A. is here just to hold the Cherokees down, or do you think they are here to someday let the Cherokees take over their own?*

G. O.: *I don't know. I know what they're supposed to be here for. They're supposed to be here for guidance or just more or less for the record, not to run their affairs or tell them what to do or how to do it. They're just more or less to be a guidance. Seems to me like they do more than that.*

I.: *Do you feel that the "chiefs" downtown hurt or help the image?*

G. O.: *Now I don't believe they're hurting. I believe they will give a more understanding for the people who don't know what Indians are like. All they know is what they see on television. By*

*these Indian "chiefs" out there, I don't think it's
a hurting thing, but it is letting the people know
more how the Indians do live. That is if they get
up and talk to you.*

I.: *Then you feel that they can better prepare the
tourists for what the Indians are really like,
other than just what they see on television?*

G. O.: *Yes, because 75 percent of them don't know
what an Indian is. They don't pay no attention to
an Indian walking down the street if he don't
have feathers on him. They don't know the difference. They want to know where the Indians
are at, just because they don't have feathers on
them.*

I.: *Are our young people being better prepared today?*

G. O.: *Oh yes, very much so. They are just as well
prepared as you'll find them anywhere else,
because they've got ability in the different walks
of life. You've got them in all walks of life and
trades. They do have the same abilities as
anyone else has. I think they are, yes.*

I.: *Do you think they are better prepared today
because they have more opportunities?*

G. O.: *Oh yes, they have more opportunities, and
they're getting more interested now than what
they were in those days. They are getting away
from that backwardness. They're going to school
and learning something, whereas in the old days
they were bashful and backward about doing
things.*

I.: *Do you think they were really bashful or if society said they were bashful?*

G. O.: *Well, some were really bashful. Of course, now,
it could be that some just didn't have the opportunity to mingle with much.*

I.: *What was family life like in the old days? What
do you remember about your family life?*

G. O.: *When I was a kid, father was the boss of the
house and the children were seen and not heard
and even seldom seen. When company came you
disappeared, went out to the woodshed, the back
room or out in the yard somewhere to play and
didn't stand around with the company. If you
had company for a meal, the children waited till*

75

the grownups were through before they came to the table to eat.

I.: *Did you speak Cherokee in the home?*

G. O.: *Yes, Cherokee was spoken and English. Both were spoken in some of the homes, in some homes just Cherokee was spoken.*

I.: *Where did you go to school?*

G. O.: *I went to Cherokee and I went to grade school.*

I.: *And college?*

G. O.: *I went to Boston, Massachusetts. It was a radio training. It was a special course, not like going off to school.*

I.: *Did your training help you later in life?*

G. O.: *Yes, that was the trade that I took up after I'd been in the service 30 years.*

I.: *How did the service help you in life? Did it make you more open?*

G. O.: *Well, yes. I got to see different kinds of life the world over.*

I.: *How was courting done when you were young?*

G. O.: *Well, I imagine it was the same, but it was more chaperoned than it is today. You didn't get out and run around or get in a car and go somewhere all by yourself. You stayed with the parents and didn't go off fishing somewhere by yourself.*

I.: *The parents were always around?*

G. O.: *Yes.*

I.: *Has religion changed much?*

G. O.: *Well, it was the same as it is today or practically the same. It's more modern now. We had just a little church with maybe a dozen or so in the church where now there are big churches. We just had a little frame building or a log cabin or something that we went to Sunday School and church in. Now there are big buildings. We didn't have electricity or gas heat.*

I.: *What do you think are the most outstanding changes between your life then and life today?*

G. O.: *I'd say education, because education gives broader knowledge and more opportunity. They*

76

are taking it up and getting more advance in different ways of living than in those days.

I.: *Do you think that today's children in the family life are disciplined as much as you were?*

G. O.: *No, nowhere near it.*

I.: *Do you think that in that sense they should go back to the old way?*

G. O.: *Maybe not entirely, but I believe that's up to the parents. If they wanted to or didn't, that's their business.*

C. H. — Cherokee Male

I.: *Could you tell me about how many people you encounter during the season?*

C. H.: *Oh, put it this way. I have my picture made about three million times a year.*

I.: *What is the average age range of these people and where do you think they are from?*

C. H.: *The general age range of the people who take my picture are between 25 and 95 and are from all parts of the world and United States. I'd say that 40 percent of them are from out of the United States, Germany first, England second, and I've had my picture taken with people from every country in the world.*

I.: *Did any of them leave a sizeable tip for the privilege of having their picture made?*

C. H.: *Well, I'll put it this way. Germany tips better than any other country in the world. India tips worse than any country in the world. The Soviet Union tips better than India will. Germans tip better than any other people, in any part of the world. In fact they tip better than American people.*

I.: *I wonder why.*

C. H.: *I don't know. I've been told that salaries are better, higher pay in Germany than they are in America.*

I.: *How long is the chiefing season?*

C. H.: *From Good Friday until November 1, seven days a week and about eight to ten to twelve hours a day.*

77

I.: When did chiefing first start at the Qualla Boundary and under what circumstances?

C. H.: Carl Standingdeer, the first Indian to ever wear the feathers, called it chiefing. Moses Walkingstick was the second, Ramsey Walkingstick was the third, and Henry Lambert was the fourth, known as Chief Henry. I've been at it for 19 years now. Carl and Moses are both dead. Ramsey's still alive, but he only works one day a week. There are lots of us others. I've got my picture on 43 different postcards, including the 3-D postcards. That's the reason I claim I'm the most photographed Indian in the world. Estimated number of pictures taken of me is 43 million.

I.: Over the 19 years?

C. H.: Yes.

I.: And they were the first ones, the ones you mentioned? Are they all called Chief Henry?

C. H.: No. They were all called Chief and then their first name. Chief Standingdeer and Chief Walkingstick used their last names, and their names were Carl Standingdeer and Moses Walkingstick. They were the first to wear the feathers, and they wore the headdress only. However, I was the first to ever wear the full dress costume with tailpiece and headdress and decked out in 10,000 feathers, plus all your beadwork.

I.: How many of the members of the tribe participate in this profession?

C. H.: When I first started 19 years ago, there were five of us then. The other members of the tribe would make fun of us because Indians didn't wear feathers, Cherokees at least. This past season there were about 400 of us and everybody made fun of everybody who didn't have a feather on. Nineteen years ago they made fun of you for having a feather on.

I.: How did you get established?

C. H.: Twelve hours a day and $3 a day and long hours and hard work.

I.: Was it voluntary?

C. H.: No, I was out of work and needed a job. Carl Stanford, when he owned Pioneer Trading Post, I went to work for him, $3 a day, 12 hours a day, posing for pictures and tips. Better known then *as . . . Well, it has changed names nine times since that time, the shop. It's changed owners about six times since Carl had that shop.*

I.: *You stand in front of that shop every year?*

C. H.: *I stood in front of that shop while Carl had it, and then I worked for Monty Young for three years, then worked for Autry Steward, Western Photos, for three, then I had my own place for two, then I worked for Bruce Pruett, then I worked for Jimmie Morris for five. I guess next year I'll be with whoever pays the most. I'm unemployed.*

I.: *Do the stores play any role in promoting chiefing?*

C. H.: *When I first went to work, they furnished the costumes, plus a salary. Now I work by the hour's salary and I furnish my own costume. I make my own costumes and work by the hour. Then I work for the store as an attraction for the store. I invite everybody to stop into the store and keep them parked straight in the parking lot.*

I.: *You make your own costume. You don't have to remake it every year do you?*

C. H.: *If it's an eagle bonnet, you make it over and over again, but if it's a turkey bonnet, after a couple of years, you throw it away and start all over again.*

I.: *How does chiefing benefit the American Indians in general, and the Cherokee Indian in particular?*

C. H.: *Well, if you know your job, you can benefit yourself. If you don't know your job, you can't. If you know what you're doing, you can make a good living at it, chiefing, you can make so much that you quit working construction jobs at time and a half. But if you don't know your job, the shop is just going in the hole by having you out there.*

I.: *Knowing your job, you mean . . .?*

C. H.: *Knowing what you do, wearing the feathers, and how to attract people's attention. I can touch any kid, no matter how scared he is of me, as long as the parents keep their mouths shut and give him five minutes with me. I can have him smiling and sitting on my knee. But I can't if they say*

79

*you better be good or that Indian's gonna get
you. That's just like if a kid gets lost and they
send a policeman out to get you, and the
policeman's out hunting a kid. That's the wrong
thing to tell a kid because when a kid gets lost
the policeman's gonna hunt him, and if he sees
that policeman he's gonna hide from him. Right?*

I.: *Yes.*

C. H.: *You know who's got a belt buckle like that.
Merle Travis. Identical. He's got one on just like
that on his last show. I loaned that one to him
for his last show. I've also loaned Bobby
Goldsboro a couple of pieces. I looked at Merle
Travis taping that show and I looked at the belt
buckle, and I said, "Damn, I believe it cost him
. . ." A beaded band with two feathers in my
hair would be a full chief costume and on the
Tennessee stallion, that's like Tennessee Walker.
I'll be a riding him while in the costume. (regard-
ing visit to "Hee-Haw" taping session)*

I.: *Are you excited?*

C. H.: *(reply to this was not coherent)*

I.: *Do you enjoy horseback riding?*

C. H.: *That's the first damn horse I've ever been on in
my life. I have two horses, a black Tennessee
Walker and a Appaloosa. I never ride them. My
daughters ride them.*

I.: *Do you feel that many tourists come to
Cherokee with false images of the American Indians and Cherokees?*

C. H.: *Yes. Ninety percent of the tourists who come
here look for Indians who live in teepees and run
around naked and hide between trees, ride
horses. Very few people who come to Cherokee
expect to find the Indians as they live today, and
the only ones who do, have been here before and
know what to expect. I think there should be a
program set up, not by the Cherokee, probably
by the federal government, teaching people
overseas, foreign people, of how Indians live today. Not that they live in teepees and ride
horses and act like savages. Ninety percent of
them that come from Germany think we live in
teepees and that we'd scalp 'em if they don't tip
you. I believe that's so.*

I.: *So, you don't tell them any different.*

80

C. H.: *I work with a barrel in front of me with TIPS on the front of it and if any of them don't speak English, I point at the barrel. They know when it comes to reading TIPS.*

I.: *What are some unique and unusual experiences you have encountered?*

C. H.: *Oh, yes. I have at home many scrap books of every state. When I first started out, I'd ask people what state they was from, or what country they was from, and I have letters sent back from every state in the union, every country in the world, and I've started one on every county in the states, and it's gotten to where it's taken up more room than I had room for. I just dropped it. I have every state in the country and every country in the world, including Red China and Russia, before they signed the peace treaty with the U. S. In fact, I was sent a book that looked like the* Life *magazine of the U. S., but it's the* Life *of Moscow, and when I first got that book, I had the FBI check that over three times over that book, and I finally give them that book. It showed the parades in Moscow and all that. Men from the embassy out of Washington, D. C., thought I was an agent or something or other.*

I.: *That was unusual.*

C. H.: *But I have all that and I decided what the heck, why keep records. I keep daily records of the weather, how much I make, temperature and whether it's raining or snowing, and I keep that and have since the day I start until the day I quit, and I have that for seven years. But I quit keeping. People say, "I'll send you a picture," and at first I recognized that as their tip. But when I got a picture from every country in the world and every county in the district, I think a little tip in the barrel would be better. I just come out plain and say this, which I didn't want to start with. A lot of people feel offended if you don't tell them. I've had a lot of them ask where the barrel is or where I put my tips. After I got everything I wanted from overseas, I set this big barrel out there, and I figured anybody could see. But I had to ask even after I put the barrel out there. You hate to charge for your services, but you hate to do it for nothing.*

I.: *So, you have lots of pictures.*

C. H.: I have seven scrapbooks at home that cover every state in the union and every country in the world. I had my picture made with a lot of famous stars and different people. In fact, the last three months I've posed with Johnny Cash, Tammy Wynette, George Jones, Loretta Lynn, the Hee-Haw bunch. I've posed with all the top Nashville stars within the last five months, which was good 'cause they bring in good money. I worked with Tammy Wynette before she ever became a star, and I think she worked with me because she figured she owed me a favor or something.

I.: I guess a big experience would just be meeting all those people. You're bound to learn a lot.

C. H.: I put it this way. I enjoy my work as chiefing more than any other job. I worked construction in the wintertime, underground construction, worked in California, Chicago, Canada, Washington, D. C. and Chattanooga for the past two years. But I'd rather see one happy kid's face than 14 happy superintendents' faces. And all kids, regardless of where they're from, no matter if they're rich, poor, middle class, they all know what an Indian looks like, and if you can make him smile, it's worth a week's pay on construction. There's been many days when I haven't made anything, but I've made a few kids happy because they seen an Indian in costume and had their picture made with them. I made something, but as far as money or salary, there was nothing. I'd rather do it and make a few kids happy than do it for the money. I know that even working in the spring and fall, we have some local counties who bring the Head Start kids in, and they have never seen an Indian in costume. They ask all kinds of silly questions, and when you see this, you know that kids in Germany have really no idea of a real Indian. You have to like to do it. You can't get drunk and do any job, and you can't get drunk and be a chief. You have to enjoy your work and do it right. I don't know, if you see one happy kid, you can look over what you should have made and what you didn't make. Do you understand what I mean?

I.: So, it's rewarding.

C. H.: That's what I've always said. If I see a kid who's screaming his head off 'cause he's afraid of an In-

*dian, and if the parents keep their mouth shut
and give me five minutes with the kid, I'll have
him sitting on my knee and laughing and talking.
I've told a few of them that I wasn't an Indian,
that I was a bear and the Indian was further on
up the road. When I first started, Ramsey Walkingstick started 23 years ago, and he had two
years on me, and he worked across the road
from me. Everything he done I did and done it
better than he did. If he posed for a picture, I
posed for a picture, and I'd either kiss the kid,
shake hands with the men, and kiss the ladies.
Then I got where I set them on my knee, and
then he got to copying me, and then I got to
where I opened the door for people. Whether
they took my picture or not, I'd open the car
door for them and ask them inside. He wasn't doing that, and I got a jump on him. Then, we
worked together. When I went to work at the
same place, he was getting $6 a day and I was
getting $3, and when I quit, I was getting $9 and
he was still getting $6. Then I went to work by
the hour at $1 an hour, then $1.25 an hour, $1.50
an hour, $1.75 an hour, and this past year I got
$2 an hour and this was straight time, no time
and a half. A man can still make a good living
just working by the hour 'cause you can put in
24 hours a day if you want. I put in 18 hours a
day this past summer.*

I.: *If you are chief, no one comes in and takes your
place. Or is it up to you?*

C. H.: *That's an agreement I have with the shop, up to
the shop and the Indian, and as long as he's good
enough where he produces what the shop wants,
there'll be no other Indian come in. But I always
make it a point and people know me, Ed knows
me, any shop owner agrees that wherever I
work, they don't need another Indian, and I
make it a point that there will be no other Indian as long as I fulfill my job. The more Indians
you got, the less money you will make. You
make the same salary, but less in tips. Because if
there's some foreign people from Europe around,
they want all the Indians in the same picture.
So, it's all the Indians posing for one quarter or
one dollar or whatever the tip is. But if there's
only one Indian out there, that's one quarter or
one dollar for one Indian. No matter if there's a
dozen down the street, he works this one spot.*

83

I.: So, you make that clear?

C. H.: Yeah, I make that clear from the start in the spring, that I'm the Indian of the year until you fire me. If you fire me, you can hire all the Indians you want. If you don't fire me, I'll be with you until the end of the year and I'll fulfill my contract, which isn't a written contract, just verbal agreement. I don't believe in a signed contract because if a man got sick then he'd have to furnish an Indian to fulfill for him. And where in the hell can you find an Indian to fulfill for you. I believe in having a verbal contract and agreement and knowing what's expected of you and them, and ain't nobody who will hold you to a contract if you're sick and can't come to work. They know you're losing too if you don't show up.

When I first started, I rented my house, didn't have nothing, worked construction for Dillard Construction Company in Sylva. I still don't have any money, but I own my own home and 23 acres of land, my wife owns a '73 Oldsmobile car, and I own a GMC pickup truck and my kids are in public school. All the furniture in the house is paid for. I just got through paying the federal government $1,740, but I still don't have any money. I'd have $1,740 if they hadn't hit me in August.

I.: I guess that was an unusual experience.

M. T. — Cherokee Female

I.: What do you find is different today and when you were growing up?

M. T.: A lot of difference, children for one. We were made to mind. We didn't stand back and sass our parents. There is a lot of difference.

I.: Did you grow up right around here?

M. T.: Yeah, right up around yonder. Me, Johnson, David, Becky and Emmett grew up yonder.

I.: Are the churches the same as they were?

M. T.: No, they're not. All the Indians used to go to church all the time. They all went. In my generation there are a lot of them don't go to church. Since I've been sick, I don't go to church too much.

I.: Were most of the churches around here Baptist churches?

M. T.: Most of them, mightly (sic) few Methodist churches, and that's the only two kind of churches there was.

I.: Did any of your ancestors have any other kind of belief than the Christian belief?

M. T.: No.

I.: They didn't have no Indian belief?

M. T.: Yeah, they had Indian belief. They worshipped the ancestors and on ahead.

I.: Do you know anything about what they used to worship?

M. T.: Well, they just talked to God just like the rest of us. They spoke in their own language. That way they had their own belief. Jesus was their savior. That's as far as I know about back yonder away 'cause I'm not too old. I know mightly (sic) little about it. They used to come around and talk in the old language. Nowadays, I can't get no one to preach in the Cherokee language. If you want to hear any preaching, it's always a white man a preaching.

I.: Why do you say that? Do you understand more in the Cherokee language than in English?

M. T.: Yeah.

I.: When they speak of Christ or Jesus, do they refer to the same man as the English do?

M. T.: Yes.

I.: How much education have you had?

M. T.: I ain't had too much but fifth grade.

I.: Did your parents make you go to school?

M. T.: Yeah, they made me go to school, but I didn't learn nothing.

I.: How far did school go then?

M. T.: Ninth grade.

I.: Where did you have to go if you wanted to go to school after that?

M. T.: Caryle or Haskell. You went from the ninth grade to the twelfth grade. And then later on they went to the eleventh grade. Davy went to the eleventh grade. He pretends like he can't understand Indian too much, and that's all we was brought up with was the Indian language. Well, of course, I make a lot of mistakes in my Indian language when I start talking.

I.: *How much education did your mom and dad have?*

M. T.: *Well, I think Mama went to the third grade and Daddy went to the second.*

I.: *Did they go to school here?*

M. T.: *Yeah, they went down there. There was a boarding school down there.*

I.: *How long has that boarding school been down there?*

M. T.: *The boarding school was there when I went to school, and it was there when they went to school. It was just a small house, because there weren't too many who went to school. Most of the Indians were wild and they wouldn't go to school.*

I.: *They just wanted to stay in the woods?*

M. T.: *Yeah, they just wanted to stay away from the lawman. They'd go in the front door and out the back.*

I.: *Why didn't they like school then?*

M. T.: *I don't know. They just wanted to stay around home, I reckon. They wanted to be around their parents. They didn't know what school was and what it was to be away from them.*

I.: *Was the school run by the B. I. A.?*

M. T.: *Yes.*

I.: *Was it that the atmosphere was too different?*

M. T.: *Yes. There was a lot of difference in it.*

I.: *Did they ask you not to talk your language when you went to school?*

M. T.: *Yes. We got punished if we talked Cherokee.*

I.: *Did they ever tell you why they wanted you to talk English?*

M. T.: *No, they never did, but they said we could get around better in the world if we talked English.*

I learned pretty fast. I learned pretty good. Me and Mama got into it one day. I was having trouble in school. I could have gone back if I'd wanted to, but I didn't go back.

I.: *Did kids get married early in life?*

M. T.: *Yes, some of them got married when they were 13 years old.*

I.: *Was this what most of the people did?*

M. T.: *That's what most of the people did. All the Indians did. You see, they didn't have papers to show they were married. They just went out and got a girl and came home and lived with her just like man and wife.*

I.: *Did the man usually go live with the woman?*

M. T.: *The woman had to go live with the man.*

I.: *So, you say the man just went out and got the woman. Was there any ceremony?*

M. T.: *No, no ceremony or nothing. He just picked her up and took her home with him.*

I.: *What kind of work did most of the men do?*

M. T.: *When I was young, most of the men didn't do too much of anything. They liked to hunt more than anything.*

I.: *Was the hunting good through here?*

M. T.: *Well, I reckon. My Daddy used to bring in wild turkey and stuff like that. He never did kill no bear that I know of and no deer.*

I.: *Was there any kind of industry in this area? I know there was logging industry. But was there any other kind of industry?*

M. T.: *Well, the only industry I know of was the men used to sell logs and make cross-ties and make boards for house roofings. Daddy done a lot of that. He made boards for people to roof their houses with.*

I.: *Shingles?*

M. T.: *Yes. I wouldn't mind having a shingled house. They last longer.*

I.: *Did the Indians then have much of a drinking problem?*

M. T.: *Yeah.*

I.: Did you find the problem with your parents?

M. T.: My Daddy did, but my Mama never did.

I.: Where did they get their alcohol?

M. T.: I never did know where Daddy got his. If he got mad at Mama, he'd take off and find him a pint or two.

I.: Was it still liquor or store bought?

M. T.: Yes, it was still liquor. Wild whiskey they call it. That's all there was around here in them days.

I.: There was a lady last week telling me that at one time the government had a still around here. Some of the Indians worked on it. Did you ever hear of the government or the B. I. A. having a still around here?

M. T.: No, well, I heard about it, but it was out in Kentucky and like that where it come from.

I.: Have tourists always been coming into this area?

M. T.: No, never been bothered with tourists until I was raising my own children. That's the most white people I seen, and then they made the roads going across the mountains and the fancy cars. See back yonder there wasn't nothing but rough road.

I.: How long did it take you to drive to Bryson City and back?

M. T.: If you left early in the morning, you wouldn't get back until after dark.

I.: Since you can remember, has the B. I. A. always been here?

M. T.: No, the B. I. A. didn't come in until not too long ago.

I.: Who had the school at that time?

M. T.: The government put up the school for them, but the Boy's Club run the school. The government was the one furnished the school for the Indians to go to school to learn to talk English and get along with white people.

I.: Do you think that it has been a help for the Indians to learn English?

M. T.: Well, in a way, sometimes I think it has been a lot of help and then again I think to myself, if I just spoke plain old Indian language all the time, I wouldn't understand what a white person said about me and what the Indians say about them.

I.: Do you think a young Indian man today could get along better with his friends if he spoke English and Indian both?

M. T.: Well, in a way he could.

I.: Since you speak English and Cherokee, do you think you can explain things in one or the other better?

M. T.: Well, I can do both pretty well.

I.: The reason I asked is that some people say Cherokee has some quality that you can be more explanatory in it.

M. T.: Well, I can do both pretty well myself, but in a way . . .

I.: Then you don't particularly see this quality between them?

M. T.: No. You can get with a white man and he'll fuss from here to Bryson City.

I.: Do you think the white man took our language away from us?

M. T.: Yes, they did, and they killed them along the way.

I.: Do you think the Cherokees could have prevented this?

M. T.: No, you couldn't resist because when they told you to go, you had to go because they wanted your land because on account of gold and silver. That's all they wanted, gold and silver.

I.: But don't you think the Indians could have joined together?

M. T.: After so many were gone, our ancestors that hid in the mountains, they fought back after they hid in the mountains. The white people couldn't go into the mountains and get them because they knew how to hide their families. People didn't talk.

I.: What do you think of the Indian money that you're supposed to be getting?

89

M. T.: *In a way I think they owe it to us.*

I.: *Why do you say they owe it to us?*

M. T.: *Because they took our money.*

I.: *It's like building a dam. If we needed electricity in Cherokee but in order to get that, we have to build a dam, do you think it would be wise for us to go up where we're going to build a dam and tell all those people we want to pay you for your land and for what you have on your land?*

M. T.: *As long as they give them a place to live.*

I.: *If there is one individual up there who doesn't want to leave, do you think we should go up there and evict him?*

M. T.: *Yes, that's what a lot of people done when they built that dam down at Fontana. Some refused to give up their land. Then there was nothing they could do about it.*

I.: *Do you think people should move aside for progress?*

M. T.: *I think they should.*

I.: *Do you think the Indians should move aside if the white man wants their land? Do you think it was right for them to take the land?*

M. T.: *Well, in a way. Like right now, they're going to build a highway right through here and evict me off of my place. I'd have to move out and give them the rightaway. I'd either move further up the mountain or down to the river.*

I.: *Do you know anything about your ancestors that went to Oklahoma?*

M. T.: *Well, I got kinfolks in Oklahoma, my great grandfather. My grandfather, it was his father who hid out up on the mountain. That's where we come from.*

I.: *Your dad, was he a medicine man? I've heard some people say he could do some medicine.*

M. T.: *Yes.*

I.: *Did he ever try to teach anybody?*

M. T.: *Well, he tried to teach me, but I wouldn't learn because I didn't believe in it. You can't do it, you can't learn it.*

I.: *Did someone have to teach him this?*

M. T.: *He had to learn it from someone else, his daddy or maybe someone else.*

I.: *How did they handle the spell?*

M. T.: *They handed it down from generation to generation.*

I.: *Did they pick certain ones?*

M. T.: *Well, they picked out the ones that didn't talk too much.*

I.: *So, would you call it witchcraft?*

M. T.: *Yes.*

I.: *I heard some people say that long time ago there used to be a guild called conjuring witchcraft. Have you ever heard of this?*

M. T.: *No, I haven't heard of it.*

I.: *Did you say he's also given some medicine? Did he mix medicine and conjuring witchcraft together?*

M. T.: *Yes, he'd talk to them before he'd administer medicine. He'd have to talk to it before it'd be any good. Only the right kind of people could enter his room.*

I.: *So, only certain people were allowed to be around?*

M. T.: *Yes, only the older generation.*

I.: *You were talking about some of the people from the South Pacific Islands. When a young woman first starts the time of her life, this was the point where they were considered young women. Was this the same belief among the Cherokee at that time?*

M. T.: *Well, as soon as a girl started her period.*

I.: *Did they have to wear anything such as a necklace? Was there any way that a young man was supposed to know?*

M. T.: *Yes, they had to wear different kind of clothes after they reached womanhood.*

I.: *What kind of clothes did they have to wear?*

M. T.: *They had to wear skirts all the time, or dresses, or whatever. The Indians didn't start wearing those clothes until my mother was a young child. That's when cloth come into North Carolina.*

    I.: When was this?

M. T.: About early 1800's.

    I.: If you could go anywhere in the world, where would you go?

M. T.: I wouldn't care about going anywheres now. When I was growing up, I used to want to go to Oklahoma.

    I.: Why was that?

M. T.: I wanted to go see some of my ancestors there.

    I.: While you were growing up, did you do any traveling?

M. T.: No, the only traveling I done was after I was widowed from my first husband.

    I.: How far away from Cherokee have you ever been?

M. T.: I've been to Alabama. That's as far as I've ever been.

    I.: You've never been outside of the United States?

M. T.: No.

    I.: What did you think of man walking on the moon?

M. T.: I don't believe it.

    I.: You don't think that they did this?

M. T.: In a way I don't.

    I.: Do you think that the government just made it up and put it on television?

M. T.: I believe that's what it is. Then again I think they might have been to the moon on account of the weather changes so much. The weather is not like the weather used to be when I was growing up.

    I.: How has it changed?

M. T.: Well, you see, we don't have winters like we used to.

    I.: We don't have severe cold and a lot of snow like we used to.

M. T.: *We don't have severe cold like we used to . . . and in the months of November and December. Our worst months were in November, December and January. Towards February it starts getting warmer and warmer all the time. Nowadays, March is the one that gets cold. In the late part of February, it didn't snow, it used to. And they get snow way up here a lot of times when we was growing up. Nowadays, they don't get that.*

I.: *Some people say if God wanted us to be on the moon he would have put us there. Do you think that man's going to the moon is denying God's work?*

M. T.: *I believe so. I think that they're doing what they want to do. They don't go by the rule of God anymore.*

I.: *Or by the Bible?*

M. T.: *And by the Bible.*

I.: *Have the Cherokees always had a Bible, say, a copy of the King James version?*

M. T.: *Yes.*

I.: *Written in Cherokee?*

M. T.: *Yes.*

I.: *Do you find slight differences in translation between the Cherokee Bible and one written in English?*

M. T.: *Yes. They're differences in the Indian history and the English history.*

I.: *Do you know an example?*

M. T.: *Well, Indian preachers use the Indian words when he's preaching backwards.*

I.: *Backwards?*

M. T.: *I don't know what it's all about, but you know maybe that's the way.*

I.: *Do you remember the first car you ever saw in your life?*

M. T.: *The first car I ever saw was long ago.*

I.: *They pumped the gas?*

M. T.: *Yes, they weren't big, but they was high.*

I.: *When was this?*

M. T.: *Model T, first car I even seen.*

    I.: *Did it scare you?*

M. T.: *No, what scared me the most was an airplane.*

    I.: *Airplane?*

M. T.: *Yes. I was a pretty good-sized little girl then when I first saw an airplane. In 1918.*

    I.: *1918? Was it one of those big double-winged ones?*

M. T.: *Yes. It was flying low.*

    I.: *Did you run?*

M. T.: *No, I froze.*

    I.: *What came to your mind?*

M. T.: *I couldn't make out what it was until Mama told us what it was. I'd never seen one like it, and I didn't know.*

    I.: *So, that was your first experience with an airplane?*

M. T.: *Yes, and then the next thing that I knowed of was that thing that I'd be in cars but never did it scare me pretty bad. The plane was the one that scared me. It's been a long time since we seen the first airplane before the second one went by over the hill there; they seen one coming over that way, and boy, they headed for the house just a sailing.*

    I.: *They were getting out of there?*

M. T.: *Yes, they was getting out of there. It was flying higher than the other one did. You couldn't see the man's hands when he waved.*

    I.: *And the next thing was the train?*

M. T.: *Yes, the next thing was the train. I haven't seen it in so long from the roads down there.*

    I.: *Did you used to see the smoke?*

M. T.: *I seen the smoke, and I seen it coming around the curve and then to up yonder. It was going up to the gorge. When Mama was taking me to the store one day, we were walking along the road. I went with her, and Mama says, "The train's coming," and I could hear the rails making the noise. We kept walking on down the middle of the track. I seen it coming around the curve there, and I just fell over.*

I.: *You fell over?*

M. T.: *I just fell over. I wasn't uncomfortable; I just fell over. I was fixing to get up, but it seemed like I was paralyzed. Mama had to drag me off the railroad tracks, and when I got up from the ground, I took off right through the cornfields.*

I.: *Why did it scare you?*

M. T.: *I don't know. It was just making so much noise, I guess. Scared me. After a little later on, after we got a little bigger when we were coming back, we saw where that thing had gone back, and there was an old man lying there on the side.*

I.: *And it ran over him?*

M. T.: *Ran over that poor little man.*

I.: *Did the train stop?*

M. T.: *No.*

I.: *Just kept on going?*

M. T.: *Just kept on going.*

I.: *Did anybody ever do anything about it?*

M. T.: *Well, they said it was an accident. They thought the old man was deaf and just couldn't hear and must have been walking down the tracks.*

I.: *That was right down here at the curve?*

M. T.: *Yes. Right in there's where that poor old man died. Remember Mama was coming and said, "Look at that man laying there, he's dead." She said, "He's an Indian though." I asked Mama what she'd do. Well, she said she'd have to tell somebody. You could see the train had hit him. He was lying right in the middle of the railroad tracks there.*

I.: *Didn't you have a sheriff?*

M. T.: *Yes, there was a U. S. Marshal then.*

I.: *Did they do anything about it?*

M. T.: *Yes, they, I think, asked them about it, and they got a little money out of it.*

I.: *Oh, so the train did pay insurance then?*

M. T.: Yes.

I.: How did they bury people a long time ago?

M. T.: As far as I can remember they put them in a box and then buried them. My mama and them buried them in a casket, but years back, when my ancestors were up yonder, when anybody died, they just set them out against a tree and piled rocks on them.

I.: Didn't they have a setting up or anything?

M. T.: No, they just set them up yonder.

I.: The animals couldn't get to them?

M. T.: Yes.

I.: They did?

M. T.: Yes.

I.: When did they start having them sitting ups?

M. T.: Well, later on, when I was little. Mama used to take me to sitting ups.

I.: Isn't that referred to as a wake?

M. T.: Yes.

I.: This sort of came along with Christian beliefs then?

M. T.: Yes, that's what it did.

I.: After they started putting them in boxes, did they dress them up or what?

M. T.: Yes, they dressed them up.

I.: Did they just have one particular person that did this?

M. T.: Well, they had about six in Cherokee Community. They went places, like they had to go and help serve dinner to and stuff like this and so on.

I.: Did they put perfume on them?

M. T.: They give them a bath after they was dead, and then they put clothes on them.

I.: But they didn't put oils or perfume on them?

M. T.: Yes.

I.: Did they go through the embalming techniques?

M. T.: No, not that I know of.

I.: They didn't take any tests?

M. T.: No, they didn't know until later on that there was any.

I.: What did the white people do then?

M. T.: Well, the white people kept to theirselves. And then a lot of them made friends with the Indians. The Indians used to go and work for them.

I.: Farmers?

M. T.: Yes, the white people were all farmers.

I.: When the park came in, how did they do their thing? Did they just come in and tell people?

M. T.: Well, they paid people for the land. I don't think they gave them too much money for land at that time though.

I.: Did you have a hospital up there?

M. T.: They used to have a doctor who came up to the house.

I.: He went to the homes?

M. T.: Yes, and they had a place they called a hospital. It held about 25 patients, I think. If he didn't go the house, they took them to the hospital. He did that when he retired.

I.: Around 1919 or 1920, was there some kind of epidemic?

M. T.: Yes, old fashioned measles. I had a sister die of it.

I.: Did they have smallpox?

M. T.: There was smallpox way back yonder before I can remember.

I.: Were any of the Indian doctors ever able to . . .

M. T.: No, there wasn't nothing they could do.

I.: They couldn't doctor them?

M. T.: No.

I.: Around 1919 or 1920, there was something else, wasn't there?

M. T.: Flu thing.

I.: It was a certain kind of flu. Do you remember what kind it was?

M. T.: No, I don't.

    I.: Did it bother mostly kids?

M. T.: Yes.

    I.: Just another white man's disease?

M. T.: Yes, another white man's disease.

    I.: Did they quarantine?

M. T.: Yes, they quarantined themselves.

    I.: Did they do this on their own? Did someone come and make them?

M. T.: No.

    I.: So, this is something the Indians already knew themselves?

M. T.: Yes.

E. D. — Cherokee Female

    I.: What are some differences between your childhood and how it is today?

E. D.: There are a lot of changes because nowadays it seems like the children have their own way.

    I.: Who do you feel had the most influence on your childhood, your father or your mother?

E. D.: I think my father did. I thought a lot of my father. More, I guess because he raised me more. Seemed like he was a mother and a father to me. When my father was there we didn't do things that weren't right because we always obeyed what he said, but then I don't think too much about my mother because I can't remember. My daddy was the only one there and I was with my daddy so much that I guess everything I learned was outside ways just watching him build and trying to help him, because there wasn't any boys or anyone to help him. They were all married and gone just me and Mandy there. I had to do more of the outside work, trying to help him, cutting wood and all that and I wasn't around my mother. Most schools today, you can't teach them hardly anything. I mean, they have to be taught first before they can learn anything. In that time, though, everything I learned was by watching older people, even my grandmother when she'd come. Even cooking. My mother didn't teach me how to cook. She didn't say you

98

cook this this-a-way or cook things like this way. I learned it the hard way because I was very small when Mama left. I just had to learn all by myself. I guess maybe that's why I think more of my daddy. I always thought he was more like a mother too and I was always with my daddy. Mama would be gone for a month, maybe two or three weeks, maybe till one of us got sick.

I.: *Do you feel closer to his people than you do to your mother's people, or is it about the same?*

E. D.: *I don't know because my mother didn't have any people, she just had one sister. My daddy had more people than what my mother had. Grandpa's people, I don't know who they are. In one way his brother, Ned, seemed like a daddy to me too. Anything that's wrong, he was always there. Just like as if he was our own daddy. And same way with my aunt, and my daddy's mother, she was always there too. I guess she took the place of my mother when Mother was gone.*

I.: *It's different today, because you all back then showed more respect for the older people, is that true?*

E. D.: *Well, today there's people, they don't claim one another like they used to. You know it go way back to the third or fourth generation; they thought maybe they were so close kin to one another. And today, now, it's different, even their own first cousins you see them going out together. Then, they always told us who our people were. Today, they don't claim one another like that. They don't seem to care none. Even their own brothers and sisters don't care none about it. Just like I say it's not like it used to be. We don't love one another like we used to. I can remember a lot of things that happened when I was a kid. Our people went about going to people when someone was sick try to help them. Now if you're a sick person, no one will come to help you or come to see them or like that. Back in those days I can remember people come even when my daddy was living. After my daddy died, well people quit coming then. People from Wolftown, Birdtown and all the way out and down to Robbinsville. People would come and see my daddy. They would sit on the porch and talk and talk, in their younger days. Now people don't come like that anymore.*

99

I.: When did you first become aware of Christian beliefs? Was this introduced to you by your mother and father? Can you remember how far back it was when they told you this was the way rather than the old ways when the Cherokees just believed in a supreme being before the missionaries?

E. D.: I guess when I was about fourteen or fifteen years old. They never did tell me until after this old man went around preaching. That's when I learned about being a Christian and all that. I don't remember when I was small; I don't remember Mama telling me about what was gonna take place later on and all that till after the preacher came around preaching to people. I don't remember way back when I was a little kid about being taught what I should do and how to live.

I.: Do you feel that the Christian religion is different today from when you were younger? That is, as far as the respect the Indians have for the Christian religion.

E. D.: I think so. There's a lot of difference because way back, older people always thought more of going to church and all that, had more respect. But today, now they've got so much of these laws they go by, and in that time they didn't. They didn't have all that as far as I remember, like today you go to church they have certain rules that people are supposed to do, and they made another rule and they're supposed to go by that.

I.: So you feel the Christian religion was stronger back then than it is today?

E. D.: Yes.

I.: Tell why you would take the herbal medicine now and why you would take it back then; how is it different?

E. D.: I guess the medicine you make today, seems like it, I don't know maybe back in that time we used our own more, like I've had children, I raised all my children and I never had them in the hospital, even if they had a cold or flu or something like that. I never did take them to the hospital. I've got my own medicine for them, good for a fever or something like that. And then we had the Indian doctor. Today they're

100

always taking their babies to the hospital. Seems like they don't even have no use for the Indian medicine.

I.: *You do agree that you have to believe in it, though?*

E. D.: *You have to believe in it. Just like you can believe the Lord's going to do something for it; it's the same thing. And then you'd hate so much ugliness and sickness then you use the Indian medicine. Well, back in the old days you have to use it, take medicine, like if somebody brought you medicine, you take it for about three or four days, and then about three days they bring you some more medicine and you take that for three, four days, and in a few days they come again they bring you more for four days, and you take all that. And after taking the second medicine they bring you, you can feel the difference. But you've got to believe in it.*

I.: *Do you feel that back then they felt that if you used the herbs and went to a white doctor that it wouldn't work?*

E. D.: *They said you could just use one thing, because it wouldn't work because you believed another doctor.*

I.: *Do you feel that the herb medicines that the Indians used helped the people more than the medicines they get from the public health hospital? Do you think the people are healthier when they used the old way of doctoring?*

E. D.: *I think so, because people didn't have all the sickness like they do today.*

I.: *Did you go to the boarding school that they had?*

E. D.: *Yes.*

I.: *Tell me some of what you remember about the boarding school. What's the most outstanding memory you have about going to boarding school?*

E. D.: *I don't know, because I didn't go to boarding school long enough to learn a lot. I know there was a lot of change in it from that time when I went. Just like I say now, I wish when I was in school it had been like it is today. Today, children have more things to be interested in, but they still don't like to go to school. When I*

101

*went to school there was nothing like that
because we had to stay in boarding school, and
stay there and don't know what was going on or
what took place, except the older children. The
smaller children, we never knew what was going
on. All we'd do was just go to school and go back
to the auditorium and stay there and play
around there. And then on the weekends we'd go
to Sunday School on Sunday morning and that
was all.*

I.: *How far did you go in school?*

E. D.: *I guess, I don't know if I finished half of the
third grade or what.*

I.: *You didn't go back at all after that?*

E. D.: *No.*

I.: *Do you think that by going to school to the third
grade that it helped you at all?*

E. D.: *Well, I think so. But then, after I quit school,
after learning more.*

I.: *Back then they didn't stress going to school as
much as they do today?*

E. D.: *No.*

I.: *Do you think that education today is a necessity
in life?*

E. D.: *I think so, because now you can't get a job
without an education. Back in those days, maybe
people learned how to work more than what
they did today. A lot of times they have to be
trained, but in the older days they knew how to
work; they didn't have to be trained.*

I.: *So you think society today is making it important to have an education; whereas, back then, if
you had a skill, or even if you didn't have a skill,
you could survive without an education.*

E. D.: *Yes.*

I.: *How about the Christian religion today. Why do
you feel this is necessary for the Cherokee people?*

E. D.: *Well, the way I think most people are is not
believing and getting out and doing things,
because it is almost time for the end of the
world to come, and people are not living like
they ought to, and then they're believing like*

the white people are doing, taking more interest in the things of the world. They learn bad things, mostly the white people in everything they do, getting out and doing things they're not supposed to do. It all comes from the white. I know it's not from the Indians, because everything they do is from the white, and then they learn that, and they turn themselves over; then they forget about their religion, and then it's hard for them to go back and become as a Christian, and they just fall away.

I.: Do you feel that when the Cherokees were influenced by the white people, other than helping them, it hurt them?

E. D.: Yes.

I.: Just tell me how you feel about that, why and how that happened.

E. D.: Well, lots of times some of our younger Christian people are always doing something; like today our younger boys have found out that they can take this weed and smoke it and get drunk-like on it, and the Indians could not do that, and now they say that this weed that they smoke now has been growing in these mountains all the time, and that this weed was what they used for something, I forgot what they said they used it for, and said that's the same thing that they smoke today. And most of our young boys take to it, and it just ruins their lives, and even some boys get killed and fight and drink and all that.

CONTEMPORARY SOCIAL ISSUES

Do Cherokees Receive Death for Public Drunkenness?:

Laurence French and Jim Hornbuckle

Three young adult Cherokee males were found hanged in their cells at the Jackson County (North Carolina) jail within a 21-month period from early 1974 through 1975. No non-Indians have suffered a similar fate during recent times. Needless to say, many members of the Eastern Band are concerned about Indian treatment at the hands of the all-white, county sheriff's department. The fear of "red neck" justice has prevailed since Removal (1838) when whites forced the Cherokees off their traditional land. Since then, animosities have existed between those few Cherokees remaining and their new white neighbors. Somehow, an unusual and complex legal situation emerged, whereby the Cherokees, although living on their own 55,500-acre federal reservation, must cooperate with the county sheriff's departments regarding incriminating activity, even when these acts occur on the reservation itself. This is largely because no jail facilities exist on the reservation.

Although the reservation has its own police force, the Cherokee Police Department, these Indian officers are compelled to be deputized by both Swain and Jackson Counties' high sheriffs to qualify officially as law enforcement officers. The irony here is that the high sheriff's office is a political and not a professional position, while many of the Cherokee officers have undergone rigorous professional police training. Having no "holding facility" of their own, the Cherokee police must transport all apprehended suspects to the appropriate county jail (the reservation is split by Jackson and Swain Counties) to await official arraignment, again before a local white district judge. Coincidentally, the district judges are elected just as the county sheriffs are.

Given the ultra-conservative political and social environment of white Southern Appalachia, many Cherokees realize that "justice" is certainly an elusive concept within this system. While many Cherokees have long been aware of the injustices of the local white court, the three recent deaths of young Cherokee men have disturbed most Indians. Perhaps, this is because many question the nature of these deaths. First, they ask why Francis P. Jackson, a 23-year-old ex-Marine and construction laborer, would take his own life for public drunkenness. It cannot be attributed to the shock factor of being jailed overnight, since he had repeated this experience several times. Or, what about Donald E. Lambert, a 33-year-old married man, who dropped out of high school only to return later and graduate? His self-motivation was high. And, like many young males in the area (both white and Indian), he was no stranger to overnight jail. The most recent death, December 28, 1975, involved 23-year-old Johnson L. Littlejohn, who worked the tourist circuit during the summer and logged during the winter. Again, his only previous contact with the law was for public drunkenness.

Granted, no one can accuse North Carolina of being a liberal state. In 1976, it held one-third of our nation's death row inmates (101, of whom five were Indians). The state still has an "outlaw" statute, where a local judge can proclaim an escaped criminal an "outlaw," signifying that any citizen can then hunt him down and bring him in dead or alive without fear of legal reprisal. North Carolina was also one of the last states to abandon the "chain gang," doing so in 1956. It still carries a miscegenation statute outlawing mixed racial marriages, although a higher federal law curtails its enforcement. Yet, in spite of this record, one would think that more courtesy would be given these dead Indians than a phone call to the Cherokee Police Department, curtly stating that these men were found hanged in their cell sometime during the night, apparently between checks by the night jailer. No further explanations or justifications were offered, and no investigations were initiated. The Cherokee Police Department then had the difficult task of notifying the next of kin. And even if these deaths were, in fact, suicides, why have not measures been taken to prevent them from occurring again and again?

The probability of three Cherokee males, jailed overnight for a minor misdemeanor, committing suicide within a period of 21 months (January 26, 1974; April 2, 1975 and December 28, 1975) defies logic. First, Jackson County has a population of 21,593 permanent residents, 6,000 of whom are students at Western Carolina University, and only 1,863, or 8.6 percent, are Cherokee Indians. What is the likelihood that this minority group would be so overrepresented, especially in an act of self-violence which is not traditionally associated with young Indian males just in their prime? No similar deaths have occurred in Swain County, which has the bulk of the reservation population with 2,564 Indians, or 32.6 percent, of the county's total population.

The sorrow associated with these deaths goes beyond the victims' families and friends. The deaths unjustly reflect on the tribal organization, whose hands are tied in these matters. The Chief's Office, Tribal Council and other tribal agencies (Community Services Committee, Law and Order Commission and the Health Board) have all worked hard to improve the quality of life on the reservation. New health facilities being planned or constructed include a new hospital and a home for the aged, and the Tribal Council has passed a resolution approving plans for a "multifaceted community treatment center" called Cherokee House. Cherokee House would have as one of its functions a local holding facility for detaining public drunks and other suspects awaiting arraignment. The Cherokee House proposal states:

> As the situation stands today, Cherokee youth and adults with legal or emotional problems are handled by county, state or federal agencies. And when institutionalization results, Cherokee clients are placed in off-reservation facilities, along with non-Indian inmates. This places the Cherokee at a distinct disadvantage due to (1) his minority representation among the inmate population and (2) his different cultural heritage.

Cherokee House offers a viable alternative to the current situation. Here the Indian client would remain on the reservation, close to friends and family, and without being subjected to an alien, often hostile, cultural and social environment. The facility would be staffed by Indian professionals. Hopefully, Cherokee House will soon be a reality for the Eastern Band of Cherokee Indians. Certainly, something has to be done to avert future situations like those involving Francis, Donald and Johnson. These deaths provide a sad commentary on the reservation system, where Native Americans are compelled to live within restricted social, cultural and physical boundaries in order to "protect the larger society from them." Yet, they, in turn, are not protected from the abuses of that larger society.

Postscript

The story of the Cherokee jail deaths gained national attention following its publication in a leading Indian periodical, *Wassaja* (Vol. 4, No. 5/May 1976). This publicity led to an investigation by the U. S. Civil Rights Commission. As a result of the federal investigation, Jackson County was compelled to install a closed circuit monitoring device in the county jail and to provide 24-hour surveillance of the cells. In essence, the United States Government served notice to the sheriff that they did not want any more of these "accidental" deaths to occur.

Another change, which many attribute to this situation, was the transfer of Cherokee law officers from state (county sheriff) to federal jurisdiction. Cherokee police are now federally deputized, with the director of Cherokee's community services (police, fire and sanitation departments) holding the status of Deputy U. S. Marshal. All other Cherokee law officers are special federal deputies. In the past, the Cherokee police were deputized in both Jackson and Swain Counties, so that they had to transfer Indian suspects to one of these jails, depending upon the section of the reservation in which the arrest occurred. Although these changes were definitely needed, somehow the cost of three human lives seems a high price to pay for progressive justice.

SOCIAL PROBLEMS AMONG THE CHEROKEE:
Laurence French and Jim Hornbuckle

The Eastern Band of Cherokee Indians is an interesting cultural group not only within our larger society, but also among Native Americans. Historically, they did much to aid in the development of a positive American Indian image, one that portrayed the Indian as something other than a savage. The highly developed Cherokee Nation of the early nineteenth century is well known, and some of the most articulate and highly respected Native Americans were Cherokee—John Ross, Major Ridge, General Stand Watie, Will Rogers, and so on. And, the Cherokees' profound influence on American society did not end with the 1838 Removal. However, the Cherokees, notably the Eastern Band, have also played an important role in maintaining the general Indian stereotype. Approximately eight million tourists visit the Qualla Boundary each season to see either the reservation or other sights, such as the Great Smoky Mountains National Park and the Blue Ridge Parkway. Consequently, the Qualla Cherokees are the most visited Native American group today. Yet, due to tourists' demands, they present not the true aboriginal Cherokee culture, but a vulgar image of the Plains Indians. During the tourist season, two dozen "full bloods" play the role of Western-type "chiefs," standing in front of shops wearing full-feathered bonnets and colorful garb. This confused image has had its effect on contemporary Cherokees, especially within the last 15 years. Since the advent of tourism, many Cherokees have experienced cultural ambiguity.

In the past, the most striking facet of the Cherokee culture was the suppression of any expression of overt hostility in interpersonal relations. Other aspects of this distinctive personality structure include a high value placed on independence, a resentment of authority as well as a complementary hesitancy to command others, and a reluctance to refuse requests made by relatives and other Cherokees. Contemporary field workers recorded similar attributes among the Big Cove Cherokees. This indicates that contemporary, conservative Cherokees continue to adhere to the Harmony Ethic, while middle class and marginal Cherokees do not. Overt aggression is typically lacking in conservative behavior, with physical encounters occurring infrequently and then only when alcohol is involved. Even then, alcohol is seen as being the culprit. This reasoning exempts the individual Cherokee from direct responsibility for his actions. Kupferer (1966) noted that aggressiveness is also absent among the conservatives in the areas of business and academic competition, much to the dismay of the Bureau of Indian Affairs and other white administrators on the reservation. Again, this attitude contrasts with the strong emphasis placed on individual aggressiveness and competition fostered by the Protestant Ethic.

Prior to the current "Indian Pride" (Pan-Indian) movement, the middle class Cherokees were more susceptible to ambivalence regarding their self-image. This stemmed from the fact that they knew that, although their reference group was the larger white, middle class culture, they would always have the stigma of being Indian. This did not affect the conservative "full bloods" as much, since they had a strong sense of in-group solidarity channeled through the Harmony Ethic. Hence, the conservatives felt somewhat secure in their accommodative situation. Probably a third of the current 7,000 members of the Eastern Cherokees could be considered "full bloods," with strong concentrations in Snowbird, Wolftown and Big Cove communities. Middle class Cherokees account for a much smaller proportion of the rolls. A significant number, in fact, fall somewhere in between. These are the marginal Cherokees.

Fifteen years ago, the middle range Cherokees had two distinctive models with which to associate — conservative Indian and middle class Indian — both providing the necessary control to regulate excessive behavior. Since then, the picture of the contemporary Cherokee has altered considerably, from that of avoidance to more and more aggressive forms of behavior, many of which develop into "social problems" in terms defined by the larger, dominant culture.

Concerning these emerging social problems among the Eastern Cherokees, certain behavioral patterns are predictable and explainable in terms of past cultural traditions. This involves the occasional incident of personal violence among the conservative Cherokees, the exceptional incidence of tax or business fraud or related business property offense among the middle class Cherokees and alcoholism, which seems to affect a broad cross-section of reservation members. These problems are explainable in socio-cultural terms, which suggests that they are social-situational rather than indigenous to Indians or Cherokees *per se*. That is, any group of people caught up in a similar social situation would manifest similar behavioral patterns regardless of race or ethnic affiliation.

Frustration-aggression theory could be used to explain occasional outbursts of personal violence such as murder and aggravated assault. The internalization of frustration by the conservative Cherokees appears to result from the sanctions of the Harmony Ethic and the lack of traditionally acceptable outlets, such as wars and ball play. Some members of this group internalize frustration to the breaking point, directing the resulting aggression toward a person or thing which they perceive as constituting the frustration. Accordingly, the pressure for business and personal success provides an explanation for the sporadic charge of fraud or income tax evasion among members of the middle class Cherokees.

Alcoholism, as a problem among Indians in general, is probably best explained by Reasons (1972), who suggested that dominant federal paternalism is the primary cause of alcohol-related problems among the subordinate Indian population in this country. By establishing a double standard, one applicable to the white culture and yet another for its Indian wards, the paternalistic federal government prohibited the use of alcohol among Indians by the General Indian Intercourse Act of 1832. Even when the Act was repealed in 1953, the Bureau of Indian Affairs and other federal agencies continued to encourage and support abstinence indirectly through local control agencies. This double standard prevented Indian groups from developing norms for self-regulation of the use of alcohol. When one has a lack of regulatory norms coupled with a need for escapism, as is often the case among many Indian groups today, then one has the type of problem that now exists.

Unique patterns of alcohol use and abuse are experienced by the Qualla Cherokee. The middle class Cherokees seem to share drinking habits similar to those of their middle class white counterparts, while the marginal Cherokees seem to manifest similar drinking patterns associated with other racial and ethnic marginal groups attempting to escape the realities of their social and cultural environment. An unusual drinking pattern, however, does exist among the conservative Cherokees. These Cherokees do not drink regularly (daily) like the middle class drinkers, nor do they drink publicly like the marginal drinkers (usually on weekends). Instead, the conservative drinks sporadically and privately, usually with close family members or friends. During these drinking sessions, large quantities of alcohol are consumed, while little or no alcohol is used during the periods between drinking bouts. It is during these drinking situations that violence occurs among the conservative Cherokees. Perhaps the major alcohol problem facing the Cherokees today is an increase in the marginal population. Public drunkenness, driving while intoxicated and public brawling while intoxicated are not only on the increase but also represent behavior quite contrary to the Cherokee Harmony Ethic.

In addition to the above mentioned social problems, other overt behaviors seldom expressed in past Cherokee traditions have emerged among the Eastern Cherokees. Criminal assault charges have increased. In 1973, there were 1,067 laceration wounds reported to the Health Clinic, and these probably represent only the most severe cases since home care or medicine men are usually consulted for lesser wounds. Another category, "accidents, poisonings and violence," accounted for 2,645 incidents during this same period. Breaking and entering, larceny, truancy and disorderly conduct are other frequent criminal and delinquent charges being brought against Cherokee defendants in unprecedented numbers. In addition, nearly 1,500 mental disorders were recorded, including functional psychosis and neurosis, as well as conditions requiring institutionalization.

Mental illness and alcohol-related problems also cannot be easily separated from the domestic scene. In 1973, it was estimated that 6,000 members of the roll (over 80 percent of the tribe) were economically deprived and earned less than $3,000 a year. Of this group, 594 were involved in severe family disorders stemming from excessive use of alcohol; 416 were heads of households. Desertion, abandonment, separations and divorce are quite common on the reservation, although this seems to be a traditional and common pattern for the Cherokees. Another traditional domestic pattern, that of unwed mothers, again only serves to complicate the contemporary situation. It is estimated that one in four births is out of wedlock. This also contributes to the high incidence of female heads of households.

It seems that among the contemporary Cherokees self-imposed restraints and controls are weakening. Increasingly, Cherokees are resorting to behavioral patterns deemed unacceptable by both the Harmony and Protestant Ethics. What the contemporary Cherokees seem to be facing is a situation whereby numerous secondary controls are being imposed upon their lives. And these controls not only represent the larger white culture, but are administered by middle class whites as well. Many programs have been implemented during the past 15 years designed primarily to curtail Cherokee primary controls and to replace them with dominant, white secondary controls. These programs often conflict with the home environment, causing young Cherokees to be torn between the family and the school. What ensues is a state of confusion for many Cherokees, both children and adults. This is ironic since traditionally the Cherokees have enjoyed considerable latitude regarding personal decisions and behavior. But, as secondary controls become more and more a part of their social lives, the more difficult it is for them to adhere to the individual dictates prescribed by the Harmony Ethic. Other current factors further confuse the contemporary Cherokees. These include the popular Pan-Indian movement and its search for a common Native American ethnic image and the Qualla Cherokees' promotion of the movie Indian image.

If full assimilation into the dominant white culture is possible and desirable to the vast majority of Eastern Cherokees, then the situation today can be viewed as merely transitional. This, however, is quite questionable. First, there is no indication that the larger white culture is, or ever has been, receptive to real assimilation. Second, the new Indian awareness movement raises the possibility that many Indians will not want to be molded into the white culture even if the opportunity avails itself.

An intelligent approach to the many social problems does not seem to be an easy one, yet it is quite apparent that some workable solutions among the Eastern Cherokees, and other Indians as well, are needed. Any viable solution, however, will require both Indian and white participation. What obviously will have to change are current perspectives on these problems.

REFERENCES

Bereday, George
  1967 "Reflections on Comparative Methodology in Education,
       1964-1966." *Comparative Education* 3, no. 3: 169-187.

Brembeck, Cole S.
  1966 *Social Foundations of Education.* New York: John Wiley
       and Sons, Inc.

Bromeld, Theodore
  1957 *Cultural Foundations of Education.* New York: Harper
       and Row Publishers, Inc.

Burger, Henry
  1968 *Ethno-Pedagogy.* Albuquerque, New Mexico:
       Southwestern Cooperative Educational Laboratory.

Coleman, James Samuel
  1965 *Adolescents and Schools.* New York: Basic Books, Inc.

Coombs, Philip
  1968 *The World Educational Crisis.* New York: Oxford
       University Press.

Dreeben, Robert
  1967 "The Contribution of Schooling to the Learning of
       Norms." *Harvard Educational Review* 37, no. 2: 211-237.

Friedenberg, Edgar Z.
  1965 *Coming of Age in America: Growth and Acquiescence.*
       New York: Random House, Inc.

Goffman, Erving
  1961 *Asylums.* Garden City, N.Y. Doubleday and Company,
       Inc.

Gruber, Frederick C., ed.
  1961 *Anthropology and Education.* Philadelphia: University
       of Pennsylvania Press.

Hargreaver, David H.
  1967 *Social Relations in a Secondary School.* London:
       Routledge and Kegan Paul, Ltd.

Havighurst, Robert J.
  1968 *Comparative Perspectives on Education.* Boston: Little,
       Brown and Company

Hodkinson, Harold
  1962 *Education in Social and Cultural Perspectives.*
       Englewood Cliffs, N.J. Prentice Hall, Inc.

Hollowell, A. Irving
  1960 "Some Psychological Characteristics of the North-
       eastern Indians" in *Man in Northeastern North
       America.* Andover, Mass.: Phillips Academy Press.

113

Holzinger, Charles H.
  1961 "Some Observations in the Persistence of Aboriginal Cherokee Personality Traits" in *Symposium on Cherokee and Iroquois Culture*. Washington, D. C.: U. S. Government Printing Office.

Kupferer, Harriet J.
  1966 *The Principal People*. Washington, D. C.: U. S. Government Printing Office.

Mooney, James
  1972 *Myths of the Cherokee and Sacred Formulas of the Cherokees*. Nashville: Charles Elder Publishers.

Reasons, Charles
  1972 "Crime and the American Indian" in *Native Americans Today*, (edited by Bahr *et al.*). New York: Harper & Row Publishers.

Redfield, Robert
  1955 *The Educational Experience*. Pasadena, Cal.: The Fund for Adult Education.

Reid, John P.
  1970 *A Law of Blood*. New York: New York University Press. Rosenthal, Robert and Lenore Jacobson
  1968 *Pygmalion in the Classroom*. New York: Holt, Rinehart and Winston.

Snyder, Charles R.
  1958 *Alcohol and the Jews*. Glencoe, Ill.: Free Press.

Thomas, R. K. and A. L. Wahrhaftig
  1971 "Indians, Hillbillies and the Education Problems" in *Anthropological Perspectives on Education* (Murray L. Wax *et al.* editors). New York: Basic Books.

Wax, Murray, L. *et al.*
  1964 *Formal Education in an American Indian Community*. Monograph #1, The Society for the Study of Social Problems.

PART TWO

CHAPTER I

Cherokee Heritage And Folklore

STORIES BY CARL LAMBERT, CHEROKEE HISTORIAN:

Karen French Owl

The stories and anecdotes in this section were told by Carl Lambert, a noted tribal historian and storyteller. As Mr. Lambert related this folklore to his niece, Karen French Owl, the stories and anecdotes were recorded and transcribed within the oral tradition.

Story #1

Cherokees believed highly in the little people. They lived in certain areas, and the Cherokees more or less were forbidden to go into the areas because they were inhabited by the little people. Right at the upper end of the Big Cove section in the gorges is one of those places. Jerry W. told me about a story his father told him. His father was Owen W., brother to Joe W., up in the Big Cove. Their father and mother told them not to go up into the gorges because it was inhabited by the little people. One time the old folks were away from home, and they decided to go up there and see for themselves. They said it was a clear day and there was not a cloud in the sky. When they went up into this area in the gorges, they thought they were struck by lightning or something. They were stunned by something. When they came to, they got out of there. They did not see any little people, but they did not have to be told to stay away from there anymore.

Story #2

When Rob B. got married, he moved from Graham County to Big Witch. They lived in a log house with a puncheon floor in it. The little people were serenading him and his wife one night. They were under the floor dancing, and when they were dancing they were causing the floor to move up and down. He got up and went outside with a light; he looked under the floor, but could not see them anywhere. As soon as he got back in the house, the racket started again. He said you could hear them chanting in Indian, like they were dancing around a campfire.

Story #3

In the town of Robbinsville, some men were digging a water line a few years ago into some of the sections that did not have water, and they ran into this tunnel that was about 18 inches square. They could not imagine why this tunnel was down in the ground. They turned a fire hydrant on and ran a hose in there. They let it run all night; the water just went on somewhere else. To this day, they do not know where it came from or where it goes. When asked if Rob knew anything about the tunnel, he said that tunnel was dug by the little people. When they had that stockade there before the Removal in 1838, Fort Montgomery was there where the town of Robbinsville is. The little people bored a tunnel under that thing trying to get there so the people could escape. The tunnel was so small that the people could not fit into it.

Story #4

At the 32,000 Acre Tract where Gene O. lives, there is a creek that goes by his house, Fish Trap Branch. There was an Indian who lived between Gene O. and the Tuckaseigee River. The Indian's house burned down; he built it back, and it burned down again. So, he went to see some Indian medicine man on Conley's Creek. He told him about the situation. The medicine man told him he would have to move the house over because he had built the house in the path where the little people came down off the mountain to the Tuckaseigee River to fish, and the little people were the ones burning his house down. So he moved it to a different location. And it still stands. It was the third house that was built, and it was being burned down by the little people because it was in their path to the river.

Story #5

At the mouth of Pigeon, Mollie and a friend walked out to the river. She showed him a rock that was a sheltering rock. This is where the little people had saved this Indian's life. There, he got caught in a bad storm in the winter. The little people got him under the rock and covered him up with leaves and saved his life. All the people believe the story about the little people.

Story #6

Irma and Joe went to the mouth of Blackrock. They went to visit a lady up there. They thought she was at home because the door was open. They thought she was out around the place, so they went out walking around above the house. They walked up Blackrock Creek. It was not running or anything, but the creek started coming down muddy. Joe told her, "We had better go back, the little people are up here, and we don't want to disturb them." So, they turned around and went back.

"The west entrance to the reservation via the Blue Ridge Parkway."

"The north entrance to the reservation along highway, U. S. route 441."

"The main entrance to the Cherokee Historical Association's tribal enterprises, the Cherokee drama and the Oconaluftee village."

"The Quall Civil Center, a popular community activity center and home of the tribal library."

"The Cherokee High School, a model of the BIA's recent educational endeavors."

"The Cherokee Museum, a cultural facility operated jointly by the Cherokee Historical Association and the tribe."

"One of the many tourist attractions located on the reservation."

"Cherokee homes located in the more isolated communities off of the
well traveled tourist route."

"BIA Superintendent, Jeff Muskrat, in a relaxed mood sitting on the stairs at the Tribal Council house."

"Doc Sequoya, tribal medicineman from the Big Cove community."

"Cherokees displaying their traditional cultural skills at the Oconaluftee Indian village."

Cora Wahneetah, noted Cherokee potter.

"Posey Long, one of the few skilled Cherokee stickball carvers."

"The annual stickball game played at the Cherokee Fall Festival. Here the Western (Oklahoma) Cherokees play the Wolftown team representing the Eastern Cherokees. This is a highly competitive game for both the teams and individual players. The men with the switches are the team coaches whose role it is to stimulate their players to perform at their best."

Story #7

There are caves across from the rock crusher as you are going through Nantahala Gorge. When the old men used to go hunting, they never would pass that area with any game without leaving part of it for the little people. It was bad luck to pass the caves and not leave part of whatever you killed for them. Certain areas such as Big Cove, Tallulah Falls Gorge . . . Tallulah Falls means other people . . . were supposed to be inhabited by the little people. It was taboo for anyone to go into that gorge. The little people are to the Cherokees as the Leprechauns are to the Irish. You did not want to cause them wrath; you wanted the little people to be on your side.

Story #8

The rattlesnake to the older people was a sacred thing. The older people never killed a rattlesnake because it was supposed to be a good omen if you saw a rattlesnake. The rattlesnake was part of their culture or religion. They more or less worshipped the rattlesnake. It had certain powers that they respected.

There were lights that used to be on Rattlesnake Mountain. Lights were caused by swan gooses. It was an illuminous light. It drifted up into the holler. The Indians thought it was the rattlesnake. It would drift off to the south. With all the cars and street lights now, that has dried up.

Story #9

The storyteller was one of the most important people in the village. Before Sequoyah invented the alphabet to where they could write stuff down, at all the various festivals and stuff that they had during the year, the storyteller repeated all these stories to the younger people. And, of course, someone who had some special talent who could remember and who could tell things accurately was one. They would take lessons under the old storyteller. One of the things they did, they did not exaggerate. Usually when we tell things today, everytime someone tells it, it gets a little bigger.

They did not have any way to write it down. These things had to be told accurately. They had to be told exactly the same way every time. The stories were passed down from one storyteller to another. This is how we got some of our history.

Anecdote #1

The Cherokees spun off from some of the Indians on the lakes: the Iroquois, Mohawks and Senecas. They did not come directly from the lakes down here. That is one reason the Cherokees were so far advanced. In moving, they naturally came in contact with other tribes and probably intermarried. They probably picked up some of the culture of the different tribes. The Catawbas were just south of us. Some of the good pottery making came from them. The Catawbas were setting on a good clay bed. The Cherokees did not have too much good clay to make their pottery. They made pottery, but it wasn't the same. There were the Overhill Cherokees and Middle and Lower Cherokees. When you compared the pottery, the Lower Cherokees made better pottery. This was because they had better clay to work with, and they were right next door to the Catawbas who were the best potters.

Anecdote #2

The Middle Cherokees were not affected by change as quickly as the Overhill or Lower Cherokees. The migration of the white settlers came from Virginia by Bristol and the Tennessee Valley. The English settling in came from Charleston, South Carolina, and came up through that area into the Piedmont and Georgia. The Lower Cherokees were more in contact with whites. Even before the white settlers came, the tribes were fighting the lower and Overhill Cherokees much more than these in here. This was because they were in a pocket and were protected by the Overhill and Lower Cherokees. It was too much trouble for a war party of any size to get very far. They would have to come through either the Overhill or Lower Cherokees to get in here. The Middle Cherokees were not changed very much. The Lower Cherokees were not understood by most of the other Cherokees, but their language was a bit different. They pronounced their words different. They were down there with the Catawbas and the Creeks and a lot of the names in north Georgia were Creek in origin, not Cherokee.

Anecdote #3

When DeSoto came through here in 1540 near Franklin, Indians were living in log cabins. Evidently, when they got into this area they had settled, and they decided that was it and started building homes and farming. They set down roots here. But the Cherokees, like other tribes, at first must have been a nomadic tribe. There is nothing to prove that they came directly down here from the lakes. There are some theories that they might have gone down into Central America and then wandered back up into this area. They may have wandered around literally thousands of miles before coming here to put roots down.

Anecdote #5

One legend the Cherokees had concerned a place in Brevard. Indians had been living there for over 10,000 years. The legend had it there was a blond group of people of a smaller stature than the Cherokees. When they came, they were a group of people with blonde hair who lived in that area in Brevard. It was definitely a different origin of people, different from the Cherokees.

Anecdote #6

The Judaculla Rock about Cullowhee is the largest rock with picture writing in the United States. We do not know the origin of the rock. It might have been there before the Cherokees came. There is a legend about a giant named Judaculla who was supposed to live up there at the top of Balsam. Up above Caney Fork in Tuckaseigee, there are some fields that are known today as the Judaculla oil fields. That is where he did his farming, right up on top of the mountain. He was supposed to live up on the top of Balsam Mountains. The oil fields are there today. There are some bushes and shrubs growing there now since the Blue Ridge Parkway took it over. The mountaineers used to range their cattle up in there. They used to talk about the Judaculla oil fields.

Anecdote #7

The myth of the Cherokees in the Mooney book must be the correct myth on creation passed down through Swimmer from our ancestors.

Anecdote #8

Most Indian tribes in general are very creative. This is inherited. The Indians had to be close to the land. They had to make use of whatever material was available to them. They utilized the white oak and cane. Some of the northern tribes used maple and ash and some other woods native to that area for making their baskets.

Indians were quite adaptable to their environment. If they had to go into a strange territory, they could easily adapt to that area. The Indians were natural conservationists. Their whole livelihood depended on their being conservationists, not killing off all the game or just using part of the animal. They used all of it. They knew they had to have a constant source of game and fish. They only took what they needed. They never killed more game than they could use or caught more fish than they were able to use. They knew they would have to come back another day or another month for more. They used fish traps to catch fish. They would use a dugout canoe to chase the fish into the trap. They would take out the big fish and throw back the smaller fish. That was the Indians' thinking; they always looking to the future, instead of taking everything in sight. They designed their fish traps so that they would only catch the big fish and let the small ones go on through. But, once in a while, something would get caught in the traps, and they would catch the smaller ones.

Anecdote #9

That was one of the things that spooked the Indians when the white settlers came. There was not enough land. It was just that their guns killed off all the game and what they did not kill, they spooked with their guns. It took the Indians longer, and they had to go farther away from home to get their meat. This made the Indians more angry than them taking the land; it was the fact they were destroying the Indians' food supply.

Anecdote #10

Two hundred years ago the whites were surprised to see the Indians with gardens and fruit trees. They were living quite modern 200 years ago. One village at that time had 200 houses, 100 on one side of the river and 100 on the other. They had cattle and horses. Some whites ate with one chief whose wife even churned butter. The Cherokees had adopted a lot of the white man's way. One of the reasons was because they were not nomadic; they were staying put, putting roots down where they were.

The idea they got where the women do all the work around the village was because it took a lot of able-bodied men to go out and hunt and bring in food everyday. The rest of them were out patrolling the borders to keep out intruders. This had to be younger people or older people, and the women were about the only ones left in the village. It was not because they wanted their women to do the work; it was just that the women were the only ones left to do the work around the home. Tending the garden and making baskets and pottery was hard work. And, some of the women also were looking after the older people who were unable to take care of themselves. The Cherokees are one of the more progressive tribes and have always been.

CHEROKEE DANCES:

Amy Walker

Introduction

Dancing and song were for the Cherokee people the very heart and soul of life; they also represented another contact with nature. The Cherokees had songs and dances for good health, for making the crops grow and for good hunting. There were also songs and dances for war, peace, victory and thanksgiving. Many dances and songs were bequests of the sacred Stone Coat Monster. Others believe that the Cherokees had their own language and songs since God scared the people and gave each a different language at the Tower of Babel. Here is one of the legends, as told by Will West Long, about the Stone Coat Monster.

The Legend of Stone Coat

Long ago, a creature whose name was Stone Coat lived among the people in human form. In his natural state, he was covered with scaly armor sufficient to protect him from any attack, an invincible monster. He lived among the people; no one knew his identity. Furthermore, he could make himself invisible, and he went from place to place wherever the people did not suspect him, killing as often as he needed food in order to secure their livers, for human livers were his sustenance. Finally, he came to a Cherokee Indian village where he took the form of a little lost orphan boy. The man who found him took pity on him and brought him home to rear. One morning soon after, one of the man's children was found dead. They examined the body and found that its liver had been taken out. Such a sorrowful event caused a deep sorrow in the village. This was the first time that anyone had died. They consulted the medicine man to see what could be done. The people wanted immediate action to punish the supposed killer. The medicine man advised them to wait, lest they make a mistake, and see what would happen next to guide them in taking the wisest action. No one suspected the poor orphan boy of having anything to do with the deed.

For a few days, nothing happened; then one morning another child was found dead from the same cause. Although they had kept watch to see if anyone had entered the settlement, no intruder had been discovered; and so when they took council over the death that had come upon them, it was decided that someone among their own people was the cause. Finally, the grown people would be killed for their livers and all would perish unless the cause was found and removed. When another of his children was found killed in the same manner, the man who had adopted the

123

orphan boy suspected him of the deed. He noticed that the boy had no appetite for regular food after the death of each child, so he went to the Council of Chiefs and medicine men who were now holding serious meetings to determine what might be done for relief and told them of his suspicions. Some advised that they attack and slay the boy at once. Others advised caution, saying this must be a powerful spirit in disguise and that to attack him outright might result in failure, arousing his anger and causing him to destroy them all. They finally agreed to lie in wait to watch him. The medicine man might then devise some means by which he could be disposed of without danger. The monster was so powerful that it was thought best to allow the death of a few more ch'ldren before the people took final action. At that, one of the medicine men declared in council that he had found a way to entrap and slay the killer. He ordered that they secure the aid of seven women whose menstrual periods came at the full of the moon. They went to lie in wait along the path taken by the killer on his journeys to and fro across the mountains in search of victims, for he had discovered that this was one way to weaken and destroy the killer.

The women were found and the plan carried out. With their legs uncovered, they lay along the path where the victim was supposed to come. Stone Coat, who was the killer in disguise, came by. He saw them and said, "Well, well, beautiful women." All at once he felt queer, began to vomit blood and grew weak, and as he passed each woman, he vomited more blood. Finally becoming so weak, he lay down unable to move. Then, the people who had been waiting for the results came to where he lay stretched upon the ground to see the dying Stone Coat. Then, knowing he was about to die, he called as many of the people as could possibly be gathered about this place, saying, "Build a fire around me and burn me up."

It was done as he commanded them. The Cherokee came from distances to witness the sacrifices. When they lighted the forest, Stone Coat began to talk, telling them that while he was burning and the smoke and smell of his burning flesh rose to the sky, there would issue forth a series of songs. These, he told them, were his offerings to the people to aid them in all branches of life. As the songs came forth, he commanded the people to learn them and to teach them to their children to be used forever by the Cherokee. The dying Stone Coat also told them that if they had tried to kill him by force in the beginning, they would have failed because it was ordained that they should not have relief until they had learned what suffering was. Knowing the depths of suffering and the joy of relief would make them value the songs they were now to learn and the medicine they were to gain by his death and sacrifice. He said, "You kill me so I'll leave disease in the world behind me, but my songs will cure that." He also told them that besides leaving behind the magic songs, the dances, the fulfilling of their social life and the song formulas, he would leave them a quantity of powerful medicines in the form of pieces of stone forming his stone coat, which would be found in the ashes after the fires had consumed his body. Then, they burned his body and watched him all night. He kept on singing different songs all the time he was burning until he died. When he became silent, as his spirit arose to the sky in the morning, the singing still came forth and could be heard until out of hearing in the highness, and the people gathered around the sacrifice and learned all the songs. Some, they employed for dancing when they were all together and others were used by people when they were alone for hunting, war and other purposes such as medicine.

After the ascent of Stone Coat's spirit, they examined the ashes and found pieces of stone all broken up by the heat of the fire. These were the particles of his stone coat. The men gathered up the pieces, and as each took a piece, he decided what line of life he would follow. Some decided to be bear hunters, some deer hunters, some buffalo hunters, some fishermen, others chose to be handsome for women. Whatever pursuit was chosen and followed became the life calling of the people and their descendants, with the songs and medicine for each purpose in life.

Cherokee Dance Instruments

The three main instruments used to accompany the dances are the hollowed out water drum, the gourd hand rattle and the box tortoise shell rattle. The drum is made of a section of buckeye trunk about eleven by eight inches, hollowed by gouging to leave a two-inch bottom with walls about one and a half inch thick, colored with clay and sumac stain. The head is a woodchuck skin held down by a hickory hoop three-fourths of an inch wide. There are perforations on the lower parts for rainwater when the drum is not in use. A drumstick is usually made of a hickory stick. When ready to use, the drum head is soaked in water and stretched sufficiently to make it ring when struck lightly and enough water is left in the bottom of the drum to enable the operator to remoisten the head by shaking the drum or turning it upside down. It requires some experience to keep the drum head tuned all night.

The gourd rattle is made of hollowed dry gourds perforated at each end with a long axis. The gourd neck can be used as a handle, or a hickory stick handle is put in one end if the gourd handle has been cut out. Sometimes the gourd is punctured with an awl to improve its tone.

125

The turtle shell leg rattles are clusters of four or five whole shells dried so that the plastron and carapace firmly encase the pebbles. The shells are tied to a strong cloth with tie strings at the top and bottom for attachment just below the knee. The leg rattles are worn only by the women. The woman enters the dance behind the leader and produces the rattling sound only at specified passages of the song or dance; by skillful movements she can hush the rattles or pound out a vigorous rhythm. At each dance, they also have a driver. The driver is the leader of the dances, usually appointed by the host. He keeps order, urges participation and also acts as a sergeant at arms. This office is only for a single night. He is also known as a starter or forcer. There is a driver to help with all the dances. The names of the dances are the Booger, Eagle, Bear, Victory, Friendship, Beaver, Buffalo, Horse and the Corn Dance.

The Booger Dance

The Booger Dance was used before the coming of the white man to drive out sickness and to keep sickness and death away. With the coming of the white man, this dance took on a different meaning. It is thought that the anxieties of the people brought about the change and that it became a symbol of the invader and of their insecurities in their dealings with the white man. They could not cope with the white invaders as men, but by portraying the invading whites as mythical animals and frivolous demons they felt more competent to deal with them. In the Booger dance, the people usually covered themselves with quilts to remain anonymous. They made their own masks out of buckeye wood colored with clay and pokeberry or black walnut and they used other things such as possum tail or any other kind of animal fur that they had to put on the mask. One mask might represent a white man with eyebrows, a moustache and goatee of black paint and maybe it would have woodchuck fur on the forehead and skin. A dark red face might represent an Indian with heavy dark eyebrows and black stain under the nose, and another could be the face of a Black man with white possum hair, eyelids and lips stained with pokeberry juice and teeth carved like a cone.

Participants could be ten or more masked men and occasionally a couple of women. They usually represented people from faraway places such as Germans, French, Chinese, Negroes or even alien Indians. The names given by the maskers or Boogers lend an obscene, dramatic element to their individual acts. Some of the names they used were Black Buttocks, Frenchman, Big Testicles and Rusty Anus. Then, at another dance, the names were usually Southerner, Northerner, Spaniard and Chinaman, and thus the name and their acts represented the character of the people they wanted to portray.

126

This is one version of the Booger dance described by a person at one dance. A masked person, led by a spokesperson, boisterously enters a house where the night dance party is being held. The maskers are systematically menacing on entering. Some of them act mad, fall on the floor, hit at the men spectators as if to get at their wives and daughters, and chase the girls to the crowded walls. The maskers then quiet down and take seats on the board or log bench along the wall. Singing by the musicians and the house party precedes and accompanies the entry. The host of the house party announces the arrival of strangers and inquires for the leader of the masked men, who is pointed out by his company. The host then converses and whispers with the leader, asking who the visitors are, whence they come and where they are going. He interprets the answers aloud to the house party, who are surprised that they are from a distant land and are going north or south. Next, the host asks them what they came for and what they want and the response is decisive and candid. Girls, the Boogers want girls; oh, they are after them, chase them around. There is more surprise and agitation on the part of the host's company. The Boogers may also want to fight. Both these demands are associated with European peoples. The host says they are peaceable people and do not want to fight. Next, the Booger leader says the members of the house party want to dance, and to this the Cherokee leader agrees.

The host of the house interprets the Booger masks in Cherokee to the gathering and then adds a few remarks intended to divert the Boogers from their purpose. He announces to the gathering that the Cherokee would like to know who these strangers are by name, then he goes to the Booger spokesman and whispers his question. The leader of the Booger whispers his masked name to the leader upon request, and the host speaks the name aloud. Then the singers of the house party, four to ten in number, the head singer with a drum and the others with rattles, commence the Booger dance-song proper. The name given by the Booger is taken from the first word of the song. The song is repeated four times while the owner of the name dances solo in the open space, stomping with both feet, bending body forward, dancing alternately on the right and left feet with body centered and the other leg nearly horizontal. He performs awkward steps as if he were a clumsy white man trying to imitate Indian dancing. Each time his name occurs in the song, the whole company applauds and yells. At the conclusion of the song, the masker resumes his seat. After he has given his name in a whisper and has had it loudly announced, each Booger dances for about five minutes until all the masked visitors have drawn applause for their obscene names and clowning. The maskers themselves do not scream or yell but indulge in exhibitionism, making dashes to the corner where the women and children are grouped. Usually, after this part of the dance, there is an interlude in which they have smoking and different games.

Next, the singers initiate the requested Eagle dance. This is a distinctive dance of the Boogers, and the dancers perform to the accompaniment of the singers and the house party. A number of women dancers, equalling the number of Boogers, join in on the line as partners during the second song of the dance. One woman wears her turtle leg rattles and assigns herself as partner to the Booger leader. The women are nicely dressed in the Cherokee style, and their entry is a symbol of the submission of the Indians to the will of the invaders and the gratification of their carnal demands. The erotic display is more overt when the Boogers have called for the Bear dance than when the Eagle dance has been chosen. As soon as the women join the dance, the Boogers begin their sexual exhibitionism. They may close up on a woman from the rear and mimic intercourse by using some protruding object made of gourd necks, which they thrust toward their partners with appropriate gestures and body motions. The women proceed serenely, and the Boogers do not insist upon touching them throughout the rest of the dance movement. The dance continues circling around the corn mortar in the center of the room until the song is ended. The Boogers now crowd noisily through the door and depart on their mysterious mission; but upon breaking forth on their new adventures, some of these errant gallants dash towards the women and clumsily try to drag a struggling victim outside. The women laugh and the girls scream and off go the Boogers.

The Eagle Dance

In the Eagle Dance, the equipment is the eagle feather wands. These are made of a wand of sourwood approximately 20 inches long and ½ inch wide to which is lashed an arch of the same material to serve as a frame for fine bald eagle feathers about twelve inches long. The feathers are fastened by inserting the quills through the holes in the arch so that they spread out like a fan. Sourwood is sacred to the Eagle rites and prevents contamination when handling the bird and its feathers. Each male dancer has a gourd rattle for his left hand, and the leading woman dancer has tortoise shell rattles in the first and third movements of the dance. A singer with a drum is at one side of the group, and there is a fire at one side of the site if the dance takes place at night outdoors. Participants, an equal number of male and female dancers on opposite lines running east and west, face each other in pairs. The dancers advance a pace, turn, retreat and circle counterclockwise, stop and resume. Steps range from a dignified walk to a usual shuffling trot, posture varies from stooping to crouching on one knee. There are three movements in this dance in which men and women in opposed pairs keep time with the drum by stepping one pace forward and then back to place. The dancers alternately pass the feather over their partners' heads with a lateral fan-like motion, holding the fans horizontal. At the change of songs, the dancers freeze, change positions and continue waving wands; then they return to the first position, alternating this until the end of the song.

During the second movement, the dancing pairs continue slowly waving feather wands over their partners' heads. They advance toward each other and withdraw over a space of about ten feet. The opposing dancers then circle about halfway, men to the right and women to the left, changing partners. During the third movement, the dancers turn, facing outward, and wave the feather wands to the sky in time with drumming and song. In this movement, which lasts about ten minutes, the men and women approach and separate back to back. During the concluding movement, the dancers face to the right and form a single column, men followed by the women, circling counterclockwise and moving feather wands up and down. The wand is held vertically in the right hand, the rattle in the left as in the first movement. Sometimes the women carry empty baskets, symbolizing the provisions of the feast to be partaken of by those present at the dance. It is the feeding of the eagle to compensate him for the taking of his feathers, and it is said to prevent malevolent medicine men from using the bird as a medium for working evil and causing sickness.

The Bear Dance

The dancers circle counterclockwise around a mortar in the center of a room or a fire outdoors. At one side of the circle is a singer with a drum, who may be aided by another with a gourd rattle. During the first movement, the men shuffle and sway their bodies imitating the leader, who growls like a bear. The dancers respond with a growl when the leader raises the tone of the song and shakes his rattle. With the second movement, the women enter the line ahead of the men, face partners and dance backwards several times. Then they reverse, and the men put their hands on the women's shoulders. The representation of the dancers as bears, potentially as mates, has a certain sexual significance. At one point, the dancers raise their heads and tear the air over their shoulders in imitation of the dance presumed to be performed by bears. It is believed that old bears have a dance in which they circle around a big hemlock tree, leaving tooth marks on the bark at head height. The bear dance that is symbolic of the bear hunt may be given as an independent performance. It is usually a major unit in a larger series of dances.

War Rites

The equipment is wooden masks with coiled rattlesnakes carved on the forehead or crown, a gourd rattle and one or two sets of turtle leg rattles. One example of a mask used is a medium red one representing an Indian. The eye holes are bored and black with grey fox fur on the top and sides of the head. Coiled rattlesnakes, the rattles inside the coils, are carved in high relief on the forehead, and teeth are carved in the mouth. Another Indian mask has a snake carved on the crown with rattles showing plainly. There is woodchuck fur on the head, and no teeth are represented. During the first movement of this dance, a warrior wearing a snake mask dances counterclockwise around the fire with a slow march step. Behind him is a singer, a woman with turtle leg rattles and other warriors. In the second movement, the warrior takes a position behind the woman with leg rattles, the singer leads the file and carries the song burden, while the others sing an accompaniment. The dance dramatizes the warrior's defiance of human enemies, of witches and ghosts. The mask in the image of a rattlesnake symbolizes his fearlessness. This is probably an enlistment dance, an encouragement to others to join in the war party.

The Victory or Scalp Dance

In the first movement, a line of warriors, each with a feathered wand in his right hand and in wartime a scalp in his left, circles around the space. A singer carrying a drum is near the center of the line, and the warriors give intermittent whoops. In the second movement, the songs cease, and the dancers walk behind the warrior at the head of the line while he recites and acts out a brief account of his exploits. The dance leader then gives his feather wand and his place to the next warrior in line. In the third movement, the victory dance song is resumed with the second warrior at the head of the line carrying the feather wand and the scalp. In the fourth movement, the warrior at the head of the line recites his exploits and then relinquishes the feather wand to the leader and goes to the end of the line, leaving the next man at the head. The movements are repeated until all the warriors have been conducted around the circle and have taken a turn at reciting their exploits. Much whooping and sustained yelling takes place at the beginning and at the end of songs and recitations. The drumming is interrupted during the recitation of exploits. At the conclusion of the dance, the feathered wands are collected and put away by the leader. This dance is an historic and boasting pageant of warrior exploits. The eagle feather wands are a symbol of victory and courage. The rites are analogous to "counting coup" of the Plains Indians.

The Formal Rites Dance

In the formal rites dance, they have the beginning dance. In this dance, the equipment is a gourd rattle for the leader and turtle shell leg rattles for one or two women. In the first movement, the dancers form a single line with sexes alternating, circle counterclockwise and then advance. In the second movement, the men face the women, dance backwards once around and then swing partners. The women dance backwards, reverse and then resume the first position. During this movement, the men engage in innocent acts of familiarity with the women partners who have drawn the file. The men sometimes hold the women's hands or clasp them palm to palm or place them on their shoulders. This dance, which resembles a friendship dance, opens a series of annual rites or social dances and is formally a social introduction. It dramatizes hospitality, first as neighbors and then as partners in the dance. In the friendship dance, the equipment is just the turtle shell leg rattle worn by the women, who follow the leaders. The men form a single file and join the women, who dance with them as partners. During the song, they dance counterclockwise with a shuffling trot, and, in the intervals, they walk in a circle. The dance is accompanied by a series of songs. During the second song in the series, when the leader begins to insert words suggestive of intimacy, the humorous gestures and acts of the pantomime begin. The intimacy sequence begins with partners facing each other. Then, partners dance side by side with hands crossed, dance facing each other and putting palms upon partners' palms, place hands upon partners' shoulders and place arms over partners' shoulders. Then, they dance side by side and the men place hats on their women partner's heads. Again, facing each other, they stroke their partners on the chin, put their hands on female partners' breasts and, while dancing side by side, touch and take hold of their partners' genitals. During the last two phases, the crowds fall together, partially to conceal these familiarities. These phases are usually omitted when whites are spectators.

During the song, the leader may raise his hands — palms in — imitating the male dancers who then dance backwards, facing their partners. At the conclusion of the song, the partners hold hands; at the change of song, they zigzag; while at the next change, they reverse directions. This is a social pantomime of the course of intimacy between the sexes, beginning with acquaintances made at the dance and developing through various stages of familiarity, intimacy, courtship and sexual intercourse. The words are sung by the various leaders selected by the driver; choral responses are made by the assistant leader and the male dancers.

The Beaver Dance

In the Beaver dance, each dancer carries a peeled sumac stick. In the middle of the dance floor is a bottle of fur or a stuffed beaver skin; and if they do not have that, a bundle of rags with feathers attached may be used to represent a beaver. In the first movement, the men and women circle counterclockwise with a shuffling step, holding the stick horizontally in the left hand. The end of each stick touches the next one, with touching ends being covered with a hand grasp. The sticks thus form a cordon or ring on the inside, supplemented by the dancers' hands. With the change of song, they change the sticks to the right hand, forming a ring on the outside of the dancers. In the second movement, the dancers carry their sticks on the left shoulder like guns. A man and woman representing hunters dance inside the ring, repeatedly striking the stuffed beaver inside the circle. During this movement, the man cries "Here!" to the dancers, and the dancers answer back. The beaver is attached to a string so it may be jerked outside the ring at the moment the dancers strike at it. This is a pantomime of a beaver hunting expedition by the hunter and his wife. The sticks represent beaver clubs or guns. Four times during the dance, they cry, "Beaver, beaver!" and the leader answers. If the dancers repeatedly hit the beaver, it is a sign of good luck; if they miss, it means bad luck. The dance lasts about half an hour.

The Buffalo Dance

In this dance, there is a singer with a drum and, at one side of the group, the women behind the leader wear turtle leg rattles. In the movement, a file of men, followed by women, circle counterclockwise with a continuous shuffling and stomping. The buffalo is symbolized by holding the fingers crooked upwards at the temple to represent horns. The Buffalo dance is preceded by a series of night dances and a formally prepared barbecue feast. The features usually associated with the Buffalo dance in other areas, such as the jostling of the female dancers by male dancers, cows and bulls respectively and the eating of corn mush from a bowl, are lacking. Furthermore, the dance is not restricted to a society of hunters; all are admitted. It is interesting to note that the dances persisted, even in this attenuated form, in spite of the disappearance of the buffalo from the Smokies.

The Horse Dance

To clear a square space for the movements, the dancers take out the mortar from the center of the room. In the first movement, one or two straight rows of men abreast face northward toward the fire, near which is a singer with a drum. The dancers move forward with slow time and small steps, imitating the walk of a horse and occasionally whinnying. At the leader's whoop, they about-face and return to the initial position, yelling at each turn. This is repeated four times to four songs. In the second movement, a woman wearing leg rattles enters the row and dances next to the man in the center of the row. The dancers, including the woman, hold hands and repeat the first movement in fast time, stomping hard with short steps imitating the trotting of horses. They advance and return four times to four songs, and formerly the men were said to have kicked at the women in the manner of horses.

The Corn Dance

In the Cherokee language, "Shallou" is also the proper name of the mistress of corn, known as Corn Woman. The instruments are gourds, and the women wear turtle leg rattles. In the first movement, while advancing with a shuffling trot behind the leader, the men and the women circle counterclockwise around the mortar in the center of the circle, dipping or pouring corn or meal into a basket or bowl held in one hand. The second movement has a change in the song. The women with the turtle leg rattles lead the other women from the line. They circle the mortar and dance sideways facing outwards, surrounded by the men's line. The men face the women and dance around the mortar for two or three turns, all continuing the hand motions. In the third movement, the men and women change places and continue the hand movements, making two or three circuits. In the fourth movement, the lines of the men and women mingle again and repeat the first movement in pouring corn from a bowl or basket of plenty. The dance expresses supplication and thanks for the abundant corn crops.

CHAPTER II
Cherokee Poetry

Introduction:

Laurence French and Jim Hornbuckle

Nothing conveys the intensity of human emotions quite like poetry. Poems move, stimulate, elate, sadden. They allow us to empathize with the feelings of the poet or to provide our own significance to these clusters of words. Cherokee poems, especially these written by young Cherokee poets, provide the reader access to the Cherokees' very special and cherished inner feelings. Some are informative, others are humorous, while many reflect deep sorrow, thought or anguish over the Indians' lot.

Sixty-one poems by sixteen Cherokees are presented here. Twenty-two poems are the work of Pam Conseen Taylor, a very talented young Cherokee woman. Also we have sixteen of Lloyd Owle's poems, five each from D. Chiltoskie and Marilyn Crowe Johnson, two from Carol Cucumber and a number of contributors with one poem each. Please read these works carefully, for they say much, often with deep emotions, allowing much to be learned and shared by all of us regardless of our race, sex, age or ethnic origin.

Bows and Arrows

Bows and arrows,
Flaming headdresses,
Tomahawks, and
Pottery.
Today's idea . . .
Of yesterday Indians.

Pam Taylor

To Be An Indian

The lines of age,
Cross my face.
Through the years,
Much has been experienced.
The happiness of belonging,
To the earth.
The love found by giving
Thanks, through dance.
The many passing of moons,
As one grows wiser.
Why then . . .
Is it so wrong,
To be an Indian?

Pam Taylor

New Yesterdays

The years of life are passing
We are growing
Around us, yesterday dissolves
Into only a memory.
A "remember when."
We grasp tightly,
Feeling insecure.
But know
We must make
New Yesterdays,
With the wisdom
Acquired.

Pam Taylor

To the Great White Father in Washington

You have turned your back
On the Redman,
When he came to you in
Peace.
He asks the Great Spirit to bless
You.
And give to you, understanding,
And knowledge.
He was only asking, for you
To listen,
To the cries of "your children,"
But . . .
What were we to expect . . .
Your children in New York City
Are crying too.
As you dine in your chamber,
As your family walks beside you,
I hope that you'll leave no tracks,
For anyone else to follow.

Pam Taylor

I Feel Red

I feel the soaring eagle,
As I climb the mountain top.
I feel the grouchy, rough bear,
As I too search the earth for food.
I feel the swiftness of the fish,
As it swims against the current.
I feel the fleeing of the deer,
As a strange being approaches.
I feel Red,
Just as the clay of the earth.

Pam Taylor

An Indian Feeling

Over on that mountain top,
*   Is a house so large,*
Down by that valley stream
*   Someone builds a barge.*
Up the road I'm quite aware
*   Of that new man-made lake.*
On the land we once used
*   To garden, for living's sake.*
Sometimes, more often than not
*   I wonder if they really know*
What we felt like, when we
*   Had to go.*

Pam Taylor

To Die in Peace

Yesterday we cried for land,
*   Yet from Florida,*
To California we lost it all.
*   Today we cry for rights*
But from Washington,
*   We hear, of glorious promises . . .*
For a tomorrow.
*   Tomorrow we will be asking*
For survival.
*   Just to let us alone . . .*
To die in peace.

Pam Taylor

Little Did We Know

We got together,
A long time ago,
And we decided . . .
We will be as the eagle—
Soar with pride, and keep the
Mountain tops as our shelter.
We would live by the streams—
So that the fish would serve as food
And to keep pure the water,
So we might drink freely.
We would walk the winding trails—
So not to destroy the vast forest—
And the secrets shared by the many
Bird songs, the animal language
And the whispers of the wind.
And we decided . . .
That what the Great Spirit had granted—
Would be taken care of in His honor,
And each living thing would have a meaning
And each deceased thing would rest in peace.
Little did we know . . .
The white man would try to destroy us.

Pam Taylor

Tears

Columbus, "discovered"
Washington, "stressed"
Lincoln, "fought"
Jackson, "possessed"
and the
Redman, "wept."

Pam Taylor

I am Indian, I

I suppose some people believe,
That we should have no race,
That the beauty of my deep bronze skin,
And the blackness of my hair,
Should carry no pride.
But I don't believe this is the truth,
Because . . .
Just as the Great Spirit
Created the
Fair skin of the Europeans,
The black skin of the Negro,
He created me Red.
So as long as there is air to breathe,
Water to drink,
And a place to rest,
I will look!
I will walk!
I will talk!
As an American Indian.

Pam Taylor

Yesterday

Yesterday . . .
I always speak of yesterday
Only because . . .
We then had a chance.
We lived in peace,
As a nation
Who belonged . . .
Only to the earth.
Now as yesterday . . .
We belong—as a Nation
Only now, it's to Washington.

Pam Taylor

Thanksgiving

The sounds of the drums
  Beat heavy in my mind.
The sounds of many chants
  Burn meaning in my soul.
The steps I take when dancing.
  Go always forward, not back.
And the reason, is for
  Thanksgiving,
Not, assistance.

                    Pam Taylor

I Am Indian, II

Red as the sunset,
As tall as the Sequoyah,
As thoughtful as an owl,
As sly as the fox,
  I am Indian.

                    Pam Taylor

Ironic Laughter

The laughter I hear,
Comes the pale one.
He laughs because,
The language I speak
Is not of his tongue,
The color of his skin,
Is not the shade of mine.
And his beliefs,
Are not in tune with mine.
Why laugh? My pale one.
Who wears the pleasant face?
Who wears the false one?

                    Pam Taylor

140

Belonging

The feel of belonging
To the earth,
Made my life
Worthwhile.
My hair swayed
In the wind,
Just as the trees,
Following a pattern.
My eyes as brown as
The mountain bear.
In search together for food,
From the ripened
Fruit trees.
The reddest bronze skin was as
Sunset.
On a warm autumn evening.
I am Indian,
I belong to the earth.

Pam Taylor

Indian Walk

We walked daily through
The fields,
Filled with the warmth of
Nature.
The sun at our back, our
Moccasins making tracks,
In the dandy fields.

Pam Taylor

The Wind's Tracks

The mild wind whispers
Softly,
Look behind you,
You made no tracks . . .
No one saw you come this way.

Pam Taylor

Indian Prayer, I

OH GREAT SPIRIT,
FATHER OF ALL,
Can I dare ask,
What color are you?
DOWN ON MY KNEES,
MY FACE TO THE DUST,
In gratitude.
That I will know it not.
The importance lies not in
Color alone,
But in the way you find
To wear it.

Pam Taylor

Indian Prayer, II

Oh Mother Earth
Hear my plea
Speak to me
Through the whispering pine,
And tell me,
Who am I?
Please give to me,
The answer
Through the bubbling brook,
About where I am to go.
Give to me I cry,
Through a sunshine ray,
A path to follow
So my moccasins will not fail thee,
A way to hear,
An identity of my own
And a path to lead me
To a hunting ground of love.

Pam Taylor

I Ask

I lay down my knife
Beside your gun,
And ask . . .
Is it good, that we not fight?

I give you my blanket,
In return for your coat
And ask . . .
Is it good, that we exchange?

I give you my land
In return for your progress
And ask . . .
Is it good, that we advance?

I share with you my beliefs,
In return for your beliefs,
And ask . . .
Why . . .
Is it good that we lose our identity?

Pam Taylor

I Honor Them

It's hard to understand
   A broken and harsh voice.
But many the years,
   They've had to speak.
It's hard to understand
   Why they weep and wander,
   So easily.
But there are so many memories,
   Behind them.
It's hard to take them shopping,
   Because the clothes are mismatched,
   And the travel is slow.
But after all,
   The clothes they've made,
   Have yet to wear out.
   And they have many miles,
   On those moccasins.
It's all right my elderly friend
I understand and honor you.
And I am looking forward to filling
   Your moccasins . . .
   If I ever can.

Pam Taylor

I'm Proud

My skin is brown and I'm proud
My cheekbones are high and I'm proud
I carry in my blood drops of courage from Junaluska
And love for my people like Tsali.
I walked along adding to the many during the Trail of Tears.
I carry the burden that every Indian carries—
The white man—
I'm an Indian and I'm proud.

Pam Taylor

144

The Oconaluftee River

Where the searching eye is caught
By the glitter of shifting sand
As clear destined water flows
Through the forgotten Cherokee land
Where flowers burst in bloom
As birds begin to sing
Along green shady banks
Small voices of children ring
Where time lingers amazingly
With shadows edged with silver
Tis a wonder of the Cherokee world
The Oconaluftee River.

Lloyd Owle

Indian Shoes

These shoes are old and worn
These shoes are old and torn,
These shoes have seen many miles
While tears haunted Indian styles.

These shoes have seen the years
These shoes know the Trail of Tears,
As many wore away
These shoes realized the need to stay.

These shoes are old and pitiful
Their roads were cruel and scornful
These shoes have walked in pain
They endured life with nothing to gain.

These shoes are Indian shoes
And as the end of life nears
These shoes will fade away
They walked the Trail of Tears one day.

Lloyd Owle

145

Friends Lost

I'm going out by the wall
To sit and watch little birds play,
I'm going out by the wall
And scare the birds away.

I'm going out by the wall
To count my little friends,
As their instinct begins to call
And they drift away again.

I'm going out by the wall
To throw things in life away,
As by the open gate
I will probably stay.

I'm going out by the wall
Where my friends are slain,
As doom met their lives
While they cried for mercy in dreadful pain.

I'm going out by the wall
Now I can walk through the pain
My soul has died once
And by the wall I'll die again.

Lloyd Owle

Mountain Life

The mountains pull at me
The trees stroke my eyes
The wind brushes by
Pulling down the sky.

The flowers tug at me
The streams wash me down
Life drives at me
I fall and hug the ground.

Lloyd Owle

146

Mountain Life

Whether I be down in the valley,
Or high on a hill,
I hear the lonely call,
Of the old whippoorwill,
Oh, I love mountain life!
To me it's so dear.

As the mountains reach so high,
And attempt to pull down the sky,
It's all so wonderful,
As a billion flowers . . .
Create such fragrant smells,
Oh, I love mountain life!

Lloyd Owle

Clingman's Dome

Where the mountains are so blue,
Below Clingman's Dome,
The people of Cherokee,
Make the valleys their home.

As clouds drift so free,
And tumbling thunder roars,
A new life seems to develop,
Through an opening in Nature's doors.

Where green plants flutter,
In the gentle breeze,
And bees buzz wild flowers,
With true life and ease.

Where one looks,
Out into the hills,
And visions are stolen,
With breathtaking trills.

Where many many tribes,
Of Cherokee Indians have roamed,
In the beautiful valleys,
Below Clingman's Dome.

Lloyd Owle

The Meadow of Eternity

I'm in a field of daises
Standing in the green green grass,
I will live here forever
My life will endure,
The flowers will never wilt
Color will never fade,
Rich is my heart with love
Femininity is softly around,
As I hold to life
Warmness will never end,
I'm in the meadow of time
I'm in the light of life
I'm in the house of love
I'm in the endless shadow,
Reaching through the stars
I'm in the meadow of eternity.

Lloyd Owle

The Puzzle

I'm working on the puzzle of time
And it is sad to realize
That the puzzle has missing pieces
Pieces unheard of and unseen.
As a heart weakens and dies
Why doesn't someone hear its cry?
As a life wilts and erases in time
Why does time fill so many spaces?
Why doesn't someone love one in youth?
As they cry for love in truth,
Why does life come so cold?
As blood is soon to grow old,
Why can't life be with everyone?
In a life of beautiful fun
A life of delicacy and joy.
If cold hearts could become warm
And love would dominate the world,
In an understanding life
And all people would sing together
A song of the stars
To hush the voice of the sea
And remove the cry of pain,
Then it would solve the puzzle for me.

Lloyd Owle

The White Ghost

The white ghost of winter
Creeps into the valley
It drifts over the hills . . .
It sweeps through the trees,
Rivers turn to ice
The Indian sees death near
It drifts through his home
As snow blows inside
Its scream is heard outside
Children cry from cold
Small bodies become numb,
Everything is still,
Then the wind comes again
A small child hushes his cry
His tender life is gone now
His mother cries of pain
The white ghost continues to rage,
Slaying all it nears . . .
And the Indian is its prey
They took his home and land
And left him in the cold,
To face the white ghost of winter.

Lloyd Owle

Nature's Picture

Take a paint brush
And a pail of Nature's paint
Then we'll go out into the world . . .
And paint so beautifully.
We'll paint in the valley
We'll paint the meadow's grass
Then we'll paint the flowers . . .
On the ground and on the trees.
We'll paint and tame the wildlife,
We'll paint the birds
We'll paint the bees.
Then we will welcome the yellow sun,
We'll bring in the rain,
We'll paint a valley of happiness
A valley of love and romance.
Then we'll paint ourselves . . .
In the middle of the valley,
And live in the ecstasy.

Lloyd Owle

Indian Turtle Shells

As Indians dance
The turtle shells rattle
To create a rhyme
A rhyme the Indians dance by.
As the Indians dance
Empty shells begin to rattle
The turtle's life is gone
The turtle rattles of death.
The Indians dance
The turtle shells rattle
Who cares for death
This is a happy time.

Lloyd Owle

151

Let's Go Logging

Come! Let's go logging,
I heard the old man say,
Come let's go logging,
Let us go today.

Let's go to the hills,
And take in the forest,
Come let's go logging,
You be my guest.

Come let's go logging,
Where tall sturdy trees stand,
Come let us see Nature,
As we listen to the whispering wind.

Come let's go logging,
I heard the old man say,
As I looked at him I knew,
He'd logged his life away.

Lloyd Owle

Race Forgotten by Time

The American Indian has been
  Kicked
  Stepped on
  Robbed
  Murdered
  Beaten
  Cheated
He has been unmercifully tortured
He has been promised everything
Every promise has been broken
He has been downed in every phase of life
He has been blinded in soul
  Robbed of is heart.
After all this
The Indian is kind and gentle
He tries with all his heart
He still has pride and hope to build a new way to live,
To restore his own traditions
Which knew
  Honor
  Love
  Consideration to all things
Oh, to reach for the stars
Which the Indian dreamed of.

Lloyd Owle

A Winter Poem

A Winter Snow!
    Crystalline mantle
    Draped gently
    'cross the shoulders
Of earth's brown winter dress.

Flakes seem to float,
    Almost in reluctance,
    Slowly, to their downward destiny.
    Some caught, at times,
    By baby gusts of wind,
    Swirl round and round
    As if at play.

Some flakes are interrupted,
    In their fall,
    By reaching arms of trees.
Spared from the common ground,
    As if their purpose
    Is something special.
    It is!
    They outline branches
    Against the blue of sky
    When the snow has stopped.

                    Lloyd Owle

Happy Hunting Grounds

The Happy Hunting Grounds
    With all hearts joined
Warm hands touching
    With the forgotten race—The American Indian.

                    Lloyd Owle

Indian Traditions

With a crown of feathers
The Indian man stood,
He could color the world
If he only would.

He was asked why
There he only stood,
He said he couldn't change
And he wouldn't if he could.

Lloyd Owle

I Pray

Oh Great Spirit
Help me, guide me
Each day of my life.
I want to learn as much as I can
Of the white man's ways.
I want to use these things
For the benefit of my people.
I want to be able to withstand
All elements of His world.
I want, Oh Great Spirit,
To retain the past
Cultivate the present
And create a better future
For all future generations.
Oh Great Spirit
Stand beside me, give me strength . . .

D. Chiltoskie

Holy Mother

Oh Holy Mother

> *Help me to find what I am seeking*
> *Guide me between right and wrong*
> *Teach me all I need to know*
> *Concerning these white men.*

Oh Holy Mother

> *Make my heart strong*
> *To beat only for my people*
> *And endure all the hate and injustice around me*
> *Make my body strong*
> *To endure the pain and hardships I face.*

Oh Holy Mother

> *Help me to speak out*
> *For changes that have to come*
> *I am small but make my voice loud.*

Oh Holy Mother

> *Give me strength to go on,*
> *And always look toward the sunrise.*

D. Chiltoskie

Termination

An end to the life we have known,
  Just like before.
How long will it be before you try
  Again to end our existence?
Once we asked only to share
  What you eventually took and what we had.
What had we done then
  To make you act the way you did?
You didn't listen then
  And you're not listening now,
  You only tell us what we should do.
You say you want what's best for us,
  We had that once and you took it.
How do you know what is best for us
  When you don't know what is best for you?
No, we can't change the past
But you're not trying to make
  The future any better for us,
  You're only trying to push us
  As far away from you as possible.

D. Chiltoskie

157

The New Indians

The New Indians
We're here, we're strong
We've been suppressed too long
Now it's our time, to rise, to speak out
And to be heard.
The white men
They've tried to change and mold us
After them, but our spirits are too strong.
The New Indians
We're tired or being pushed, shoved,
Lied to, spit upon, and pitied.
The New Indians
Yes, it's our turn now
They can't stop us, we've got to be heard.
The white men
They've got to listen to us now
And they will!!

D. Chiltoskie

Our Tomorrows

We are their tomorrows
*   Their hopes their dreams.*
Today we start, today is our beginning.
We can fulfill our dreams and hopes
*   But we must fulfill theirs too.*
Will we let them down,
*   Will they lose, like so many times before?*
Are we brave enough, to leave,
To try in the white man's world?
It's a big challenge
*   How many will take it and succeed.*

D. Chiltoskie

158

Beginning

Little is really known about the American
Indian, or what links our human soul
with the earth, we believed that
this land was created for us by the
Great Spirit and that it would
be ours. . . . . .forever.
The new world . . . this is what the
white man, called our land, but it was
not new at all . . . The Redman. . . . . .
inhabited America for centuries.

Carol Cucumber

To Be Free

The struggle has begun
A new hope has been born
Our sunny day will come.
Look up into the sky as the
Wind whispers in the trees, atop
A floating cloud that echoes
To be free . . .

Carol Cucumber

Brothers

My Brothers
    I
am an
        Indian
The world and Universe
are my Brothers
    I
Have been told and
    I
    Know, but sometimes
    I
Wonder if the people in
This world and Universe are
My Brothers also.

Jackson

Vietnam Tears

I stood and I watched as a mother cried,
When she had heard that her son had died,
He didn't die because he was sick,
Or he didn't die because he was in a wreck,
He died doing what he felt was right.

I watched a father try to hold back his tears,
His son had lived only a scant 19 years,
His son had died nine thousand miles away,
And what was there left for a father to say?
He got down on his knees and said a prayer,
His brave son knows his father did care.

I stood and watched as a little girl cried,
She didn't understand why her brother had passed on,
Why he never again played with her on the lawn.
Looking at the little girl's tears I knew,
That her big brother died
Fighting for me and you.

Henderson Climbingbear

160

Boys, Girls, Beads and Hair

Lovebeads and long hair now are in.
But tell me, what will they win?
The war on poverty, peace for the world,
No boys, only a girl.

Boys, the girls think they are ever so keen;
By running around and being so mean.
By doing this they do not know,
That one day they will hurt some so and so.

Their minds are not on the Peace of the World,
Only on their hair when it is uncurled.
If only they would consider exactly what for,
Even though we love freedom, there is still so much war.

So stop and think all of you teens,
Just what being a leader means.
Picture yourself in greater heights
Then you will know something about our Civil Rights.

Florence Ross

Nineteenth Century Law

If a man commits murder,
A crime punishable by death,
Let him be made to eat ramps,
Till he expires by his own venomous breath.

Cecil Johns

Love

Look around, do you see?
The war hawk, the dove,
Something reaching for me;
Below and above,
Everyone's searching for that little thing
called love.

Sharon E. Bradley

Death Spirit

The old Indian dies.
His folks missed him not.
But his ghost will proudly rise
And it will be sought,
But never in this world will his spirit be caught.

Dinah Swimmer

Tomorrow

Maybe tomorrow,
Maybe there will be freedom
For all our sake, no?

Johnny Bradley

Life

Can you use a weapon
To live in this world?
Forever are you weeping
To kill a squirrel?
You just go around once in life; give it a whirl.

Stephen Queen

My Wish

My wish
When I die
Place my body in a tree
Where the winds can blow
Through my body and carry
On my beliefs.

Bambi Armachain

Winter Snow

Tiny flakes of white
  Fill the air in multitude,
  Serve to insulate this place
  'gainst man's alien sounds,
  Brought about
  When he loses contact
  With his inner self,
  A natural quiet.

If you will listen,
  As you watch in wonder,
  And witness heaven's open windows,
  You'll hear all of Nature
  Hold its breath,
  As it's dazzled by the miracle
  Of another Winter Snow.

Homer Crowe

Indian Love Song

Why do I walk the white line alone,
  Playing a lover's flute?
By the road I shall fall as a crumbling stone,
And shall wait there as mute.
I walk the white road to the
  Blood-red moon,
Lifting my mourning cry,
She who was lost comes here to me soon;
I have willed that I die.

Blackfoot Song

163

Ending

He was born in early morning
his mother all alone
his name yet to be chosen
destiny already known.

The last of many brothers
the first of those to come.

He is growing very quickly
how fast the time has gone
the teachers say he's bright.
Sure to lead his people—
as sure as time goes on.

The last of many brothers
the first of those to come.

He never had the time
to learn all he could.
His dreams of betterment
and college
ended when his father passed away.

With his mother unskilled and
no work for those unlearned,
the boy forgot his dreams
to support his family in any way he could.

Yet he hopes the future
holds more for his son,
but deep inside he knows
before his son's life has begun,
He's the last of many brothers
and the first of those to come.

Marilyn Crowe Johnson

Hunger Versus Inflation

What is for supper
what are we having today?
Will we have beef, chicken or
shall it be fish?
We know the answer
It's beans and potatoes
cornbread and mush,
soups or gravies, easy to fix
without any fuss.

It's not the meal fare
that gets me depressed,
it's the weight that will double
and the zippers that will pop
when I try to dress.

The waistline once showing
the hours I've spent
exercising my flesh,
has turned completely from firm
into a mess.

The lettuce and tomatoes
the boiled meats I once had
have increased price,
and it makes me mad!

Instead of ranting and raving
and being sad
thinking of delicacies long
ago I once had

I shall hunt up some
Indian chow
that grows in the wild
since a long time ago.

Wild salad greens
shall it be for me
field cress, mushrooms and
assorted things,
it's a bit of hard work
in the woods and the hills

But it sure beats beans
for a good healthy meal!

Marilyn Crowe Johnson

165

For God's Holy Name

In the beginning, the white men
came to the new world, to
worship in peace and freedom and
to share the Lord's holy name.

Teach the heathen Indians
about the word of God.
Tell them of His wonders,
miracles he performed.

Mention that we came here
to praise His mighty name,
to worship Him in freedom,
to teach others so they would do the same.

Then ask them very kindly
to let us live near them,
that there is room for all—
'tis for God's holy name.

The Indians are useful
teaching us what they know
about living in the wilderness,
surviving in the cold.
The days are filled with glory
freedom for us all.
We've built, grown and prospered
we need no one else at all.

Time has flown by so quickly
things are not the same
the Indian must move
for they are in our way . . .

You can't find them?
the others refuse to move, you say!
They absolutely must go—
for it's here we mean to stay!

166

What? Won't move again?
Won't let us have more land?
Kind of selfish and savage now . . .
We'll have to deal with them today!

We've moved them once, we'll move them again.
In the future it'll be the same,
We do this not *for us*
But for "Gold's" holy name.

They are few and weakened now
but still proud and untamed
(they surely must be insane).
Yes, move the others also—
way out onto the Plains.

Nicely done, so few of them remain—
Guilty? For what?
We did this all for
"Gold's" holy name.

Marilyn Crowe Johnson

Peace

The loud cry of the War Chief
echoes through the night.
Rise, avenge your brothers!
We must fight!

A still soft sound barely heard,
whispered by a single man.
No. Have you not learned?
Then quieter softer he whispers —
still —

Your anger and hatred kills.
The redman and white man die.
Must you bend to vengeance's will?

The War Chief has many followers.
The Peace Chief sits alone.
Few have heard his words.

Again comes the cry for war!
Again and again comes the plea for peace.
Still again and again plus many times more —
has anyone heard?

Marilyn Crowe Johnson

Changing

Unobstructed view
from windows in my home
of sunsets in evenings
with oranges, pinks and blues.
Created with many beautiful hues.
The grass turning bright
vividly green.
Light, dark and many shades in between
pines almost black.
Within the light of the waning sun
mountains in the distance.
Clouds lofting above.

Dark purple and gray.
The river now darkened
nearly black and foreboding.
Totally different from earlier today
when in the bright sun
it's noisily moving
was constantly gay.
Soft breezes one can only feel
gently lifting the leaves.
Nudging scattered flowers to nod
lulling small birds
to sleep in the trees.

What a shame
this incredible beauty must end
to give way to blackness
without end.
Alas, I cry,
but to behold—
stars now showing in the expanse above.
I discover a new cycle
of the Great Spirit "Love."

Marilyn Crowe Johnson

CHAPTER III
Cherokee Arts And Crafts

INTRODUCTION:

Laurence French, Jim Hornbuckle, Reuben Teesatuskie

and Elsie Martin

Arts and crafts are by far the most popular of all Native American artifacts. The demand for both aboriginal and contemporary Indian arts and crafts is incredible, with these objects being found throughout the world. The recent Pan-Indian movement has done much to increase the American Indians' sense of self-worth and self-pride, and this is evident through visible means such as appearance and attire. Consequently, Native Americans have pooled their combined heritages sharing their "Indianism." Sioux braids, Navajo headbands, Plains Indian headdresses, Navajo, Ute and Zuni jewelry are worn by many Indians regardless of tribal affiliation, while ojos (God's eyes), fans, turtle and gourd rattles, Indian baskets, spiral pottery, beadwork, woven blankets, wood and stone carvings adorn Indian homes.

Included in this chapter is a section on the origin of Cherokee arts and crafts and the contemporary preservation of these arts and crafts by the Eastern Cherokees. This is followed by a section on the sale and display of Cherokee arts and crafts, with particular attention paid to the Qualla Co-op, the "Medicine Man Shop" and other local cooperatives. The third section looks at particular Cherokee craftspersons and their works, including the art of basketry, wood and stone carvings, pottery, beadwork, sash weaving, mask carving, bowl making and jewelry.

The last section is unique in that it presents the art of Cherokee food preparation. Traditional foods still play an important role in the lives of many Cherokees, especially the more conservative families living away from the tourist route. We used the interview method, letting the Cherokee woman explain, in her own words, how she prepares her Indian meals. Having attended such meals, the editors can attest to the enthusiasm generated at an "Indian dinner," the atmosphere being similar to that commonly associated with white Thanksgiving, Easter and Christmas feasts.

THE ORIGIN OF CHEROKEE ARTS AND CRAFTS:

Laurence French and Jim Hornbuckle

During aboriginal times, prior to the advent of white contact, the Cherokees lived in permanent agricultural villages without the benefit of the more technologically sophisticated implements utilized by their European white counterparts. Yet, the Cherokees seemed to manage well without advanced technology as the thousand-year survival of this system indicates. The early Cherokee way of life necessitated innovative uses of the natural environment, and in doing so, the Cherokees fostered the talents and skills associated with the production of these implements. Moreover, this way of life required a complex apprenticeship educational system in order to enable future generations to preserve these skills.

Looking back in time, envision an early Cherokee village with its centrally located seven-sided town house surrounded by forty or so log homes, while beyond the village's fort-like log perimeter lie the communal garden plots and fields and pastures. Within this setting, the Cherokees virtually lived off the land, improvising shelter, clothing, food, tools, weapons, household utensils and ceremonial and religious objects. Vegetation, wildlife, minerals, ores and even the soil itself provided the raw material from which these things were constructed. Once viewing the completed objects, one realizes that it is the craftsmanship which accounts for this transformation of common place natural sources into objects of art.

Trees were felled with stone axes, wedges and hammers and shaped with stone chisels and adzes. Most garden tools were made of either stone or wood including stone spades, hoes and knives and wooden rakes, pitchforks, planting and threshing sticks. Similarly, dugout canoes were used for both transportation and fishing. Early Cherokees were quite adept at the art of fishing, devising both traps and nets in addition to the common hook and line method. River cane basket traps were employed in capturing large quantities of fish. Here, the traps would be placed at strategic points downstream; then Cherokee males, joined by hemp rope or grape vine with long strands of ropes with stones attached hanging from their waists, would form a line across the brook or river upstream. Moving downstream, the Cherokee men would shout and pound the water, driving the fish ahead of them into the traps. Fish nets, on the other hand, were usually dragged across a stream or were used in a similar fashion as the fish trap method described above. When a family needed only enough fish for themselves, then a male would go down to the nearby stream and cast his line with its carved bone fishhook. He might also go out on a larger body of water with the family canoe and repeat this process.

All domestic utensils and clothing were produced from their natural surroundings. These included baskets, bowls, knives, spoons, rugs and clothing. Common household objects were ceramic bowls for cooking and storage of water or liquids. Early Cherokees made coiled pottery using the natural clay from the area. Most of these vessels were of a coarse texture due to the use of crushed stone and mussel shells, sand, mica, quartzite and straw as reinforcers. The color of the ceramic object was determined by both heat intensity and time of firing, this being done either over an open flame or in a ceramic oven. The popular black texture was obtained by using a moderate heat for a long period. The colors varied from a light sand color to a glossy black. The pots were first air-dried, then fired. Cherokees decorated their ceramic vessels with stamping paddles consisting of flat wooden devices with designs carved upon them. Only the earlier pots were straw-tempered, these dating to over a thousand years ago. Straw-tempered clay, however, continued to be used for chinking between logs and stones as a reinforcement for this common natural mortar. Bowl carving, either from soapstone or wood, seemed to complement the Cherokee women's household.

Baskets, too, were an important aboriginal artifact. They were used to gather, store and prepare foods. They also served as back packs and as decorations. Native dyes, made from broomsedge, apple bark, marigolds, bloodroot, dahlias, walnut bark, hemlock, touch-me-nots, madder, indigo, black wood and pokeberries, provided a variety of colors for the Cherokees. Baskets were usually dyed with black walnut root for dark colors and with bloodroot for reds. The material itself, river cane, maple sugar and oak splits, contrasted these colors with their natural yellow hue. Early Cherokees had bread baskets, fish baskets, pack baskets, hanging baskets and hominy sifters in their homes. Some baskets had handles and some were ribbed, while double-weave baskets were so well prepared that many claim they could hold water. The Cherokees and Catawbas shared a unique basket design in which the baskets were rimmed with a thin oak hoop, bound with hickory fiber.

Although animal skins, especially deer and bear skins, were widely used by the early Cherokees for clothing and blankets, woven material was used as well. Blankets, clothing and hemp rugs were all constructed on a simple frame, while sashes, scarfs and belts were made by the fingerweaving method.

Weapons demanded equal skills in their making. Early Cherokee weapons consisted mainly of war clubs, knives, spears, the bow and arrow, blowguns, gorgets (body armaments) and shields. These weapons were used either for hunting or war parties or both. War clubs were carved from stone and affixed with bear gut to a sturdy hardwood handle, while knives were chipped from flint or quartz with the handle bound in rawhide. Similarly, spear points and arrow heads were also chipped from flint or quartz and then fastened to their respective shafts with bear gut. River cane was used for spear shafts, while the smaller switch cane was employed for arrow shafts. Bird feathers adorned the opposite end of the arrow shaft, serving the two-fold function of identifying the owner and maintaining accuracy in flight. The bow itself was carved from a single piece of locust or mock orange wood five to six feet in length and strung with deer sinew. Blowguns, used mostly for hunting small game, were made from sturdy river cane and measured eight to ten feet when completed. Some skilled craftsmen even filed the interior for greater accuracy. Locust shaft darts tufted with thistledown and often dipped with a mild poison were the projectiles shot from these weapons. River cane animal traps and hemp snares were other implements used by the early Cherokees in their hunting endeavors.

Body armament consisted of strings of shell, bone and animal teeth made into neck collars, arm and leg guards and chest and back plates. These were probably quite effective defenses against glancing blows from spears, arrows, knives and clubs but were rendered useless once the white man introduced gunpowder to the American Indians. Some evidence suggests Cherokee warriors used hand-held shields as well, but these, too, were ineffective against firearms.

Finally, we come to ceremonial objects, which were used in a wide array of activities from birth to death and all sacred and festive events in between. Typically, ceremonial ceramics included large clay pots, opened at both ends, used in burying infants and children. Clay peace pipes and effigy pottery were other sacred ceramic objects used by the early Cherokees. Each figure, whether it was a frog, turtle, bird, animal or human image, had a sacred significance in itself, as did carved stone pipes and stone and wooden effigy figurines. Larger carved ceremonial objects were the "Willum Ollums" or wooden totem poles representing an abstract pictorial history of the Cherokee it honored. Other wooden artifacts include the Cherokee ceremonial masks used in all major festivals, and during funeral, hunting and war party rituals. Cherry, black walnut, buckeye and holly are the woods most commonly associated with Cherokee masks. Many were adorned with animal fur and parts, especially those used in hunting rituals. Perhaps the most unusual mask is the Booger mask used to ward off evil spirits. Interestingly, the serpent was a major symbol of evil during aboriginal times and often adorned the Booger mask. After white contact, the Booger mask took on the

173

face of the devil, again often with the serpent intermingled in his horns. Medicine bowls, wedding jugs, ball sticks for the seasonal stick ball competition, ornamental necklaces, collars, bracelets and turtle rattles were other ceremonial objects used by the early Cherokees.

The advent of the white man and the influence of his culture and religion greatly altered the aboriginal way of life. Yet, in spite of these changes, many of the early arts and crafts have managed to survive to the present. The following section looks at Cherokee crafts today.

Cherokee Crafts Today:

Laurence French and Jim Hornbuckle

Many of the traditional Cherokee arts and crafts have survived to the present. This is mostly due to the long isolation afforded the Cherokees, which provided an environment conducive to the preservation of many of their cherished cultural traits. Yet, even in the short span of 30 years, from the end of World War II when the Boundary first experienced significant outside influences until today, many of their traditional customs, notably the arts and crafts, have been threatened with extinction. Fortunately, efforts have been made to preserve these Cherokee practices, so that today their arts and crafts are world renowned.

Although these practices no longer have their early, aboriginal significance, they do serve four important functions today: economic, therapeutic, recognitional and cultural. The economic function is obvious. Skilled Cherokee craftspersons can augment their income with the sale of their work. And it is for this reason that many co-ops and other outlets have emerged on the Qualla Boundary.

Many must wonder how these crafts are marketed. Actually, there are many outlets on the Qualla Boundary for the collection and sale of these crafts. Probably the most significant distributor is the Qualla Arts and Crafts Mutual, Incorporated. The co-op explains its history and purpose as follows:

> *The goals of Qualla have always been to keep alive the rich cultural heritage in arts and crafts of the Eastern Band of Cherokee Indians. In the early years, Qualla made an important contribution by providing a year-round place for the artists and craftsmen to sell and market their creations, at a time when this work was the only source of income for many a family. Qualla Arts and Crafts Mutual, Inc. has consistently paid higher prices to the artists and craftsmen for their work and has provided the recognition they so greatly deserve. Qualla is located on the Qualla Indian Boundary, Highway 441, Cherokee, North Carolina, at the eastern entrance to the Great Smoky Mountains National Park.*

> *In the early 1930's the potential of arts and crafts on the Qualla Indian Boundary was recognized by the Indian artists and craftsmen, and with assistance from the Bureau of Indian Affairs under a community development project, support was provided for these talented Native Americans. As an outgrowth of this project, the first craftsmen's cooperative was organized in 1946 and ultimately grew into the present organization.*

In 1960, a building program was undertaken by the group which resulted in the attractive sales shop that the organization operates. So successful has this cooperative venture been, that plans are now being made to enlarge the sales area.

Privately-owned shops also attract these prized arts and crafts, including the Medicine Man Craft Shop, the El Camino restaurant, J. P.'s River Room restaurant and the Cherokee Holiday Inn.

Monetary gains, however, are not the primary consideration for most Cherokee craftspersons. Quality production brings peace of mind, as do all creative endeavors. Perhaps this is why the therapeutic and cultural functions are the most significant ones. The process of creating or participating in a cherished Cherokee endeavor not only directly links that particular Cherokee with his or her cultural heritage, but it brings the craftspeople considerable peace of mind and a strong sense of self-worth.

Actually, all four contemporary functions are interrelated. Quality Cherokee crafts are self-serving while at the same time profitable. Once sold, they reach the far ends of the world, bringing international recognition to the Eastern Band as a whole; in this sense, Cherokee craftspersons are the tribe's best ambassadors.

Cherokee arts, such as dancing, singing and bow and arrow, blowgun and stick ball competition are all kept alive through yearly festivals or powwows, most of which are intertribal. The fall festival is the modern counterpart of the ancient harvest festival, which was the most significant event during aboriginal times. Similarly, the fall festival is the most important cultural event for many of today's Cherokees. Great honor and recognition are bestowed upon those who distinguish themselves in the various competitive events. And equally important is the thrill afforded the Cherokee spectators who watch these events, leaving standing room only.

Forty-niners and powwows, often representing multiple tribal groups, are again staging a comeback, especially among the young people. This, incidentally, can be attributed to the new Pan-Indian movement and its emphasis on renewed Indian pride. But the young Indians are not the only Cherokees participating in these performing arts. The "Trail of Tears Singing" draws both Eastern and Western Cherokees to the Snowbird community for an emotion-laden weekend of singing and interaction involving Cherokees of all ages. Even Cherokee senior citizens have their own choir in which they perform regularly for the general Indian population, singing in the native tongue.

There are a number of crafts still practiced today by the modern Cherokees including basketry, beadwork, bow and arrow making, blowgun construction, bowl making, jewelry, Indian stick ball construction, Indian dolls, pottery, sash weaving and stone and wood carving, to mention the most popular.

Cherokee baskets are collector's items today and with obvious reason. In addition to the traditional river cane, oak and maple splints, a new plant introduced by white settlers—honeysuckle—has become popular among contemporary Cherokee basket makers. Emma Taylor, considered to be one of the Eastern Band's most gifted basket weavers, learned the skill from her mother when she was just seven years old. Emma makes both single and double-weave baskets and works equally well with river cane, oak and sugar maple splints or honeysuckle. She describes her work as follows:

> When I make white oak baskets my first trip is to the woods. There, I go to get my white oak, bringing back young saplings which I then split into quarters. I then sit down and take out the splints with the grain of the wood. I then scrape them on both sides until they are smooth and flexible. I then weave them into a basket. Once I start, it takes me three to five days to complete two or three baskets. I then take them to market.

Crucial to basket making is the dyeing process. Again Ms. Taylor describes the process:

> I will explain first the use of the walnut bark. You take the walnut bark from the tree and place it in a big tub with the splints that you want to dye. You fill the tub with water. Then you build a fire so the splints can boil. You let the splints boil from eight to nine hours. The fire must be kept going all the time. After they are dyed I take them out of the tub and rinse them in cold water and dry them off. They are now ready to use.

> The second type of natural dye I use is the yellow root. This can be found by the river bank. After you have all the yellow root sticks that you need, you scrape the outer bark off of the root. Then, they are placed into a clean pot with the splints. You then place the water in the pot and add some salt to it. This is to keep the splints from fading after they are dyed. You leave the splints in the water for approximately an hour. Then you take them out and dry them off. When they are dry, you can start your basket.

> The bloodroot that we use grows in the woods, too. After you dig up the root, you cut it up and place it in a clean pot. Then you add the salt when you add the water. You also let it set for awhile. To get the orange color, you must leave it for two hours. After you take them out and dry them, you must let them stand for half a day before using the splints.

Equally adept at basket making are Ms. R. Bradley, K. G. Reed, P. Junaluska, J. Taylor, E. Wolfe and many more. A difficult task is that of making the plaited river cane in double weave. Actually the double weave required the skillful art of weaving one basket inside of another, doing so in one continous weave of the material. Ms. Eva Wolfe is one of several Cherokees who makes the double weave, and her skills have earned her numerous prizes and national recognition, including first prize for one such basket exhibited at the United States Department of Interior in Washington, D. C. In addition to baskets, plaited honeysuckle vine mats, plaited white oak flower baskets and plaited river cane purse baskets are common and popular items as are many other basket products.

Beadwork has gained popularity among the Eastern Cherokees with the advent of dozens of gifted craftspersons. One of these is Ms. Lula Nicey Welch, who learned the art over fifty years ago from her mother. Commercial glass and plastic beads, as well as the introduction of the corn bead, have provided the modern Cherokee with a vast supply of materials, a situation not shared with their ancestors. Ms. Welch explains the beadwork process as follows:

In doing the first beadwork we would use the corn beads which are sometimes known as Job's Tear. These are also used today by our people. The plant was not native to our land. It was imported. It was probably one of the many trade items from the white traders. The stalk grows from two to six feet tall, and the beads are formed on the tassel rather than on the ears. The plant comes up in early spring, and it looks like grass. When the beads turn black, they are picked. You may put them in a cloth bag to dry. They become gray color, and if they are dried out in the open by the sun, they are a white color. The tassel is then pulled out of the bead, and this leaves a hole for the needle to go through.

Our ancestors would use the corn beads along with commercial glass beads to sew decorations on men's trousers or on the hems of the women's skirts. Apparently they did not use them to make belts as they do today. The thread that they used was the fibers pulled from the Indian hemp weed. After the introduction of thread, they used the flax thread. Today, they make all different types of beadwork. The pony beads are used to make belts, while the smaller glass beads are used to make bracelets, rugs, neckties and bolo ties. They may also use a loom today. In doing this they would go up over and under the thread on the loom. In making the belts they go through the bead twice, picking up only one bead at a time.

178

As Ms. Welch stated, belts, earrings, rings, bolo ties and necklaces, as well as beadwork used to adorn clothing itself, are very popular among today's Cherokees. Ms. Dorothy Swimmer explains how to make a belt:

In working with the large beads, we make belts, necklaces, headbands, and in working with these beads, say to make a belt, we start out with a solid row of beads and then work back through until we come out with an uneven number. You pick up one bead at a time, and it is sewn on to the next bead. This is called solid beadwork. The needle will go through each bead twice so if your belt should break, it would be a clean break, and it could easily be mended, usually without losing any of the beads. And, in doing the beadwork with these large beads, we make up our own designs as we go along. When the beadwork is completed, you overcast the edges and then you sew on strips of buckskin which serve as a tie. Belts are made in different lengths and widths and this determines how long it takes to complete the job. But if you really worked on it, it would take about two or three days to finish a belt.

Wood and stone carving equal basketry in popularity and demand, and although many Cherokees excel in this art, five craftspersons have national reputations: Goingback Chiltoskey, Amanda Crowe, John Julius Wilnoty, Virgil Ledford and Lloyd Carl Owle. Both Mr. Chiltoskey and Ms. Crowe have taught this art at the Cherokee High School and are viewed as the standard-bearers of Cherokee wood carving. Mr. Chiltoskey has been carving for over fifty years now, while Ms. Crowe exemplifies the academic distinctions afforded Cherokee wood carving, having earned both the Bachelor's and Master's of Fine Art Degrees from the Chicago Art Institute, as well as having been awarded the John Quincy Adams fellowship for foreign study and an honorary doctorate from the University of North Carolina.

While Ms. Crowe has earned considerable academic recognition, this is by no means a prerequisite for success, as John Julius Wilnoty can attest. John is the subject of an interview with Mr. Tom Underwood later in this section. Mr. Wilnoty is talented in both wood and stone carving and has passed these skills and talents on to his son, John Julius Wilnoty, Jr. Certainly, two generations of exceptional craftsmanship will become a legend in Cherokee. Other young artists are Virgil Ledford and Lloyd Carl Owle, who both learned wood carving under the direction of their teacher at Cherokee High School, Ms. Amanda Crowe. Mr. Ledford creates beautiful animals while Mr. Owle tends to capture human scenes from the Cherokee past. Both artists use buckeye, cherry and walnut woods.

Pottery is yet another craft in which the Cherokees display a unique talent. The early Cherokees used the coil method, and many contemporary Cherokees continue the practice today. Amanda Swimmer explains the process:

For coil pottery, start with a flat disk of clay, placing ropes of clay on top of one another until you reach the desired height. Then, you mold these coils together using your fingers. Now set the pottery out in the sun to dry for about three or four hours. When they become firm, bring them in and carve them to the shape you want. Then shine them up with smooth river stones. This gives the pottery its smooth finish and removes any air bubbles as well. On large bowls, use a paddle stamp while using seashells, small sticks or something similar for the design on smaller ones. And after you get them put on, then set them out again and let them dry till they turn a chalky white. They are now ready to be burned. First, preheat the pottery until it turns a bluish color. It then should be put directly into the fire where it remains until the fire has gone completely out. The type of wood used in the firing determines the color of the finish. For the lighter colors you use hardwoods, which give off more flames and less smoke, while for dark colors use a softwood, which gives off more smoke and less flame. Our people have never used a potter's wheel or any types of molds, and they never paint their glaze either.

The dark-finish pottery of the contemporary Cherokee craftspersons, most notably effigy pottery, is highly praised by collectors.

Many other Cherokees are active craftsmen making all types of cherished, traditional cultural artifacts. And while most of these crafts reflect the unique Cherokee culture, the skills of other Indian groups have found their way into the Eastern Band as well. Silver and turquoise jewelry are prime examples. Today, due mainly to the influence of the Pan-Indian movement, Indians of all tribal affiliations have come to adopt the beautiful Navajo and Zuni jewelry as the acceptable, universal Indian wear. In Cherokee, the three Teesatuskie brothers have mastered this art. Reuben Teesatuskie, former editor of the tribal newspaper, *The Cherokee One Feather*, explains the art of Indian jewelry making for us; he has been making jewelry for about ten years.

Turquoise Jewelry:

Reuben Teesatuskie

The process of making a ring is to first decide on your design. You make it all in single pieces. There are several different types of rings. I make rings with turquoise stones in them.

You make the ring to fit the turquoise. Most generally, I start with a plain piece of silver and make the band. If I want to do inlaid work, I get all that detail cut out first. I do this with a fine saw blade. It's about the size of a pin or needle. I then cut the silver to whatever length I want, and file and sand it, getting it all down to a fine finish. Then I put it together with silver solder. The silver solder has to be a certain temperature before it will flow. You have to heat the whole ring so it will flow evenly. You then cut your turquoise, and shine it, and polish it and then put it on a little plastic back. You then put it on, cut it and polish it, shine it and get the rough edges out of it. Next, you start making the band. Here you work with the bezel which is a fine piece of silver that looks something like the ring band. You put it on the stone to hold the stone in. Then, you fix your stone to where it will fit right, evenly and good and snug. You mash the edge of the ring band in to see if it's going to work. Then you solder it with another medium size solder. First, you start out with a hard solder, then a medium solder, while the last thing you do is to use a solder that's easy, and that is the bezel. You put that all together; then you start getting your turquoise, making sure it fits snug with no loose spots. Then you mix the glue to hold it in and push the bezel around it, to hold it in. After you get all that done, you start shining it, taking off the rough spots, and then you have a finished ring.

To make a necklace, you do similar work. You start with a flat piece of silver. Then you cut your design and put the two pieces of silver together. Next you clean it up and see what you've got. If you want turquoise inlaid in it you put your turquoise in, cut it to fit and then mix your glue. Use a real hard glue and remember it cannot be wet. Apply the glue and then set your turquoise, and you let it dry for about eight hours. Then you smooth down the edges and put on a chain. If you want to make a chain, there are several different models to choose from.

If you want to make a belt buckle with a stone in it, you again start out with a flat piece of metal. Now you have to design it. You can stamp it. Next you shape it to fit the stone. Most turquoise you get from here comes from out around Phoenix, Arizona. There are several different lines out there. You pick the size you want in the belt buckle and then determine if you want it inlaid or if you want it just to set on the silver plate or if you want a coral stone along with the turquoise. Place it where you want it, make your bezel and solder it to the belt buckle itself. Next, work on the band and bezel. Then you set the stone in and polish it and you have a finished belt buckle.

I learned to make silver about twelve years ago from a lady in Gatlinburg who taught jewelry classes in Cherokee during the summer. Her name was Miss Stevens. Now I believe she owns her own shop in Gatlinburg. I took some advanced silver training in Santa Fe, New Mexico, at the School of Indian Arts. There my teacher was Mr. Porgin, and I learned some modern techniques of inlaid works from him. I also worked in gold out there. I have also done casting. But silver is expensive to work with, and it's rough making a profit. I sell either to the Medicine Man Craft Shop or take personal orders. That way I can get some profit out of my work. When you sell silver you have to count your time, material, design and the quality of the product. I like to sell only what I consider to be perfect items. If it is not perfect or not perfect enough to suit me, it is not sold. I'll just keep it and melt it down and make something else out of it or tear it apart and design another item.

I have taught jewelry classes in Cherokee. I have also taught beginning jewelry at the Southwestern Technical College. When I teach a jewelry class, I start with the basics using a double band ring and a necklace with inlay and then go from there. I enjoy working with silver and turquoise and teaching these techniques to my people. All Indians seem to be wearing this type of jewelry now. It has come to represent Indian pride and solidarity. I guess we have the Southwestern Indians to thank for this craft and for sharing it with all other Native Americans.

Comments on the Work of John Julius Wilnoty:

Tom Underwood and Jim Hornbuckle

I.: *This morning we are doing an interview with Mr. Tom Underwood, owner of the Medicine Man Craft Shop. Mr. Underwood has on display here many of the native crafts, ranging from basketry to jewelry to carvings, and so forth, the whole line of Indian-made crafts here in Cherokee.*

Mr. Underwood, I notice that you have a rather large collection by a rather well-known artist, Mr. John Julius Wilnoty. Would you care to comment about this collection and about some of your dealings with Mr. Wilnoty?

T. U.: *Well, Jim, I've been dealing with John Wilnoty since he first started working; rather, I've sold John's work since he first started working at 20 years old. He is now 35 or close to 35. He has been a stone and wood sculptor for about 14 years.*

When John started out, he started out making little head pendants out of stone and selling them. The first ones, at his suggestion, we sold at $1.50. There were only about five or six

182

pieces in his first series. Then he came back to see if I had sold the first series, and I had. Then we decided to double the price of what they had been going for. So we raised the price to $3.00, and they sold out right away.

At that time I was managing and directing the Museum of the Cherokee Indians. When John came back I began to realize that John had exceptional talent in sculpturing and carving. I suggested to John that he try making stone pipes, because in ancient times the Cherokees had been very fine stone pipe makers. He said, "Well, I never have made a stone pipe in my life." I said, "Well, if you'll come down to the museum I'll show you some of the old, old Cherokee pipes and some that are even older than the culture itself." So one day he came on down to the museum and we looked. There are cases in the museum of all the stone pipes, and we looked and he said, "Well, I can make a better pipe than any of them," and sure enough very soon he brought in one or two pipes and they were beautifully done, the very first ones he had ever made. So he started making pipes and made a series of pipes that were very fine pipes. Then he began to make other things. He at first made the head pendants and then made the pipes, and he branched off into many things.

The exceptional things about John Wilnoty today are that he does the whole spectrum of stone sculpture and art, and he follows the most acute sense of line proportion and design of any living sculptor today. He has an eighth sense that tells him when a thing is right. He sees rhythm in the piece itself, the natural lines of what he's creating. He is able to take a piece of stone and accentuate a man's head or a woman's head or a certain part of the body without seeming to distort the rest of it, because he can take a piece of stone and project a face so that when you look at the piece, the face, and that is what he wants you to see, that is what you see. He will do the rest of the body, but it won't be distorted. It will be made in such a way that it looks natural and it looks great. And that is one of the rare, rare talents that he has.

He also has the ability to do design pieces, his multiple image pieces, that is, he will have multiple images. You can turn his work and find multiple imagery all worked and seeming to

183

mesh one into another. This is a rare and unusual talent too. Most of us would be able to carve a three-sided piece, but one would not have anything to do with the other. But John seems to be able to mesh them into each other, to integrate them.

He also has the ability to pick up a piece of stone and live with it until he sees in his own mind's eye the imagery in that stone, and he simply removes the surplus of what he doesn't see there. He removes that to make the image. He himself has said that is what he does; he sees what is in the stone and just removes what doesn't belong there. And in his Eagle Dancer he was able to so look into the graining of the wood or to visualize the graining of the wood to design the Eagle Dancer so that the muscles of the body, even the eye in the Eagle hood, the muscles in the face, the kneecaps and the whole imagery were brought out. The muscles, all the muscles in that man's body, were brought out in the natural grain of the wood. It seems an impossible task, yet before he started that piece, he brought that piece of wood right into this store before he had ever cut a chip out of it and told me that was what he was going to do. He had to know that was what he was going to do, to start with.

John—a lot of people think that John doesn't do much work, but John is the kind of artist that— 95% of what John does in sculpture is creative. Occasionally he'll make a stone axe or a bird stone or something that we don't consider creative work; we sell it as non-creative, but even that is exceptionally beautiful. He seems to have a magic touch with what he does in wood and stone.

He was talking to another local craftsman and sculptor one day, and the man showed him his piece of work and asked him what he (John) thought of it. John said to him, he said, "Well, it would be all right if you'd finish it." And this is typical of John's work; he completely finishes what he does. When he picks up a piece of something, even to make a stone axe and it has no imagery or any obtuse carving to it, he will finish it perfectly. And it is one of the things that has made his work so great.

John himself wouldn't go to school much when he was a young boy; he has no formal education.

*He makes no bones about it. He reads about on a
third grade level, but John doesn't really need
to. He can do—he is a genius in more respects
than one. He's a mechanical genius. He can put
mechanical things together that you wouldn't
believe and make 'em work. He maintains his
own truck, does all the mechanical work on his
own truck, and quite often helps other people
with theirs. He also does beautiful leather work
and holsters for guns. He does all his leather
work on his pipes. His embossing, his sewing, his
stitching, and there just isn't much mechanically
outside of his stone work that he can't do.*

*He also is handicapped by being a narcoleptic,
which is a form of sleeping epilepsy. They think
when he was a boy, just a young child, he might
have fallen off the bed or got some lick to his
head that caused this narcolepsy, and he has to
take an awful lot of medicine to be able to function normally. What he takes normally in one
day, one of his doctors once told me, that what
John took in one day would keep me awake for a
week. So you can imagine the strength of the
medication that he takes and its effect on his
constitution. At times he just gets completely
away from everybody and everything and keeps
his family close to him and doesn't take the
medicine and just rests from the effects of it.
But he can't drive a car then or use any of his
tools that he would cut himself with or—he's
very limited in what he can do. In the past,
before he found out what was wrong with him,
he cut himself, he ran hot tools through his
hands, all kinds of things happened to him. And
of course he couldn't keep a regular job until he
found that he was really a great sculptor.*

I.: *Would you classify John as a sculptor rather
than as a wood-carver?*

T. U.: *Oh, certainly! A wood-carver is a man who
carves, who carves wood. John is a great
sculptor. He sculpts in wood, stone and bone. He
is not a wood-carver. He is a sculptor. And he
will probably go down as one of the great
sculptors of our time. Many people from
museums and all walks of the collecting world
have viewed John Wilnoty's work and have just
been amazed that a man like this would even exist in America today, that we even have one
with such unusual talent. There is no doubt in
my mind that in the future, probably long after*

185

I'm gone, John Wilnoty will be recognized as one of the great sculptors of our time, another Michelangelo. If he is able to keep well enough, to keep creating and keep improving like he has. He was great to start with.

When the people at the Pasadena Art Museum were collecting wood-carvers and stone carvers and people that did beadwork and people that did all kinds of Native American crafts, they had heard about John Wilnoty, so they came here to talk to me. And when I found out they were in Pasedena—his main collector lives in San Jose, which is not very far from Pasedena—I sent the museum to the lady who owns the collection. They went there with the intention of using four or five pieces of John Wilnoty's work. When they saw what she had—she had conscientiously collected the whole spectrum of his work, that is, his wood pieces, his masks, which you probably have never seen, his combination wood and stone pieces, his wrestlers, his bears, the whole of his work—they asked her if they could make him the main attraction in this massive display. It covered one floor of a giant building, and a very large photograph of him was placed in the entrance way. They built five individual cases for his work. They published a catalogue on his work, which they didn't do on anybody else, and they gave him a write-up in the Los Angeles Times. *The* Los Angeles Times *did a write-up on the whole show, and then they did a write-up on John Wilnoty.*

Also, something over a year ago, the museum, I believe it is in Phoenix, sent a special emissary here to get John to enter the national arts and sculpturing competition; but the way things are handled, it's very, very risky business to move John's stuff. It's fragile, small and it can be stolen easily; some of it's very, very, very, very expensive. So it's been a hard matter to let any of it out of the store. I have had quite a bit stolen since I have had the stuff. A couple of years ago I had a pipe I was offered $500.00 for, stolen right out of the case. It wasn't the loss of the money so much as it was such a beautiful piece. But this year I have agreed to let the Appalachian Consortium and the North Carolina Arts Museum in Raleigh do a display on John and borrow some of his work, and even now I have qualms about it.

186

I.: Will that include the Eagle Dancer?

T. U.: No! It sure won't!

I.: To date the Eagle Dancer *is his most famous work?*

T. U.: Well, it is his most famous piece, but it's possible that there are other pieces that are just as good or even better. The Indian Arts and Craft Board in Washington has a piece that weighs about 80 pounds. It is a massive stone sculpture called Up *from the Deep. It is a beautiful piece of sculpture and perhaps is more significant as a piece of sculpture than the* Eagle Dancer. *A lot of people that collect his work realize that he is such an unusual artist that they like his free-form better than they do his multiple-image work. He hasn't been doing free-form but about four or five years. And his free-form work is just out of this world. Again, his sense of line and proportion, his sense of design, comes into being. He never gets anything that looks odd. He never makes anything that looks grotesque. It all fits. It all is beautiful art. Even his grotesque pieces themselves never look grotesque. When you look at them, you realize that they are works of art. Even the lowest laymen, when he looks at a John Wilnoty pipe or a John Wilnoty piece, will somehow know that he is looking at a beautiful piece of work. Even the most ignorant person that you can bring into the store—if they look at a piece of John Wilnoty, especially the simplest works of John Wilnoty, his pipes and his people—they realize that they are looking at a beautiful piece of art.*

I.: They're looking at the work of an artist.

THE ART OF CHEROKEE COOKING:

Emmaline Driver and Elsie Martin

Although the Eastern Cherokees have access to much the same types of processed foods as do other Americans, their traditional foods are still cherished by many. Plants, fruits, roots and nuts, as well as game, are popular traditional foods. Sprouts such as poke, sochan, dandelion, sweet grass and bean salad, to mention a few, as well as artichokes, ramps, Indian turnip, mushrooms and swamp potatoes are common foods gathered in the wild. Later, in the fall, buckberries, huckleberries, raspberries, blackberries, strawberries, gooseberries and elderberries, plus persimmons, fall grapes, hazelnuts, chestnuts, butternuts, chinquapins, black walnuts and hickory nuts are harvested from nature; while cress is picked during the winter. These plants, fruits and nuts are augmented by wild game, the most popular being black bear, groundhog, raccoon, rabbit and squirrel and also a number of wild birds such as pheasants, grouse and quail. Also trout, bass, crayfish, frogs and turtles are common water foods. And although no longer common, many older Cherokees remember preparing and eating bee grubs and locust.

The Cherokees have a long history of agriculture going back centuries before white contact. Perhaps corn or maize represents the most important cultivated plant raised by the Cherokees. From it they prepared a flour or meal, which has remained their favorite until this day. Cabbage, a multitude of beans, as well as cultivated fruits, have long been favorites of the Cherokees. Hence, today, individual family gardens are still important to the traditional Cherokee family, providing them with their own favorite foods. Similarly, hunting of wild game and the gathering of natural foods still play an important role among these contemporary Cherokees.

Cherokee food preparation is an art in itself as the two interviews in this section attest. Many corn flour breads have survived from pre-white days to the present, including bean bread, chestnut bread, sweet potato bread, carrot bread and sweet bread. Fried bread, on the other hand, represents the influence of other Indian groups, notably the Plains Indians. It is made from wheat flour, which was not a common grain among the aboriginal Cherokees. Some Indians call this "ghost bread" or some other local name. Cherokees also enjoy pumpkin fried bread and fruit fried bread. Mush, hominy and grits are other corn derivatives. Cornmeal was stored, dried on the cob, and other vegetables, notably beans (leather breeches), as well as fruits and herbs, were dried as a means of preserving them. Some traditional Cherokees continue to utilize this process.

Game meats, for the most part, are first parboiled, then fried, broiled or baked. For example, to cook a mud turtle, you first cut off the head under running cold water, keeping it clean until you have all the meat from the turtle shell. You then place the meat into a pot of cold water and parboil it. Again you rinse the turtle and parboil it a second time. Now add salt to the turtle and boil it till it is brown. You may also bake it. Our two traditional Cherokee cooks will now expound more on the art of Cherokee food preparation.

Cherokee Cooking:

An Interview with Emmaline Driver

I.: *How is the food that the Indians, the Cherokee, eat different from the food of the white man?*

E. D.: *Well, like now you never see the white man eat like the Indian when . . . well, I can remember part of the things the Indians cooked like when they made lye dumplings how they made lye dumplings when they didn't have no sody (sic) like they do today. Well, they used ashes, you know, strong ashes, well, they'd sift it and boil it in water and maybe put about two big teaspoonfuls in with the meal and then mix it, and then I guess you'd call it they'd raise their own corn, flour corn. They didn't have to use no sody because the lye's already in there, and when they make bread they made dumplings. They didn't make lye dumplings, but they did make meal, you know, meal bread and making their bean bread. And, like people today wouldn't eat it, and when they didn't have nothing to eat for their dinner, they'd boil water, you know, boil water and then they'd mix the meal and make little bitty dumplings like, and then they'd put them in water and boil them and salt in it, and that's what they'd eat.*

I.: *Well, how do you lye the corn? You know you talk about how they make the corn.*

E. D.: *Well, you'd lye it in the ashes; you'd boil your lye and after you sift your ashes you gets a kind of like flour. After you'd sifted the lye and take all the lumps, coals, out of it and just plain lye— I mean ashes—and then you get maybe a gallon of these fine ashes, and then you boil it in water, and you just let it boil and boil, and then how you know when it's going to get strong, well, you could taste it. It gets real strong, almost enough to skin your tongue, and then after you know it's strong enough, then you put your corn in there, and maybe you let your corn stand in*

189

there 20 or 30 minutes, and that skin off of the corn—that thin skin on it—that comes off, and it—the underneath—turns light yellow-like, and it turns dark yellow, and that's the skin part after it's light, and then the light part comes off, and then you take it out and wash it, and then you beat it, and after you beat that, it gets so fine, and that's what you use. You don't have to put no sody in it.

I.: *Do they beat it different today than they did back then?*

E. D.: *Well, some of 'ems still beats it, you know, like they did.*

I.: *Is this where they take that big drum and use that beater?*

E. D.: *Yeah.*

I.: *But now, because they use the ashes, you don't have to add soda to it, it's already in there?*

E. D.: *You don't even add salt. I don't know. They never did give us salt too much at that time. The same way you do when you make hominy—one was you make it with ashes and lye, but you didn't cook it in boiling water. But you can use lye like that and hot water and let it stand in there until it gets stronger. Back at that time people burned hickory wood to make the ashes strong. Then they'd get the ashes and put it in a great big pot and shell about a gallon of corn and soak it in there about an hour until the corn turns yellow. When the corn gets soft enough so you can just about peel the skin off—and then you beat that.*

I.: *Well, did they think the difference in the wood had something to do with it?*

E. D.: *Well, what they used was hickory 'cause it made stronger ashes and they used locust and popular.*

I.: *This is the same thing used to make grits then?*

E. D.: *Yes, you just do the same thing as you do with hominy. I know there's a lot of Indians used to make hominy back then. You know, when you make hominy you beat it up; you don't cook it like you do when you make this other meal, cooking it in lye. When you use plain corn meal, you have to use soda. When I make it, I use soda and flour, two handfuls of flour—that makes*

190

quite a bit. Then you boil it in water. Have beans boiled first and then put it in with your beans and mix it up. But you never use cold water, always boiling water to get your dough all mixed up.

I.: Why boiling water?

E. D.: Cold water makes it all come apart and just mashes up, won't stay together or stick together. A lot of people don't use enough water, but you gotta have water boiling when you put your bread in. If the water's not boiling, then all the stuff just sticks together. Water has to be boiling when you put your bean bread in. My people ate mush too. Have you ever eaten any? Never ate any mush that's been made? Well, I made a lot of that stuff.

I.: Is that like the stuff that's in the pot after . . . I know Daddy will drink the soup . . .

E. D.: Well, it looks like that, but when you make mush you use meal and just kind of mix up meal and pour in boiling water. You have to add salt to it, I guess. Make meal just almost like you're gonna make thickening, and then you pour it in the boiling water, and it doesn't take much, maybe two cups full, to make a big old pot full of mush. It gets thick, almost like grits taste, but it's not that coarse. It's kind of soft and fine, not like grits. A lot of Indians used to eat that. When you bake hog meat in the stove, bake it brown and then boil it in water and make soup—that's what they usually eat with it, or maybe fish sometimes or wild meat that they cook—they have to roast it first if they're gonna fry it.

I.: I can remember when they killed pigs when Gramma was alive, she used to catch the blood.

E. D.: Yes.

I.: How and why would she do that?

E. D.: Well, she just took the blood, put salt and pepper in, mixed it up, and then poured it into whatever it is, and then some of them used to just fry it in grease.

I.: Well, didn't the Indians think this was wrong to eat the blood?

E. D.: I don't think they did; a lot of them used to do that.

191

I.: *Well, you know in the Bible it says something about the blood, you're not supposed to . . . Well, do you think this is different today? I mean, today they don't save the blood. I can remember Gramma used to do it when Grandaddy used to kill them down here. She would catch the blood, but I never see it anymore. Do you think it's because of the Christian religion that they don't do that?*

E. D.: *I guess so, or else just nobody who remembers how to fix it. A lot of people's forgotten; they don't know Indian cooking anymore. Now there's people as old as I am who don't know how to cook Indian cooking. I say it's a good thing I learned to make everything. I learned just by watching my grandmother. Well, my grandmother used to come and stay with me and Mandie and my daddy, and she would cook, and I'd watch her cook. When she made hominy, I watched her, and when I got by myself, I thought I'd try it and see if I could make it, and I'd start out making it the way she fixed it and cooked it—and I cooked it.*

I.: *Another thing that I think—well, I didn't know I've never heard of another—is sweet corn. How did they make that?*

E. D.: *Well, you just boil corn and beans, beat your walnuts and make thickening in it, and pour in your corn. But it's not like it used to be way back. I used to think when I would go into people's homes, I could always tell when they had sweet corn, seems like the whole house just smelled like sweet corn. And they didn't cook it like we used to cook it. Way back they used molasses to sweeten that with and then when they cooked it they'd put in corn, beans and pumpkin and mix it. That's what made it taste so good I guess. Seems like we don't have no pumpkins like we used to. I used to like it better . . . Maybe that's why so many people have this diabetic sugar and all that. They didn't use sugar and sweet stuff back then like they do today.*

I.: *Do you think that by the Indians cooking the way they did back then that they were healthier?*

E. D.: *Yes, because they didn't use no sugar or lard as much as they do. Lard, shortening, oil, they didn't have all that.*

192

I.: What did they use for their seasoning?

E. D.: They had hogs, and they'd save that, but they didn't use too much of it. And they didn't eat nothing fried like we do. Everything is fried that we eat today. Back in those days everything was boiled, baked and then made into soup, and that's what they ate mostly. Like when they cooked greens, maybe they'd add a little seasoning to that, but today everything is just fried in oil.

I.: Do you think greens were different than they are today—most of them?

E. D.: Well, most of them. There's a lot of other what they eat today, and then there's a lot cooked about the same. But back in those days some of the greens were dried and then later on cooked. You can dry it, and sometimes you can put it in a bucket and dry it, and in the wintertime then you cook it, and it tastes like greens yet it's dry.

I.: There's not too many people today make leather breeches. Is this the same kind of method you're talking about where you string them up?

E. D.: Yes, and that's the way most used to do it. They don't have dried pumpkin either. You ever seen dried pumpkin? My grandmother would cut up pumpkin and take the whole thing inside out and slice them about that thick (one inch), a whole ring—just enough to take the peeling off. Then she'd pick the peeling off on top, and there'd be just a big old ring. Then my daddy took two sticks (about one yard), and he'd stick them together and put nails on these poles and put sticks across these, and grandmother would string this pumpkin on these over a fireplace where it was kind of warm, and she'd hang these rings on there, and three or four days later you could tell they were drying, and they get long and just grow up. They eat that, and it almost tastes like sweet potato. You boil them in hot water, let them cook up, and after a while you take them out and season them with salt, and it tastes like fried sweet potato.

I.: And it will be pumpkin? Well, what about the leather breeches—how do they do that? I know you string up green beans.

E. D.: Well, you boil them up the same way.

I.: You cook them just the same as you would if they were just regular beans?

E. D.: *You just put them in the water; after they get done, you take them out and wash them and season them.*

I.: *You wash them?*

E. D.: *Yes, you wash them, too, before you cook them to get rid of dust or whatever and then put in clean water. Then you wash them again when you take them out of the pot.*

I.: *How did the Cherokees preserve their food besides drying—I mean their meat, hog and stuff?*

E. D.: *Well, I guess some of them canned. They didn't have cans like we do today. They had jars, and they had these little tin jars, and they used rubber bands.*

I.: *So they wouldn't be jars?*

E. D.: *Yes, they were jars, but they were funny-looking jars.*

I.: *Oh, they had tin lids?*

E. D.: *Yes. See you had to tighten the lids. You had to put a rubber band on top. They were round rubbers. You put that on top; then you had to put the lid on top. And then they used to have these glass jar lids. You have a jar, and they had a wire around them, and then you get a little old glass lid, and you put it on top, and you push the wire over to hold it down. But I haven't seen much of these, but I did see these tin lids.*

I.: *So they can just about like they do today?*

E. D.: *Yes.*

I.: *But they canned a lot more. Did they plant their food any different back then than they do now?*

E. D.: *No, I guess they plant about the same. Today they have more seeds to plant, different kinds of seeds. You know, they didn't raise carrots and things like that. They did raise turnips, but they didn't have these purple top turnips; they had these old field turnips, long roots, you know, turnips like that. And they had a lot of this cress, but I don't think they canned it.*

I.: *Did they use fertilizer?*

E. D.: *No, I guess I can remember when they started using fertilizer. That was after I was married.*

194

*It's been, I was about eighteen years old then.
They didn't use fertilizer at that time. They just
planted in the ground; they made a new ground,
cleared off a field, and just planted in there. The
ground was rich. Most of them plowed it. Most
of them just used hoeing to plant corn and
beans. They had all kinds of beans, and they
didn't have no bugs or anything like we do today.*

I.: *You mean they had bigger and better crops even
without fertilizer?*

E. D.: *Yes, and people would have a lot of beans.
They'd have piles of beans. They had a loft. You
know, they didn't have stairs like we do today;
they just had a ladder. And in the ceiling they'd
have boards up there, and they'd put the beans
up there. Just big old piles of beans and jars and
cans. When they got ready to cook beans, they'd
get a basketful and shell them and cook them.*

I.: *So they would dry them, but they would just
have them in the loft?*

E. D.: *Yes, and then the corn. They'd have cribs full of
corn.*

I.: *Would the corn get hard?*

E. D.: *Well, what was already ripened. They'd get corn
when it first started coming in; when it got big
enough to eat they'd boil it, and when they took
the husk all off, they just get to eating of it and
take the husk off and leave so much of it, and
then they'd tie it, tie them together, and they'd
boil it in hot water, and when it got done, they'd
take it out. Then, where they were tied
together, they would dry them just like pumpkin
there by the chimney. You know, they didn't
have no stove. I've ate some cooked like that,
and it doesn't taste just like real fresh, but not
real different. Then when they'd take it out,
they'd shell it. And after you strain corn, when
you boil corn, the next day it kind of withers
like. That's the way it gets; it gets hard. You
know what sweet corn is like before you plant
it? Well, that's the way it looks after it's dried
by the fireplace. After they get it, they shell it
and then boil water and put that corn in there,
and that corn will start swelling. It just tastes
something almost like lyed corn, but it don't
have that taste to it.*

195

I.: Did it taste like parched corn?

E. D.: No, it was different. It was just like fresh corn.

I.: Just like it was cut off the cob, maybe?

E. D.: Yes, something like that.

I.: Why didn't they do that?

*E. D.: I don't know. They just didn't make it like today.
There's a lot of difference in . . . Today, seems
like there's a lot of ways to cook things today.
Maybe they just didn't have the things to use to
cook with at that time. Like today they make
casseroles and all that, Indians can't make it like
that. Like today there's more things you can
cook than in that time. In the days of the Indians, when they didn't have nothing, what they
made was soup, and when they'd roast things,
like if they had a rabbit, they'd have to roast it
and maybe keep it, put it in a sack or something.
My daddy's mother used to, you know, bake fish
and put it in a sack and hang it up, and then a
little later they'd eat it. And I said, how does
that fish taste? You can eat cold fish, and it
doesn't taste good.*

I.: Did he say it tasted the same?

*E. D.: He didn't say how it tasted. He said they eat it
that-a-way. I guess that's just the way they had
to eat it. They learned that-a-way. 'Course, I
have never ate anything like that. They used to
cook fish, just fresh fish, clean and they add boiling water. They put them in there without fry-
ing them first to make soup or something.
They'd just clean them and boil them. I don't
know what all they cooked. As far as I know
what they cooked, I never did cook anything like
that except corn and make leather breeches. I
cooked parched corn and made hominy. You still
have to cook it in ashes like you're going to
make popcorn. If they have nothing to eat, they
just bake a whole bunch of potatoes and put
them in ashes instead of boiling them in water.
They taste different baked in ashes.*

*I.: Do they taste different just baked in the oven,
too?*

*E. D.: Yes, they still seem like when they're baked in
the stove they're not quite as good as when they
are baked in ashes.*

I.: The ashes tend to give them flavor?

196

E. D.: *Well, I don't know if they did or not, but anyway it tasted different. We used to cook chestnuts in ashes. They was good. You have to cut the chestnut, make a hole like with a pin. If you don't, they'll pop just like a shell when they get hot, just pop out. And they taste different.*

I.: *They used chestnuts to make bread too didn't they?*

E. D.: *Yes, and make bean bread, and use butter beans to make bean bread.*

I.: *Is this different from the other bean bread?*

E. D.: *Yes, they taste different. If you get green water beans and peel that thin skin off, and inside they're green, and you put them in bread, and that tastes different. They don't taste like bean bread, but it tastes good, just as good as fresh green beans. You know, when you make bean bread with green beans, just shell the pods.*

I.: *I don't like chestnut bread. Do you make it the same way you do the bean bread?*

E. D.: *Yes.*

I.: *But the chestnuts and beans just give it a different flavor?*

E. D.: *Yes.*

I.: *The beated bread they call it, the beated chestnut bread, is that different from just regular chestnut bread?*

E. D.: *Yes, beated bread has a different flavor. That corn meal that you get at a mill just don't taste like what you beat yourself. It has a better taste.*

I.: *It's essentially the same thing? It's just corn meal?*

E. D.: *Yes, only the corn you have to cook and get the skin off. The meal you get at the store is just dried corn ground up. The meal you make yourself you have to lye it, and it's kind of cooked off a little.*

I.: *Is that why they call it beated?*

E. D.: *You have to beat it yourself. If you cook your corn too long, it will cook up, and it won't turn into meal. It will just turn into a lump. You overcook your corn. You just have to have so long to lye your corn.*

197

I.: You have to know when to stop boiling the corn?

E. D.: Yes, when you notice that skin is coming off you take it out. Don't let it boil too long.

Cherokee Cooking:

An Interview with Elsie Martin

I.: The other night we had a very good meal. Let me just see if I can recall what we had . . . bean bread and grease, fatback grease, white morgan beans, chicken, fish, sochan greens, fatback that looked like big pieces of bacon and cornbread. That was probably the Indian food you had there, right?

E. M.: That was Indian supper.

I.: Talking to you before, you mentioned that some of these had special preparations. I complimented you on the chicken and how it seemed to come right off the bones, and you said it was fried first.

E. M.: It was fried real done, just like you do fried chicken.

I.: But was there a special batter?

E. M.: No, the flour had only salt and pepper. I rolled the chicken in salt and pepper and flour and dried it and then put it in boiling water. I let it simmer for 2 ½ hours.

I.: That created the gravy we had?

E. M.: Yes.

I.: So the salt-and-pepper-flavored flour created the gravy. Was it any special flour like wheat flour or corn flour?

E. M.: Corn flour.

I.: Do you use a particular kind of flour like white or yellow? Is there a distinction made between white corn or yellow corn for these types of flours?

E. M.: I imagine we use white corn.

I.: Now Johnston mentioned that sometimes they grind this very fine. Instead of being like a meal, it's like a flour.

E. M.: Fresh water ground.

I.: Where can you get that around here?

E. M.: We get that usually in Robbinsville or Mingas Mill in the Park.

I.: How was the fish cooked?

E. M.: It was rolled in cornmeal with salt and pepper seasoning. It was fried in deep fat. The deep fat is not a vegetable oil. We use fatback grease.

I.: You buy that in a big solid chunk, and then you put it into a pot, and it just dissolves into a liquid?

E. M.: Yes.

I.: Do you have to put anything else in there to get it going like a little water or anything?

E. M.: No.

I.: Do you bring it to a boil and then use it?

E. M.: Just like you would use Wesson Oil.

I.: Would some of that be used for your grease?

E. M.: The same.

I.: What keeps the grease remaining a liquid so that it doesn't go back to being a solid?

E. M.: It does become a solid.

I.: So that grease is hot grease?

E. M.: Yes.

I.: I noticed people used the grease on top of the bean bread. How do you make your bean bread?

E. M.: The bean bread is made from pinto beans. You cook your beans 1 1/2 hours, and you don't season them. Pour them into your corn meal. For an average-size meal I use about 2 1/2 cups of corn meal. I pour into that more than four cups of beans and water. These are cooked beans. You mix beans and corn meal together until you have a firm dough, and you make balls out of this dough. Put these into boiling water.

I.: The beans are fully-cooked or half-cooked?

E. M.: Fully cooked. They are firm. If you cook them for an hour and a half they are firm, if you cook them longer they are mushy.

I.: The whole cake is put in the boiling water?

E. M.: The balls that you have formed out of this dough are put in boiling water. The water has to be boiling.

I.: How long do they boil?

E. M.: Usually out of this cup and a half of corn meal and your bean mixture you can usually get around 32 bean balls, and all of these you place in the boiling water, and you cut your heat. Your bread is ready for the evening meal.

I.: Some people serve this cold?

E. M.: Yes, it can be served cold.

I.: I enjoyed eating the hot bean bread with the grease over it.

E. M.: That is how it is eaten.

I.: Is there any other seasoning added to the bean bread other than the hot grease?

E. M.: Salt, and they that don't like to use grease will use butter.

I.: Is the sochan a wild plant?

E. M.: It is a wild plant.

I.: Do you have a particular time of the year when you have to pick it?

E. M.: The spring time.

I.: Can people freeze it or can it to preserve it?

E. M.: You can can and freeze it.

I.: Are many of the beans still preserved through the old method of drying them such as leather breeches?

E. M.: Leather breeches are dried.

I.: If you were using one of them for your bean bread or just as supplement to your meal, how would you retrieve the dry vegetable?

E. M.: The leather breeches are green beans that you break as if you were going to can, only you string these. I think if you are going to have leather breeches tomorrow for lunch, today you would soak these beans overnight, and then you cook them the next day.

I.: Just like you would if they came out of the garden?

E. M.: Yes, like you would if you were cooking dried apples.

I.: Getting back to the sochan, was there any particular way that you cooked that?

E. M.: *It's cooked just like turnip greens. You parboil sochan.*

I.: *And after you parboil it, do you drain off the first liquid?*

E. M.: *Yes, and then you run this under cold water, rinse the greens in cold water, and then let that drain, then you dry it.*

I.: *Is a similar process used for poke salet?*

E. M.: *The same process.*

I.: *Is that sometimes cooked with some fatback in it? Some people mention that they cook some of their greens with fatback as well as some sweetening like honey or sugar or molasses. Is that common?*

E. M.: *I don't know.*

I.: *What kind of seasoning would you put on the greens?*

E. M.: *You usually fry them in fatback to give them taste.*

I.: *Do they use any other kind of seasoning? Some Anglos use vinegar on their greens. Do Cherokees use vinegar on their greens?*

E. M.: *Not an awful lot.*

I.: *I remarked to you about the consistency of your corn bread, that it didn't crumble in my hands and that I really liked it and that you had that large loaf of corn bread that people just broke off pieces and ate it with their meal. It had the consistency of a regular bread like you would buy in the store. It would sop up the juices in your plate, and this was unusual, and yet I find out this was a common way of preparing it where the Cherokees are concerned. How would you prepare it to get this consistency?*

E. M.: *I use a cup and a half of corn meal, a half a cup of self-rising flour, a dab of salt, about a teaspoon of soda and cold water.*

I.: *Do you have to knead it?*

E. M.: *No. Bake in the oven at 450 degrees for half an hour.*

I.: *Do you think it's the fine consistency of the corn meal that holds it together like that?*

201

E. M.: *I think so because you have the fresh water ground, and we keep referring to the fresh water ground rather than to the store-bought.*

I.: *So many of the kinds the housewife would buy in the store are of the bolted kind?*

E. M.: *Yes, and much of it is self-rising.*

I.: *Mr. Martin mentioned that a very popular breakfast among the Cherokee was cold beans, leftover beans with hot grease on them, and I guess most people are familiar with the traditional Anglo breakfast of eggs and bacon and orange juice. It was interesting to hear about that. Do you think there are any more unique meals that the Cherokees eat, like for breakfast, or what a man might take to the woods for hunting or fishing?*

E. M.: *When hunting or fishing they don't eat a meal. It was the practice that you don't eat before going hunting or fishing. Today I don't think it is practiced as much. As for the breakfast, it is not unusual to go into an Indian home, and I'm talking about the elderly people mainly today, as to where we do eat beans for breakfast. It isn't unusual to find a bowl of fatback grease on the table. Sometimes these being the only two things for breakfast, corn bread or bean bread. You don't have your biscuits or your loaf bread.*

I.: *Like the beans had already been cooked, and they would take them cold and put the hot grease on them?*

E. M.: *They warm them.*

I.: *And would the bean bread be warm, too?*

E. M.: *No. If you have extra dough from your bean bread, if you don't want to make that many balls, if you have dough left, you can bake it, and usually this is eaten for breakfast.*

I.: *Do some people wrap their bean bread in different leaves?*

E. M.: *Yes. This is May and the leaves are out. It is time to pick hickory leaves to wrap bread in, and usually in the fall they will use the fodder to wrap the bread in.*

I.: *Now would they wrap it before they boil it?*

E. M.: *Yes, it gives it a distinct flavor. And if you don't know any better, you can use oak leaves, the white oak or the chestnut oak.*

I.: *Someone mentioned that one of the Cherokee ways of preparing fish is that the fisherman would take his trout or whatever fish he caught and would wrap it in leaves, and he would start a fire on the stones, and he would bake it on the stones. Are you familiar with that process?*

E. M.: *I don't believe it was leaves. I believe it was fodder, not fodder but shoats from the corn. Your people do the same with corn, wrapping it in foil. You bake them in the ashes.*

I.: *Today, on the one hand, you have the young people eating junk food. What did the Cherokees use for a sweet food, or do they still use it today?*

E. M.: *I think that, from what I can gather, they used honey locust to sweeten.*

I.: *What kind of soup would go with one of these meals?*

E. M.: *You would have fish, baked real crispy until it crumbles, and squirrel soup that is baked hard, and those are the only two that I know.*

I.: *Would they be baked similarly? What kind of broth do they have?*

E. M.: *The broth is brown, very flat taste, just the taste from the fish or squirrel, and you season it with salt.*

I.: *Do you add anything to thicken it like corn meal?*

E. M.: *You can.*

I.: *Is that what they call mush?*

E. M.: *The corn meal is mush.*

I.: *Would they use the corn meal mush to thicken the soup?*

E. M.: *Yes, or they would eat the mush by itself.*

I.: *Now is that just corn meal and water?*

E. M.: *Yes, thickened.*

I.: *And it can be boiled like in a broth?*

E. M.: *The soup thickened with corn meal, or if you make your own hominy. I believe Emmaline told you about hominy. You can take this hominy and put it into your soup.*

203

I.: *What kind of wild herbs and plants could be used for medicinal purposes? Or animals? Like the other day you mentioned groundhog for ears.*

E. M.: *The oil rendered off of the groundhog fat you use for earaches.*

I.: *Are some of the different plants used like the Indian turnip root?*

E. M.: *I'm not familiar with the plants used in Indian doctoring.*

I.: *What kind of benefit would the teas have?*

E. M.: *Peach tea is to break fever; the wild cherry is for coughing. There is a certain way of preparing the tea from each one. You don't just go out and break a limb off of one. For another tea we use blackberry root for diarrhea.*

I.: *Would that be dried first?*

E. M.: *No.*

I.: *In all of these, even though they have special preparations, the basic ingredient is the root or the bark or the leaf boiled in water, and then they would drink.*

E. M.: *Today with the changes in the usages of teas, our Indian teas, they have gone to where they will sweeten the tea now instead of drinking as it once was. They were quite bitter. They will use sugar or honey. Very seldom do you find families using the groundhog recipe.*

I.: *I noticed that some of the men still consider the black bear a delicacy. They had some problem with them going into the park and hunting the black bear, which is their traditional hunting ground. Do you know anybody who still considers some of these meats to be a delicacy?*

E. M.: *They are used for Thanksgiving and Christmas and certain times of the year when they have a big feast. There are just a few families that do that.*

I.: *Is the groundhog still eaten by some of these people?*

E. M.: *It is. Squirrel, raccoon, deer also.*

I.: *A lot of Cherokees are appalled when you mention possum. Isn't that a traditional meat?*

E. M.: No.

I.: What about bird as far as game?

E. M.: The grouse.

I.: Do some of these birds have some significance like the owl or the eagle?

E. M.: The owl is not a common thing that you find around here in an Indian home. To some Indian families or to we that have been raised by Indian grandparents, it is not something that you fool with.

I.: He represents a spirit of the night, right?

E. M.: Probably.

I.: Isn't snake considered taboo? Cherokee families will not eat snake, and they don't wear jewelry with snakes on them because isn't it related to the evil spirits of the Booger mask?

E. M.: That's right.

CHAPTER IV

From The *Cherokee One Feather,*
The Official Tribal Newspaper

Reuben Teesatuskie, Editor
Patricia Panther, Assistant Editor

Not Just a Piece of Land:

One Feather Editors

The Cherokee Strip is not just a piece of land in Oklahoma once given to appease the Cherokee Nation (reclaimed later, of course). It is also the name applied to both sides of U. S. 441 as it turns through Cherokee and the Qualla Boundary. Here can be found the basic elements of present Cherokee economy.

Here are the craft shops, the quick-food stores, a few good restaurants, motels and last, but far from least, the chiefs and dancers in their feathers (THE Indians). All are engaged in as rapid an exchange of the paper dollars as possible and the focus of all this activity is the tourist — Cherokee's number one industry. The tourist is a varied assortment of humanity coming in an even wider assortment of garbs. Some are young with low jeans, bare feet and long hair. Others have crew cuts and 30 too-many pounds. Some of the women have teased their hair into perfect waves and curls, permanently glued them in place, and then added a semi-matching, glazed hairpiece for the top. This was the year of the halter top. Unfortunately, the size of the halters didn't seem to vary so much. Many were "snug"!

The tourist season gets off to a slow but gradual start in April, has a quick flurry as the streams open to fishing, increases as the schools close and then builds to an unbelievable crescendo of noise, traffic, exhaust fumes, heat and travelers by the Fourth of July. After this weekend most of the local people become immune to anything and just hang on through sheer determination until after Labor Day. Then, there is a brief lull until the October leaves are sent scurrying by the autumn winds and approaching motorists. Let no one kid you that tourism is an easy business. From the time the leaves and wild flowers bud in April until the last leaf goes, the Cherokees work as much as humanly possible. Some may hold down three jobs, simultaneously, and it is more usual than unusual to have two jobs. Many work 16-18 hours a day, seven days a week. The work is usually hard work, too, with little pay — waiting tables, cooking, cleaning motels, doing maintenance around the motels and campgrounds, chiefing and dancing. These jobs require a heavy reliance upon tips, but

Cherokee doesn't seem to attract many "big tippers." Even the children work, posing with their parents or dancing. A summer at Cherokee will fully convince you that Indian endurance and strength is no myth and completely eliminate any idea that Indians are lazy. Some jobs even require considerable tact and diplomacy because they require talking with the tourist and salesmanship.

Most tourists seem to fall into two general classes. One, the "cheapie"—he can't believe that Indian jewelry costs that much. "You don't mean two HUNDRED and fifty—why, I wouldn't pay much more than $2.50!" He also believes that Indians are "supported by the government" and live off the fat of the land in general—(and HIS tax dollar in particular) and don't pay any taxes and get everything free. However, the main thing he resents is that he isn't getting what he thinks the Indian is. Then, there is the second class of tourist. He is always part-Indian himself ("Can't you tell?"). He knows that that isn't a Cherokee headdress the chief is wearing (the tour guide at Oconaluftee Village just told him). He is always intensely interested in Indians and wants to know "how they feel" but is too involved with trying to out-Indian the Indian with his bits and pieces of hearsay to listen. Most of the Cherokees, whose major mistake was "out-civilizing" their "civilized" white neighbors during the 1800's and getting removed for their trouble and progress, still demonstrate a superior poise and courtesy. They have learned to answer the most inane questions imaginable with frankness, they can tactfully and, usually, humorously turn aside the most rude or ignorant comment, they can deliver a monotone "yes" or "no" that will effectively end a conversation when necessary and—if all else fails—they can become "impassive Indians" with no loss of face or tip. (It may be that Indians are the most impassive when they are trying their best not to laugh in your face!)

The Cherokees have demonstrated for some time that they have most of the qualities necessary to increase their personal and tribal incomes from the tourist trade. They have public interest, the area is accessible, it borders the most visited park in the nation—and the people have the necessary personal attributes—like stamina! Probably the biggest drawback is cohesive agreement as to purpose and method. Some members of the community are concerned about how to attract the larger spenders to increase business; others seem concerned about generating enough business for a winter season. Still others may be aiming for both. There are any number of things that might increase the tourism income or transform Cherokee into an all-season resort. For myself there would be two major considerations for "touring" Cherokee or staying longer once I was here (as a tourist). One would be a greater selection of desirable, quality craft shop items, better control and labeling of Indian crafts and renovation, remodeling and expansion of the shops into attractive, landscaped, mall-type areas that would be more enticing to tourists used to spending more money. More variety in the type of musical entertainment offered would draw another type of tourist. An auditorium or club with a stage, seats or dance floor would justify higher rates for the musicians and insure a crowd despite the weather (and reduce the number of near traffic fatalities). Many other recommendations for entertainment and recreation facilities have been made and studied already. The possibilities are endless.

But Cherokee might not want to practice tourism all year. Twelve months of the traffic, pressure, hard work and long hours might be impossible. Twelve months of contact with the tourists might be even more impossible! Possible changes in community life and their impact are another consideration. The Cherokees are better acquainted with the price of progress than most!

Some may well ask if the work is so hard, the reward small and the hours impossibly long, why do these people continue waiting tables, cleaning, cooking, dancing and arraying themselves in hot feathers just to exchange a few pieces of paper with a group of tourists who will never again be quite as unattrative, critical and over-exposed — until next year. The answer is very simple — it's the only show in town — and it's only on half-a-year!

Save The Cherokee Indian Stick Ball Game!:

W. David Owle

For the old timers one of the favorite pleasurable pastimes is to recall some of the big stick ball games and some of the great ball players of bygone days. Wolftown, Big Cove, Birdtown, Painttown and Yellow Hill had teams.

It was amazing and a near wonder where the players came from. Every man from every home felt it his honorable duty to represent his community. Such men as Deweise Reed, Adam Reed, Josiah Long, Joe Washington and the Queens from Wolftown were mighty men. In the Birdtown section were such men as Sampson and Epps Welch (Boss), John and Owen Walkingstick, Jack and John Taylor, Standing Turkey and a little fellow by the name of Lloyd Lambert, who could sting the big fellows like a hornet.

From Big Cove came the Welch and Wolf families, Blain and Ned Hill, June Wolf and the whitest Indian to play like a full blood was Rans Swayney. Of course there have been many later players. From Painttown the Stampers, Toonis, Crows, Standingdeers and Hornbuckles protected their township's honor.

From Yellow Hill every branch, hollow and hillside produced men like Joe and Will Saunooke, Sampson and Lloyd Owl, Catolster, Henry Lossiah, Ute Shell and the Jessans.

On the day of the game the atmosphere was charged with explosive expectations. At Yellow Hill, for example, on the day of a game, men, women and children would gather with their neighbors in the field near the old mound to await the noon hour of the contest. It was a gala occasion.

Then a long single yell stirred the emotions. It was followed by three short responses by the team and their supporters. Repeated three times came the signal that the Medicine Man had finished the ritual required of him at the water.

Both teams entered into this game with rooster-like challenges yelling until they met in center field.

The players had already spent the night "getting strong" for the game by participating in the ball dance. They were "scratched" down the arms, legs and across the back with sharp bones of various birds, animals and snakes to give them cunning, endurance and fierceness.

On their way from the "water" to the ball field, the women carried extra garments for the players to bet for them. There was no secret and no shame in the methods of barter. On the other side a player would call out, "I have a dress to bet." A woman on this side would drop off the dress she was wearing and match the bet. (On game days the women would wear as many skirts as they could.)

209

As the two teams met in the center of the field, the betting intensified—dress against dress, knife against knife, shirt against shirt and once in a while a cow against a cow. The bet loot was then removed to a wagon and guarded carefully by two men. After the game, the winners were glad. The losers could only say, "Wait until next time."

The game was started by a respected old player speaking to them, making the rules. Then with "Ha! Tuel-doquo!!" (play to 12 points), the ball went into the air and the battle royal was on.

It is no accident that there were great athletes from among the menfolk of the Eastern Band of the Cherokee Indians. A few who wore the insignia of the famous Carlisle Indians were Sam Saunooke, Johnson Bradley, Ben Powell, Theodore Owl, Jesse Youngdeer, Steve Youngdeer, Nick Bradley, Jack Jackson and Fred Bauer.

What About Saving The Cherokee Indian Stick Ball Game

1. Start with the children in each community. They can do anything. They can learn and play.

2. Write some rules that would give larger participation. Use a smaller field and have competent officials to replace the "drivers" who carry switches.

3. Develop the game into quarters and have a rest period at the half. Allow substitutions.

4. Do not try to kill each other by standing other players on their heads, or choking or doubling up players to stop their breathing.

5. Make it a fast rule to use two ball sticks in handling the ball in the game. There is no more attractive or spectacular part of the game than to see a team pass the ball from player to player in a skillful exhibition of team work. Any person can scoop the ball up with one stick, and any tough guy can bump you and overpower you, but not all can dodge and run and handle the sticks like a champion.

6. It would be difficult to change the game as it now is played by the adults, but someone with imagination and love of youngsters who is dedicated enough to the heritage of his people can save the Cherokee Indian stick ball game.

Museum to Perpetuate Cherokee History:

One Feather Editors

From the time of the Dawn Age in Eastern America, a proud people without the knowledge of metal artfully fashioned tools, pelts, money and weapons, eventually created the only Indian alphabet in the world, and slowly assimilated themselves into the new white man's culture, until they were herded like animals from their homes and deposited like outcasts on America's western frontier.

They were the Eastern Band of the Cherokee Indians, and their fascinating story and culture will once more come to life this spring with the opening of the Museum of the Cherokee Indian.

The museum is part of a rare historical trinity which, with *Unto These Hills* and Oconaluftee Indian Village, has been designed to preserve and perpetuate the history, culture and antiquities of the Eastern Band of the Cherokee.

The museum will display crafts fashioned by the Cherokees who populate the Oconaluftee Indian Village during its tour season, which will begin May 15 and continue daily from 9:00 a.m. to 5:30 p.m. through mid-October.

Under one roof, a visitor may enjoy and examine the largest and finest collection of Cherokee artifacts, displays and documents in Eastern America.

Dramatic displays include the ancient rifled blowgun with its dart, and the rare hand-carved effigy masks used by the Cherokee up until a hundred years ago to frighten away witches and heal the sick and ailing.

Pictures and painting portray the great Cherokee chiefs in their colorful costumes and the tragic "Trail of Tears," which is also outlined by map.

"Hearphone" audio equipment provides visitors with recorded messages on outstanding leaders such as Sequoyah, John Ross and Will Thomas, while library documents include rare writings by and about these great men.

And of the greatest significance is the exhibit of the historical hatchet of Tsali, the great Cherokee martyr whose story is beautifully re-created in *Unto These Hills*, the world-famous outdoor drama which will open for its 26th season on June 21. With the Great Smokies for a backdrop, Indian and non-Indian actors together relive the unforgettable saga of the Cherokee Nation. Performances by this dedicated and impressively professional troupe are scheduled nightly, except Sundays, through August 28.

The museum will be open daily from 9:00 a.m. until 5:30 p.m. in April and May when, for the summer, the hours will extend from 8:00 a.m. until 7:00 p.m., resuming the 9:00 a.m. to 5:30 p.m. schedule from September through November.

The museum is one of the three exciting attractions conceived and sponsored by the Cherokee Historical Association. Carol E. White, general manager of the CHA, emphasizes that these attractions are operated not for profit, but as a means to perpetuate the life and traditions of the Cherokee Indian, to raise their living standards and instill in them a greater appreciation of themselves and their race.

Full information and color brochures describing the village and drama are available free of charge from the Cherokee Historical Association, Cherokee, North Carolina 28719.

USET Calls for Indian Leadership Training Program

During the quarterly meeting of the United Southeastern Tribes held at the Seminole Reservation, Hollywood, Florida, delegates passed a resolution designed to promote Indian leadership on the highest levels.

The resolution acknowledges that Indian employment is encouraged by the Civil Service Commission; however, it states that the intent of the laws providing Indian hiring preference have no real meaning when executive positions are at stake.

Important jobs require qualified people.

Currently there are no large scale management training opportunities for Indian people. To alleviate this problem, USET has requested an executive training program from the Federal Government and has recommended the following steps be taken to implement it:

1. A current listing of skilled, qualified Indian personnel who, with some training, can become qualified for executive management positions shall be compiled. From such a roster the quantity of such a training program should be determined, and,

2. Said program must be put into effect immediately both in the area of apprenticeship training and formal education to qualify Indians for positions of executive authority in local agencies of the Bureau of Indian Affairs and the U. S. Public Health Service and all other Federal agencies having legislative commitments to Indian people.

3. This educational and apprenticeship program should be inaugurated immediately among the United Southeastern Tribes as a pilot effort. Toward this end, funds should be made available for a salaried apprenticeship program and for a salaried professional managerial and administrative training program on a formal basis.

4. At the same time, information should be compiled and made available on all positions within the structure of the Bureau of Indian Affairs at all levels and the BIA should immediately recruit Indians who, with training, can become qualified on the local agency's level.

5. It is requested that a conference be held immediately between representatives of the four Southeastern Tribes and representatives of the Bureau of Indian Affairs and other appropriate Federal agencies in order that plans be made to implement the intent of this Resolution.

The Federal Government is continually urging Indians to seek employment with the Bureau of Indian Affairs. They seem to be suggesting that by working for it, we will play a part in the decision-making that goes on concerning Indians. Due to a lack of the qualifications set up by the Bureau, most Indians are placed either as mailroom workers, clerk-typists or errand boys. These positions offer nothing in the way of handling affairs or making decisions.

The problems of the American Indian are like problems of other minority groups in many ways. Yet we have a whole Bureau of the government working, supposedly, on our behalf. If we could make it do what it is supposed to do, we would stop losing land, pride and independence. We would get back so much that has been taken unfairly. We must utilize the Bureau and make it work for us!

So that the government cannot use the qualifications excuse any more to keep us out of effective jobs, we must see that we are provided with an apprenticeship program which will train Indians to take the leadership positions that we must occupy. In order to get started, to break into their system, we must learn their skills. Our American society today is white, run on the basis of white beliefs, and so we must learn how to change what they have created for us by using their methods. We must take over the management of our affairs, using their offices and their government, but with our Indian attitudes and values always guiding us. We, being Indian, have a quality of understanding that Federal employees simply haven't got because they are not Indian. It is our understanding of Indian ways, and sacred, and always above any skills the white man may teach us.

The United Southeastern Tribes has passed a resolution calling for an apprenticeship program. The Federal Government will be asked to provide money and facilities. If we can get that much from them, the rest will be up to us. If we can be strong and work hard to make our lives good once again, the plan can work. But we are the ones who must make it.

Eastern Band of Cherokees has Unique Government:

One Feather Editors

On the Qualla Boundary, Election Day rolls around every two years on the first Thursday in September. The eligible voters of the Eastern Band of Cherokee Indians gather in their respective townships to elect councilmen to represent them for a two-year term. In alternate election years the people also have the responsibility of electing a Principal Chief and Vice Chief, who will guide the fortunes of the tribe for four-year terms.

The Cherokee people have a heritage of good government which is older than that of the United States of America. In fact, the founding fathers incorporated many ideas from the First Americans into the federal structure.

The six townships, Big Cove, Birdtown, Cherokee, Wolfetown, Painttown and Snowbird, each elect two members to the Tribal Council. The Council then selects one of their number to serve as Tribal Chairman. Many committees, boards and commissions are appointed by this governing body. These are made up of council members, members of the executive branch of tribal government, representatives of the Bureau of Indian Affairs and people from the community at large. Some committees administer programs; some serve in an advisory capacity, while others have specialized duties.

One of the first actions of a newly elected Chief is the selection of his Executive Advisor. Although he is nominated by the Chief, the Council must give its advice and consent to the selection.

Council House staff members appointed directly by the Council are the English Clerk, Interpreter, Messenger, Tribal Clerk, Indian Clerk, Enrollment Clerk, Marshal and Janitor.

The Executive Committee, which is made up of the Principal Chief, Vice Chief and Executive Advisor, is empowered to perform the necessary functions of the Tribe when Council is not in session. The Business Committee handles routine matters which ordinarily require agency approval during Council recess. Also working closely with the Agency Branch of Credit is the Credit Committee. Included in their responsibility is the overseeing of the four Tribal Enterprises.

When a citizen of the Qualla Boundary wants the Council to consider a proposal, he first must prepare a resolution or get an appropriate office to put his ideas into the stylized form of a Council resolution. The next step is to give a copy to the chairman of the Resolutions Committee, who will present the bill to the legislators. It is then given a number and read by the English Clerk in English and by the Interpreter in Cherokee. The discussion that follows may be in either language. Parliamentary rules are followed. The group may pass, reject or table legislation. Passed resolutions must be signed by the Chief before they become official tribal policy. Some legislation, such as the annual budget, is subject to review by the Commissioner of Indian Affairs.

Resolutions will usually name a committee, person or agency to carry out the intent of the bill.

A 4% tax is levied on all retail sales on the reservation. The income from this levy is used to support the tribal Community Services.

The Eastern Band is incorporated under the laws of the State of North Carolina; however, the tribal government is not just concerned with business. It is a unique system of local government, both simple and complex at the same time. Some sociologists are predicting that Americans crave a return to the tribal way of life. If and when they do, the Cherokee government will be there to once again serve as a model.

Over 1,000 Attended High School Dedication:

One Feather Editors

The Eastern Band of Cherokee Indians dedicated their new $7.5 million Cherokee High School with recollections of their past and challenges for the future.

Approximately 1,000 persons gathered in the athletic stadium on a sunny, windy afternoon to hear Commissioner Morris A. Thompson of the Bureau of Indian Affairs recall the history of pride among Cherokee people and how the great Sequoyah, who never formally attended school, "educated himself and developed a writing system for the Cherokee language" in the early 19th century.

Thompson, whose helicopter was parked on the stadium turf behind the speakers platform on the track, told of looking through the school, which he termed "that magnificent building" that resulted from nine years of hard work by the Cherokee people and BIA.

"There is not a mark on the new school," he said in complimenting the Indian on the care given the rock-faced structure in use since last August. "You are all to be congratulated for that."

James Ray Cleaveland, superintendent of schools in Cherokee, told the group that the school "is not an end but a beginning . . . Students are what the building is for. The true worth of the program is what you, as students, do with these facilities" in the future.

Chief John A. Crowe paid tribute to the four principal chiefs who preceded him: Osley Saunooke, Jarrett Blythe, Walter Jackson and Noah Powell, who foresaw the need for the school and set the stage for the building project. "They fought for what they thought was right," Crowe said.

Bertha Saunooke, widow of the one-time chief and a member of the school board and Tribal Council, termed the school "a dream come true for the Eastern Cherokee."

Principal Howard Patton pledged to use the facility "to strive for an educational program second to none." Student body president Noel Blakely noted that the school is located on an ancient Indian township site and that the building "has brought a renewal of the pride to the Cherokee people."

Reservation Superintendent Jeff Muskrat presented Thomas Mallonee and John Abbott. Mallonee read a greeting from U. S. Representative Roy A. Taylor and noted that Taylor joined Cherokee leaders this week in a congressional presentation for $6.9 million to erect a new hospital. Abbott said U. S. Senator

217

Robert Morgan "feels that it is fitting that this magnificent structure come to these Cherokee people."

Theodore Krenske, former superintendent here and now director of the Office of Indian Service in Washington, said the school's existence is due to "determined efforts" of the tribal leadership and cooperation of BIA. Area BIA Director Harry Rainbold also lauded the collective effort, and Tribal Council Chairman Jonathan Ed Taylor noted that a lot of labor in the building was done by the Cherokees, especially the rock work.

Commissioner Thompson said this was the first BIA school built to specifications, recommendations and desires expressed in the community, "and you are to be congratulated for your input."

"The students are to be congratulated for the concern and care they have shown for this school, and I mean all 550 of them."

"The school building is being used by all members of the community," Thompson said, "people taking college courses through Western Carolina University at Cherokee and people receiving adult technical training through courses taught by Southwestern Technical Institute in Sylva."

The high school band provided music for the program, and a quail dance was presented by an elementary dance team. School board chairman Daniel McCoy presided.

Lady Bowler Teaches Humility to Newsman

Editor's Note: Recently Lula Gloyne went to Charlotte to take part in a bowling event. Her opponent was Kays Gary, well-known columnist of the Charlotte Observer. *Here is the tribute Gary paid the 84-year-old bowler.*

I got scalped Saturday by a Cherokee lady with a bowling ball. So did Jack Knight, WIST's excuse for almost anything.

A bunch of women dreamed up the stunt to prove the already obvious superiority of That Other Sex.

It was also obvious from the beginning that the women, the North Carolina Women's Bowling Association, wanted a sure-fire set-up for the premise in choosing Knight and Gary.

Knight's bowling career matched the lifespan of the 7/8 Edsel with similar success. Gary's never began until Saturday, at which time it also ended.

Championing the women's cause was Lula Gloyne, a member of the Cherokee Qualla B's team competing here in the largest bowling event in the state's history.

Lula says she is 84, a grandmother with a 113 bowling average. She took up bowling at 79 and once rolled a 213 game.

I was afraid that even in my maiden effort I'd beat Lula and louse up a column. Knight was nervous for fear he would not beat an 84-year-old woman.

Lula took care of my fears with the first ball at Park Lanes. She rolled a strike. So did Jack. She then proceeded to make Jack's fears come true. In a half-game she beat him 74-70 and I only had 50. And she was off her game, but it was only practice.

I learned something about the game when I picked up my ball. It weighed 16 pounds. I learned that it could be a deadly weapon. Deadly for me. The sticks (pins) at the end of the lane were entirely safe.

I also learned something about courtesies of the game when once intending to be gallant, I picked up Lula's ball to hand it to her. "Get your hands off my ball!" she cried.

It seems that bad luck falls upon the bowler whose ball is touched by somebody else who is a poor bowler. If that is true, Lula's tournament efforts Saturday and today are doomed.

How did she get into bowling and why?

"The team needed a substitute for somebody who was sick and I wasn't too busy and so I filled in," she said. "I'm really not very good."

Well, the crowd cheered and cheered as well they should as Lula Gloyne's appearance had to be a highlight of this monstrous event involving 4,300 women, all nuts about this fun-and-health sport.

Lula fired a 118 in her first tournament team game — five over her average — but she had just had a four-hour ride down from Cherokee and wasn't loosened up yet. Today she'll bowl six games in individual competition starting at 8 a.m.

Impeccable in speech and gracious in manner, one senses Mrs. Gloyne is perhaps a bit piqued at being heralded for being 84. A grand dame she is but "I don't want people thinking I need assistance just because of my age."

A registered nurse and native of Cherokee, she was on active duty as an Army nurse through World War I, spent years as a field and clinic nurse for the Bureau of Indian Affairs in Oklahoma, then came back home to retire some ten years ago "but never actually retired until two years ago."

She still lends her nursing skills in emergencies to Cherokee families "but I keep busy, too, teaching classes in chair-bottoming, basketweaving and map-making, all with vines."

She lives with Annie Nick, age 92, in Cherokee.

"You take care of Mrs. Nick?" she was asked.

"Oh, no. She's as active as I am," Mrs. Gloyne said. "She just doesn't care for bowling. I'm sure she's enjoying being alone this weekend for a change."

When Millie Moore, president of the Charlotte Women's Bowling Association, presented trophies for our token appearance and told me, "You're low man on the totem pole," Lula was comforting. "Don't let it bother you, young man," she said. "Young man!"

It was a great day.

Qualla Co-Op to Host Open House for Lucy George:

Steve Richmond

Deserving recognition will be given to Lucy George, May 18 through June 30, 1970, when an exhibition of honeysuckle baskets is opened to the public in the Member's Gallery of the Indian owned and operated craft cooperative, Qualla Arts and Crafts Mutual, Inc., Highway 441 in Cherokee, North Carolina. One of the most ingenious and creative basketweavers in the United States, Mrs. George is a member of the Eastern Band of Cherokee, and was born on November 17, 1897, in the Birdtown community of the Qualla Indian Boundary in the mountains of Western North Carolina.

This exhibition, which was organized by the Indian Arts and Crafts Board and is being sponsored by Qualla, will offer to the public the opportunity to see and purchase outstanding and rare examples of honeysuckle basketweaving. It was during the depression years of the 1930's that Lucy George found it necessary to provide a way to supplement her family's income. Other Cherokee mothers were doing this by weaving baskets to sell or trade at the general store for the household goods needed to feed and clothe their families. Unlike these basketweavers, Lucy George had not been taught basketweaving by her mother and now found it necessary to learn in the early years of her marriage.

Most of the Cherokee basketweavers used river cane or white oak in weaving their baskets. Lucy George knew of only one Cherokee who used the honeysuckle vines as a basketweaving material. For this reason, she felt that her chances of helping provide for her family's needs would be better if she started weaving baskets from a material that was not in general use by the other basketweavers. There were no teachers available, and Lucy George realized that she would have to learn by teaching herself, using only the knowledge that she had obtained in visiting in the homes of friends who used river cane or white oak material and adapting this knowledge into a new basketry form.

Acquiring an impressive skill in wicker work weaving, Mrs. George began creation of a wide variety of basketry forms made of honeysuckle vines — a material previously considered of little value in her mountain community — and through her accomplishments soon developed new aesthetic dimensions in basketweaving for the Eastern Band of Cherokees.

In the mid 1940's, with the assistance of the Bureau of Indian Affairs and the Indian Arts and Crafts Board, the Cherokee craftsmen organized their own craft cooperative, Qualla Arts and Crafts Mutual, Inc. With the establishment of their own wholesale

221

and retail outlet, special emphasis and assistance were given to help the individual craft worker to improve and market his crafts. As a member of Qualla, Mrs. George's interest in basketweaving was challenged to her heights of individual design and aesthetic achievement.

Active as a basketweaver for some forty years, Mrs. George today will tell you that she is not getting old, but that her hands are. It has been these nimble hands that have enabled Mrs. George to achieve the widely renowned reputation for the perfection of honeysuckle basketweaving and the richly patterned designs of all her baskets, which are both decorative and utilitarian.

The honeysuckle baskets of Mrs. George have won numerous prizes in competition at annual fairs held on the Qualla Boundary and have been shown in many state and foreign exhibitions. In recent years, Mrs. George has found time to teach and demonstrate honeysuckle basketweaving to the younger generation of Cherokee, as well as to craftsmen of other Indian tribes in the Southeast.

Mrs. George is the mother of six children and now lives with her husband in her childhood community of Birdtown, along the Oconaluftee River. One son distinguished himself during the Korean conflict and was awarded, posthumously, the Congressional Medal of Honor.

This is the first one-man exhibition of Mrs. George's basketry, and the members of Qualla and her friends will honor Mrs. George with an open house Sunday, May 17, from 1 to 5 p.m. in a preview showing of the exhibition.

Cherokee Indian Fair Began in 1914

One Feather Editors

In the summer of 1912, Cato Sells, Commissioner of Indian Affairs at that time, made a special trip from Washington, D. C. to Cherokee. His object in coming to Cherokee was to discuss with James E. Henderson, Superintendent of the Cherokee Indian Reservation, and James Blythe, Farm Agent, the possibility of promoting and sponsoring an Indian Fair. The superintendent's desire was that the farmers of the six townships organize a club in each of the respective townships; the clubs would form a Farmers' Organization. When the Big Cove club was organized, the membership totaled 22 members. The officers elected were as follows: chairman, John W. Wolfe; vice chairman, Johnson B. Thompson; English clerk, Johnson Owl; Indian clerk, Deliskie Climbingbear; treasurer, Mary Elizabeth Wolf. The Program Committee consisted of Will West Long, Charlie A. Lambert and Arsene Thompson.

During the year of 1914 the Commissioner of Indian Affairs officially authorized the presentation of the Fair. The Big Cove Farmer's Organization had a special meeting. At that meeting a Fair Committee was elected to work with Superintendent Henderson and Farm Agent James Blythe. The Fair Committee was elected as follows: Will West Long, Charlie Lambert and Arsene Thompson. They were confronted with the problem of a place to hold the Fair; there were two prospective locations — Cherokee and Big Cove. When a vote was taken, 10 persons were in favor of holding it at Big Cove and 11 persons wanted to hold it at Cherokee. Cherokee was chosen as the location. The next decision that had to be made was what the name of the Fair would be. The two names put up for vote were "Indian Fair," presented by Will West Long, and "Cherokee Indian Fair," presented by Mary E. Wolf. The latter name was chosen and has never been changed.

The greatest wonder and attraction of the first Fair were the automobiles to be seen on the grounds. Law and order was provided for with the hiring of two Indian policemen, William Wahneetah and John Crow. The chief Marshal was Sam Saunooke, and his assistants were William J. Owl and Arsene Thompson.

By this time the Birdtown farmers had organized a club called Birdtown Farm Club. Leaders of the club were Owen Walkingstick, Hugh Nolan Lambert and Ben Bushyhead. The Big Cove and Birdtown farmers combined their clubs for the first Cherokee Indian Fair.

An Advertising Committee was appointed to promote the first Fair. This committee consisted of Sibbald Smith and Jacob

Smith. They traveled in a one-horse buggy as far away as north Georgia. Contributors of prizes awarded for exhibits were D. K. Collins, R. J. Roane, Sylva Supply Company, Asheville Seed Company and C. M. McClung Hardware in Knoxville, Tennessee.

The prizes consisted of various farm equipment. The first exhibit was held in what was then the school chapel and is now known as Qualla Hall. It created much excitement and wonder.

A singing contest was held on the steps of the Boys' Dormitory. There were three classes entered. These were Wright's Creek, Blue Wing and Big Cove. The leaders were Henry Bradley, William L. Hornbuckle and Soggie M. Hill respectively. The judges allowed only one mistake to each class. There was a first, second and third prize. The prize money was divided equally among the members of the choir. The singers were all satisified with this arrangement.

Big Cove Farmers in 1912: 1. John Wolfe, 2. Johnson B. Thompson, 3. Johnson Owl, 4. Deliskie Climbingbear, 5. Will West Long, 6. Charlie A. Lambert, 7. Arsene G. Thompson, 8. York Cornsilk, 9. Elijah Welch, 10. Adam Welch, 11. Soggie M. Hill, 12. Johnson Wolf, 13. Ward Wolf, 14. Wesley Driver, 15. William Driver, 16. Chickelelee Driver, 17. Going Bird, 18. Runaway Swimmer, 19. Thomas Swimmer, 20. Moses Powell, 21. John W. Swayney and 22. Eli Bird.

Cherokee History:

Lucian Lamar Sneed

This article is the first of a series on the history and beliefs of our Cherokee ancestors. It is my sincere desire that as a result of this series the Cherokee heritage will be preserved for future generations to come, for no people on this earth have a more beautiful heritage to preserve than the Cherokee.

The following are two formulas used by our ancestors when hunting and fishing. We must remember that the Cherokees of old, in their own way, were true believers in God, the great spirit.

When the hunter would go after bear, deer or fowl, he would use certain prayers to attract the game to where he would shoot it. These prayers have a magical quality and are sung in a low-pitched voice. When animal traps such as bear traps, otter traps, raccoon traps, squirrel and rabbit traps and bird snares are set out, they must be accompanied with certain spells to assure their success in attracting the game. In all hunters' formulas the fire is the chief diety appealed to, although the great terrestrial hunter Kanadi (sometimes called "The River"), is also helpful. Both of these beings are full of attraction for the game, and the hunter endeavors to identify himself with them.

Cherokee Hunting

Give me the wind. Give me the breeze. Yu! O Great Terrestrial Hunter, I come to the edge of your spittle where you repose. Let your stomach cover itself; let it be covered with leaves. Let it cover itself at a single bend, and may you never be satisfied.

And you, O Ancient Red, may you hover above my breast while I sleep. Now let good (dreams?) develop; let my experience be propitious. Ha! Now let my little trails be directed, as they lie down in various directions (?). Let the leaves be covered with the clotted blood, and may it never cease to be so. You two (the Water and the Fire) shall bury it in your stomachs. Yu!

In the case of formulas designed to attract fish, every device is used to cause the fish to move toward the fishhook or into the fishtrap. The fishhook may be annointed with spittle after certain leaves have been chewed which exercise an attraction power. The prayer is often directed to the fish to travel over his water trails to the trap. The following is a specimen from Mooney:

This Is for Catching Large Fish

Listen! Now you settlements have drawn near to hearken. Where you have gathered in the foam you are moving about as one. You Blue Cat and the others, I have come to offer you freely the white food. Let the paths from every direction recognize each other. Our spittle shall be in agreement. Let them (your and my spittle) be together as we go about. They (the fish) have become a prey, and there shall be no loneliness. Your spittle has become agreeable. I am called . . .Yu!

Former Tribal Officer Writes Book About N. C. Indian Land:

One Feather Editors

Fred Bauer, a former Vice Chief of the Eastern Band of Cherokee Indians, has written a book entitled *Land of the North Carolina Cherokees*. Mr. Bauer painstakingly builds his case against "dependent tribalism and reservation controls" using federal records, old newspaper accounts, state and county land records as well as eyewitness reports.

He argues for individual Cherokee state citizenship as opposed to collective ownership of land by a tribal group. According to the treaties of 1817 and 1819: "any Cherokee who owned an improvement could become a citizen of the United States by having his name registered with the government agent."

By the Treaty of 1819, the watershed west of the Little Tennessee River became the boundary, and only a small southwestern portion of our state remained to the Cherokee Nation. Birdtown, Ela, Bryson City, Almond, Judson and Bushnell, as well as the lands north of the river (now in the Park), became State land. Indian lands now in Swain and Jackson Counties were completely within North Carolina sixteen years before the final Treaty of New Echota. The Cherokee citizens owned land, and bought and sold land in the same manner as their Caucasian neighbors.

The book chronicles the relationship between the North Carolina Cherokees and Colonel William Holland Thomas. The Qualla Town trader figured prominently in the long story of treaties, lost land records and debts to the Cherokees unpaid by the federal government after the "Trail of Tears."

In tracing his history of this mountain land, Bauer discounts the Mooney Myth—a popular story of Tsali, who killed a soldier who was mistreating Tsali's wife during the removal and who later gave himself to be shot in order that the Cherokees hiding in the mountains could remain in their homeland. A series of articles in the *Asheville Citizen* by John Parris dealt with the same subject earlier this year.

"The Eastern Band of Cherokee Indians is the legal name Congress gave to those Cherokees in North Carolina who were involved in the Thomas land purchases." Bauer emphasizes that in organizing to obtain their rightful monies from the U. S. Government, the petitioners did not "relinquish their individual property rights." He maintains that they were transformed into a "tribe" by acts of Congress and efforts of the Indian Bureau.

Other subjects covered by the author are reorganization, the several rolls, the parkway controversy and a new constitution.

Much of what I read in *Land of the North Carolina Cherokees* was new to me. Not everyone will agree with Mr Bauer's conclusions; however, his book is valuable. Young people thirst for knowledge about their people and their homeland. Since we no longer pass stories by the fireside, the only alternative is put down what we know on paper.

I believe that tribalism is a better way of life than rugged individualism; however, I'm glad that, for now anyway, the country is big enough for many diverse lifestyles.

About the Author

Fred Bauer is an enrolled Cherokee who was orphaned soon after birth. He was adopted by James Blythe, his mother's uncle, and his wife Josephine, a daughter of Chief Jarrett Nimrod Smith.

He was a student at Cherokee Indian School and the Carlisle Indian School in Pennsylvania. After serving in the Air Force in World War II, he was Physical Education Director and Coach at various Indian schools. In 1935 he was elected Vice Chief of the Eastern Band and served for four years.

History of Boundary Tree:

Hiram C. Wilburn

The name "Boundary Tree" as applied to the Boundary Tree
Motor Court, Boundary Tree Dining Room and Service Station,
together with the tract of land upon which they were developed,
has interesting historical associations. The Boundary Tree itself,
better known in the legal documents as "The Poplar Corner
Tree," stood on the high bank of the road at the lower border of
the Boundary Tree Tract, some eight hundred feet south of the
service station. It was a very old tree, perhaps six feet in
diameter at the base.

The tree was first "marked" and designated as a "corner
tree," February 2, 1798, when the old pioneer, Felix Walker, obtained Grant No. 501 from the State of North Carolina and
established its beginning corner on this tree.

Grant No. 501 contained four square miles and included all
the choice lands on the Oconaluftee River three and one-half miles
up, as well as over a mile up the Raven Fork. It was upon land included in this grant at the mouth of Mingus Creek that the first
white settlement within the bounds of the Great Smoky National
Park was made, in all probability, in the year 1792.

Felix Walker was a great old character in his day. Besides
being an extensive landowner and speculator, he represented
Buncombe County, and later Haywood County, in Congress for a
number of years. He was of the Daniel Boone party that opened
the Wilderness Road into Kentucky in 1775. Walker lived for
many years on Jonathan Creek near Maggie, North Carolina. The
site of his residence is marked with a metal shield beside U. S. 19,
just east of Maggie.

In 1792 when Buncombe County was established, the Boundary Tree area was included. In 1808, it became Haywood County;
in 1851, Jackson County; in 1872, Swain County. In the 1840's
when the Cherokees were re-settled on lands in the vicinity of
Boundary Tree, this stood as a marker between them and the
whites.

When in the late 1920's the State of North Carolina acquired
all the white owned lands in the area, Boundary Tree became an
important monument between Park lands and the Cherokee Indians. In 1946 the Park conveyed a tract of about eight hundred
acres to the Cherokee Indians, with the purpose that it should be
developed as a tourist center. During the negotiations the tract
was frequently referred to and described as the Boundary Tree
Tract. The Tribal Council prefixed the name "Boundary Tree" to
its several developments, and so the name has become definitely
and permanently established. The following wording appears on a
marker at the Boundary Tree Tract:

229

PLACE OF THE
POPLAR BOUNDARY TREE
NORTH LAT. 35 DEG. 30 MIN.
ON SOUTHERN BOUNDARY LINE OF LANDS
ALLOTTED TO THE EARL OF GRANVILLE, ONE OF THE
LORDS PROPRIETORS IN 1743 BY THE BRITISH CROWN.

THE DIVIDING LINE BETWEEN BURKE AND RUTHERFORD
COUNTIES RAN HERE UNTIL AFTER 1792.

BEGINNING CORNER OF GRANTS 501 AND 502,
ISSUED TO FELIX WALKER IN 1798.

THE POPLAR WAS ON THE LINE DIVIDING THE
CHEROKEE AND WHITE SETTLERS AFTER 1940
UNTIL 1946, WHEN THE PARK SERVICE CONVEYED
THE BOUNDARY TREE TRACT TO THE EASTERN
BAND OF CHEROKEE INDIANS.

ERECTED BY THE CHEROKEE HISTORICAL ASSOCIATION,
1952

Eagle's Revenge:

One Feather Editors

When the Cherokee killed a deer in the days that deer roamed in their forests, they saved some of the meat for winter. This was cut into long strips and hung on a drying pole until quite dry. When dry it was hung in the cabins.

A Cherokee man and wife lived in the Nantahala gorge. Their cabin was directly under a very high cliff. The man would leave his home early in the morning and wind slowly up the path to a place beyond the cliff. Here the deer fed. He would wait quietly until he knew that he could kill one of the deer with only one shot. His arrow always found its mark.

As soon as he killed the deer, he would dress it. Best of all he liked the fresh liver. He would go to the point of the cliff just over the cabin and drop the fresh liver down to his wife, who would have it cooked by the time he would wind his way down to the cabin. After he had made his meal of the liver, he would put up a pole for his wife to use to dry the rest of the meat.

One night the man heard a sound as if something was pulling the meat off the drying pole. As he looked out, he saw an eagle perched on the pole stealing the meat. He shot the eagle and returned to bed. The next morning he reported this to his chief, who sent the seven dancers to get the eagle and prepare for the Eagle Dance. This was custom when an eagle was killed. Messengers called the people to the council house at sundown for the dance.

The dancing lasted from sundown to sunrise. Seven boys trained as dancers; they danced while the others sat in a circle and watched. This was usually a joyful time. Because of the victory over an eagle, they could visit and tell of interesting adventures. About midnight a strange man joined the circle. He soon began telling of his great deeds in a battle. None knew him but supposed he was a warrior from one of the other Cherokee towns, so they were glad to have him visit them.

At the end of his story he gave a loud yell, "Hi!" The people shuddered as one of the dancers fell dead. The stranger told another story, and as he yelled another dancer fell dead. This kept up until all seven dancers were dead and all the people were too frightened to move.

The stranger left suddenly as he had come. The people were too scared to go after him to punish him for the death of the seven young men. It was not until many days had passed that the people found out who the stranger really was. He was not a Cherokee warrior at all—he was the brother of the eagle that the hunter had shot. He had taken the shape of a man to get his revenge for the death of his brother eagle.

231

Folks, Fact, Fiction #1:

Ruth Smith

Do you like to think back to other days? I do. I used to go to Estella Teesatuskie's home years ago, and we would sit under a tree in the yard and listen to Jonah tell "booger" tales. Jimmie and Berdie Holland can tell 'em, too. When we used to live beside them, they would scare the daylights out of me, but the next night I was begging for more. Got to the place where I was almost afraid to look out the window at night, for fear something out there would be looking IN. When Scrub and I were kids, we used to pull down the shades at the dining room windows, close the doors, get under the table and tell ghost stories, with cold shivers chasing each other up and down our backs.

Oliver Smith's mother, Mary Melvina Smith, is responsible for a lot of old time tales remembered by Ol' Milt. He recalls her telling of living in Tennessee on the Little Tennessee River and watching the boats, the Mary Bird, Side Wheeler and Ol' Rail Stealer, as they made their trips up and down the river. During the Civil War, their garden was often visited by raiding soldiers, and it was after one of these forays that Mary Melvina found a long Dragoon Colt pistol lying in the dirt. Then there was her son, Duffy, who had been so puny he had spent some time stretched on the bedstead. This day he rose and went outdoors where a brand new grapevine swing hung invitingly. Duffy grabbed it firmly, ran a few steps and took off, Tarzan style. There was a ripping noise, the vine tore loose and down came Duffy on the wood pile, knocked completely out. He was carried back to bed, but, despite a perilous childhood, Duffy survived to the ripe old age of 85.

Folks, Fact, Fiction #2:

Ruth Smith

June will soon be over, the month of brides and roses, not to mention vacation. When I was a leetle shirt tail youngun, I fairly lived for the time when we could go down the street chanting, "No more lessons, no more books, no more Teacher's sassy looks." But we had fun in school, too. Our class was so mischievous that we went through five teachers in two years. Resignation forms were in great demand during that time. The first teacher to give up was a minister's daughter who sought the solace of tears when her pupils became too much of a handful. The first time this happened, we were filled with dismay and consternation, for we weren't BAD, just lively and full of the Old Nick. But the novelty of Teacher's tears wore off, and we used to watch for her to "puddle up" and shed some more. Her last day was to have been a surprise to us, but someone found out and told the rest of us. So at

232

recess time, Bill Dildine filled his water color pan with water and hid it behind his desk. Teacher began her "swan song," she was leaving us, and so on. Ol' Bill got out his hankerchief and dipped it in the pan of water and held it to his eyes till he had everyone's attention, then wrung the water out in the aisle. Needless to say, what Teacher meant to be a solemn occasion ended with gales of laughter from the roomful of little wretches. During this time we had a girl in the class who was older than the rest of us. Consequently she wore silk hose (probably sneaked out of her older sister's drawer). In addition to silk hose, Burdeen also possessed hairy legs. She sat behind me, and in order to enjoy a greater degree of comfort (I 'spose), she mostly had her legs stretched out in the aisle. I dearly loved to glance around, note that she was busy, get hold of a few of those ol' leg hairs and yank on 'em. The reaction would satisfy anybody. One of the male teachers that were later hired fairly wiped up the floor with a couple of the boys, then later he went to be a missionary. It was said he should make a good one, for he had had experience with heathens.

Folks, Fact, Fiction #3:
Ruth Smith

Here's an old snake tale, told to Milt by his grandma. When she was a little girl, she and her brother were sent on an errand down one of the little dirt roads so prevalent back in those days. Idling along as kids have done for generations, their eyes taking in the activities and scenes of the countryside, their attention became focused on a large black snake winding its way up a big tree some distance off the road. As they watched, they became aware of the snake's goal, a bird's nest concealed within a hollow in the tree trunk. A small, round hole in the tree trunk afforded ingress and egress. "That ol' snake thinks he's gonna have baby birds for dinner," said Little Brother. "I'm gonna wait till he's ready to go in, an' then bust him with a rock." He selected a good "throwin' rock" and waited. Round and round the tree coiled the snake, each time coming nearer and nearer to the entrance to the bird's home. Just as he was ready to stick his head in, Little Brother let fly his rock, and the snake slithered helplessly to the ground, cut almost in two by the unerring accuracy of a small boy with one good "throwin' rock."

Folks, Fact, Fiction #4:
Ruth Smith

'Twas a snappy winter morning, giving promise of a beautiful day to come. Deacon Oliver Smith rose from his downy couch and made his way to the kitchen to cook his breakfast. The oven door was open from the evening before, so he shut it and

233

turned on the heat, in preparation for baking his breakfast bread. Bustling about busily, Oliver was finally aware of strange sounds.

"Seems as though I hear something," he muttered to himself, peering under the table. Nothing there; no one in the sink; nairy crittur in the cupboard. By this time the yells were so loud he couldn't help but know that they were coming from the oven. He opened the door, and out popped his old cat. Cussing in cat language, it dashed into the bedroom and secreted itself beneath the bed. The old-time Sioux were said to be fond of boiled dog, but never does history tell that Cherokees relished roast cat.

75-Year-Old L. Calhoun:

One Feather Editors

Lawrence Calhoun is 75 years old and lives in the Big Cove Community and has lived there all of his life. He has five sisters, Katie Littlejohn, Eva Bradley, Dinah Welch, Wallie Welch and Agnes Welch; three brothers, Smathers, Walker and Henry. We asked him who the oldest was, and he said, "probably Wallie, she must be at least 100 years old," jokingly, of course. Lawrence has one daughter, Peggy, and three sons, Tamer, Alex and Earl. Tamer lives in Virginia, Alex in Oklahoma, Peggy in Asheville and Earl lives at home.

While talking to Lawrence, we learned that he has an incredible memory. He remembered names of people he had met many years ago. He recalled getting into some mischief and trouble with the law. A warrant was issued for his arrest, and he took to hiding out in Tennessee, but he heard that there was going to be a Green Corn Dance in Big Cove, so he sneaked back home. Somehow, the Swain County sheriff found out that he was home for the big ceremony and came up to arrest him. He said it was Sheriff McGurley (John) and his son, Fred, that came up to arrest him. But they never did arrest him because Deleskie Climbingbear talked the sheriff out of it, and the sheriff tore up the warrant. It's not that easy these days, Lawrence said. He went on to tell us about this particular Green Corn Dance he came home for. He said Deleskie was shaking a turtle shell rattle, and each time he shook the rattle, it got louder; on the last shake, it was real loud. He recalled two groups of men who appeared out of the bushes on opposite sides of the dancing ground with loud shouts and advanced toward the pole in the center around which they dance in opposite directions. We told Lawrence that we planned a Green Corn Dance in September, and he said that it would be wonderful if the ceremony could be revised, and he would be happy to help with the ceremony. He went on to say that there aren't too many people left that know anything about the Green Corn Dance except for the people up where they are removed every night, meaning *Unto These Hills*. He told us we could go up there and learn about the Green Corn Dance.

We asked Lawrence if he was a medicine man or if he still did any doctoring. He said, "Not much, my eyes aren't good enough to gather herbs. I doctor mostly in my dreams." He said he started learning about Indian medicine when he was seven or eight years old and he was taught by his father, Oganstota, and his mother, Sally Ann. His father was a famous medicine man and shaman. He said that his father's shamanism was never surpassed by anyone, nor his gift for Indian medicine. We told him that his father's picture was in one of the Bureau of Ethnology Reports published by the Smithsonian Institution. Lawrence seemed surprised, and I think it would be nice if he could see the picture or perhaps be given a copy of the picture. Lawrence told us of a time that his father was called upon to doctor Nessie Watty, also from Big Cove. Nessie had become deathly ill, and white doctor from the Cherokee Indian Hospital had been called to help her, a Doctor Hall, as he recalled. After Dr. Hall examined Nessie, he told the family that there was nothing that he could do for her, and she would probably die that very night. Finally, in desperation, Nessie's husband, Goliagh, went up on the mountain to ask help from Oganstota. Immediately, Oganstota went up on the mountain in search for herbs to make medicine. When he had gathered the necessary herbs, he took them to Nessie, and the family told Oganstota that Nessie had been sick for a long time. Oganstota made a tea from the herbs for Nessie to drink. Minutes after she drank the tea, she began to vomit, and particles found in the vomit looked like dirt and dust swept from the floor. The next day Lawrence's father and mother told the family they should go and check on Nessie. Lawrence said, "When we arrived there, the family was eating breakfast, and there sat Nessie at the table eating with the family, feeling much better, and Nessie lived at least 30 more years after that." Lawrence's guess was that Nessie had cancer, but his father Oganstota caught it just in time. And this made him remember the death of his nephew just that very morning that we talked with him. His nephew, Henderson Welch, died of cancer. Lawrence recalled Henderson's love for dancing at the Cherokee Fall Festival. Lawrence went on to say that cancer can be cured with Indian medicine if it is caught in time, even up to 15 minutes before death.

"I got sick one time," Lawrence said. "It wasn't much, but my legs sure did ache and my back too. I went to my brother, Henry, and asked if he knew of some medicine to help me. Henry agreed it wasn't much, but he'd try to help me. He gathered some herbs for me. Henry said it must be my kidneys. I drank the medicine that Henry gave me and in a few days I felt fine. I had already been to the hospital down there, and the doctor down there told me there wasn't a thing wrong with me and to go on home. I knew I was sick, or else I wouldn't have wasted time to go down there, but Henry helped me with his Indian medicine."

We asked Lawrence to tell us the funniest story he has ever heard which was about an old woman that wanted a short-tailed cat. One day the woman, upon entering the house, found her house cat lying on the floor sleeping with its tail stretched straight out. She ran out to the woodyard to get her axe so she could chop the cat's tail off quickly before the cat woke up. She raised the axe high above her head, brought the axe down, missed the cat's tail and chopped the cat right in half.

Big Cove people love to tell jokes and play jokes on people, and I remember a joke that was played on Lawrence a few years ago. There was a free labor group made up of people in Big Cove. The group would get together and help each other with spring planting and harvesting. They also helped each other if there was death or illness in a home. If a house was being put up, everyone would get together and help put it up. Upon completion of the house, there was a housewarming. People brought food and household items. When Lawrence was building the house he lived in before this new one, the free labor came up and helped him. When the house was finished, there was a housewarming. Many nice gifts were brought but someone brought a gunny sack full of mangy dogs. If I'm not mistaken, it was Manuel Watty that made his contribution of mangy dogs. It was all in fun, and everyone got a big laugh of the joke. He has a beautiful new home now, built for him by the Social Services Department of Cherokee. The house is located in Big Cove, high up on the mountain overlooking Big Cove. The scenery is beautiful from his porch. In the spring and winter you can see far above the Big Cove Loop and as far down as the old Blankenship place. We asked Lawrence what he thought about his new home. He said he was very proud of it, and it was very warm in the winter, much warmer that his old log house just below the new one. He said he certainly appreciated what Social Services and all people connected with it had done for him. And thanks to the Indian Action Team, a very nice graveled road winds its way up the mountain from Big Cove Loop Road up to Lawrence's house.

Rev. W. David Owle:

One Feather Editors

Alone in the dark beneath a pine tree on a hillside near Arden in 1920, a young Cherokee man prayed to God for guidance. W. (Walter) David Owle was troubled because he did not know what direction his life should take. When at last he finished his prayerful meditation, Owle knew the purpose of his life; he would give himself in service to his people—to the Cherokee and other Native Americans.

W. David Owle was unusually qualified to serve his people, for he had something few Indians had in the early part of this century—a college education.

The *One Feather* interviewed him recently when he visited relatives here in Cherokee, and he recounted the trail that led him to his life of service.

Owle attended the old boarding school until he was 16 years of age. He and Morgan Bradley both decided they had learned everything they could there and made plans to go away to school. While planning this adventure, they became influenced by Bird Galoneet, who told them they should be baptized in the river near the present location of the Drama Motel and taken into Yellowhill Church. A few weeks later the two walked to Whittier to board a train. It was September, 1912, and as telephone poles zipped by the window, Owle and Bradley, dressed in Government khakis, headed for the trade school in Hampton, Virginia.

Owle's three years at Hampton were productive. He learned the blacksmith trade, in the tradition of his father who once smithed where Qualla Supermarket now stands, and he completed a year of college. At graduation he was second in academic standing.

His desire to learn was not satisfied. Owle continued in college, going to Springfield College in Massachusetts. The college was then a physical education school, and in addition to his studies, Owle participated in all the team sports—football, baseball, soccer—plus tennis.

The first World War nearly prevented Owle's graduation from Springfield. He was drafted in March, 1918, but through an arrangement managed by Dr. Bennett of Bryson City, he was allowed to delay his service until May. After graduation, Owle returned to Swain County and shipped out for Camp Jackson. Because of his college military training, he was made first sergeant on his second day of duty. He trained troops until the Armistice and was discharged two months later.

Following the war, Owle was employed at Christ School in Arden as director of physical education. He had been there 18 months when he attended a young people's conference at Blue

Ridge, where the speaker, John Armant, urged people to dedicate themselves to serving young people. It was at this conference that Owle became concerned about the direction of his life. It was there, as he prayed under the pines, that he decided to spend his life helping Indians as best he could. The decision led him to Arizona, where he taught physical education to Pima Indians, and later to Haskell in Oklahoma, where he directed the physical education program.

At Haskell, Owle felt the call to the ministry. He went to theological seminary and became ordained. For more than 50 years afterwards, he served the Seneca Reservation near Buffalo, New York. He is now retired and living on the Seneca Reservation, but he still works as he is able, doing "free-lance" work in special cases.

The Cherokee Cultural Group Therapy Program:

Elsie Martin and Laurence French

The Eastern Band of Cherokee Indians has adopted a new therapy program designed to aid clients in their mental health and alcohol program.

The Cherokee Mental Health and alcohol program, staffed entirely by enrolled members of the tribe, has developed a unique form of cultural group therapy whereby staff members, Indian clients and other interested members of the tribe participate in informally structured Cherokee craft sessions. The objectives of the sessions are threefold: (1) to increase the client's social integration; (2) to reinforce the client's awareness of his or her proud cultural heritage; and (3) to offer constructive, positive, acceptable avenues for tension management.

Unlike traditional group therapy sessions, these are quite informal. Furthermore, they focus on the positive and not on the negative aspects of the client's life, again a major departure from most group therapy approaches. Informal communication and a shared participation in the construction of cherished Pan-Indian and Cherokee arts and crafts occur within a very congenial environment, one shared by clients, counselors and other "normal" Cherokee citizens. Only here the client is indistinguishable from the others in the program. Clearly this lack of visibility, or stigma, is the most rewarding aspect of this therapy program. All come to feel that they are one, which in turn not only aids the client in reestablishing a positive self-image, but helps dispel erroneous images the "normal" Cherokee participants may harbor against those enrolled in the mental health and alcohol program.

It has long been recognized that Native American arts and crafts provide the major link with the rich cultural heritage of the Indian groups surviving today. In this sense alone, cultural group therapy provides an invaluable service by aiding the client in establishing direct ties with his or her proud heritage.

The staff at the Cherokee Mental Health and Alcohol program realize that the contributing factor underlying most American Indian personality problems is the confusion surrounding their ambiguous social existence. They believe that reestablishing the American Indian's strong sense of cultural pride can only help alleviate the problems plaguing him.

CHAPTER V
Cherokee Profiles

By The Editors

THE EVOLUTION OF THE
"CHEROKEE PERSPECTIVE"

Early in 1973 Cherokee students at the Qualla Boundary started a student organization with the intent and purpose of improving the educational prospects among Native Americans attending non-Indian colleges and universities. Most agreed that cultural conflict played a crucial role in past educational failures among Cherokee students in their higher educational pursuits. Consequently, a priority objective of the group was to ascertain the reasons for these failures and to provide viable avenues for alleviating these sources of contention.

At a well attended community meeting, held at the Cherokee Boys Club, a master plan was drafted incorporating "cultural workshops," "special tutorial programs," "college/high school Indian student liaison programs," "adult Indian educational programs" and the like. Soon these students, including Cherokees ranging in age from elementary school students to senior citizens, became interested and deeply involved in their cultural heritage, both past and present. Many of the articles in the book are a direct consequence of this self-initiated search for their traditional roots. Whenever possible, college credits were awarded these projects further reinforcing the significance of the overall project. Clearly the rewards of this project were much more than originally anticipated, and today all those who participated have come to feel a great sense of pride regarding this endeavor.

The Editors

JOHN CROWE: PRINCIPAL CHIEF OF THE EASTERN BAND

John Crowe graduated from Cherokee High School and then went on to serve six years in the Army during the Second World War. He is married to Ollie Wolfe, also of the Cherokee reservation. Mr. Crowe served twelve years on the Tribal Council and was the Vice-Chief to Noah Powell. He assumed the Chief position following Chief Powell's untimely death in 1973. Since then Mr. Crowe has been elected twice to the highest tribal position of Principal Chief. One of his greatest concerns is the preservation of the American Indian heritage in general and the Cherokee culture in particular.

ALVIN SMITH: VICE CHIEF OF THE EASTERN BAND

Alvin Smith was elected to this office in the Fall of 1974 and is currently serving his second term as Vice Chief. He graduated from Cherokee High School and then went on to Northeastern State and Western Carolina Universities. He also is a veteran of the Second World War. Mr. Smith served ten years on the Tribal Council prior to his election to Vice Chief. He is married to Betty Sherrill and has a son and daughter. Like Chief Crowe, Mr. Smith is concerned in restoring and preserving the Cherokee heritage.

JEFF MUSKRAT: SUPERINTENDENT OF THE CHEROKEE AGENCY

Jeff Muskrat is an Oklahoma, or "Western," Cherokee. He is a retired Army officer who is now employed with the Bureau of Indian Affairs. He attended Northeastern Oklahoma Junior College, Tulsa University and the University of Maryland. Mr. Muskrat was appointed Superintendent of the Cherokee Agency in 1976. He is married to Imogene Roberts, and they have two daughters and a son. Mr. Muskrat also agrees that education is the single most important issue facing not only the Cherokees, but all American Indians today.

JOHNSON CATOLSTER

Johnson Catolster is both a Cherokee craftsperson and a respected Tribal leader. He is a graduate of the Cherokee school system and has continued to enroll and participate in adult educational programs and workshops over the years. A past Chairman of the Tribal Council and noted bowl carver, Mr. Catolster is now living in retirement at his mountain home in Cherokee. He was a strong influence to those of us who participated in this endeavor —THE CHEROKEE PERSPECTIVE.

JONATHAN L. TAYLOR

Jonathan Taylor is also a former Chairman of the Tribal Council and continues to serve on the Council. He is actively involved in all areas of tribal affairs as well as participating on a number of regional and national Indian organizations and committees. Mr. Taylor serves as the coordinator of Tribal health programs and was a prime factor in bringing the new hospital to Cherokee.

BERTHA SMITH SAUNOOKE

Bertha Saunooke is one of the leading Tribal figures, having served on the Tribal Council for nearly a decade now. She has been instrumental in bringing a number of educational and social service programs to the reservation. Mrs. Saunooke was married to the late Principal Chief, Osley B. Saunooke.

ELSIE SAMPSON MARTIN

Elsie Martin is a talented Cherokee craftsperson and community leader. She lives in the Birdtown community on the reservation and is employed by the Tribe as a mental health technician. Mrs. Martin gained national recognition for her innovative "Cultural Therapy" program which she initiated on the reservation. In addition to arts and crafts, Elsie is a tremendous Cherokee cook.

RICHARD "YOGI" CROWE

Richard Crowe attended reservation schools as well as Western Carolina University and the University of Tennessee. He has his undergraduate degree from the University of Tennessee and is currently pursuing a graduate degree from the same institution. He is a veteran of both the Army and Air Force, serving a total of seven years in the U. S. Armed Forces. Following the service, Yogi has held a number of important positions with the Tribe. Moreover, he was the prime mover for this project as well as the establishment of the Cherokee Indian Education Movement.

243

AMY GRANT WALKER

Amy Walker is a noted craftsperson skilled in both beadwork and finger weaving. She resides on the reservation with her husband and four children. Mrs. Walker served as a Teachers Aide at the reservation schools and later attended Western Carolina University where she graduated recently. Her future plans include graduate school at the University of Tennessee and a position as social worker working with her people.

HERBERT WACHACHA

Herbert Wachacha grew up in the Snowbird portion of the reservation. He attended both reservation and local schools. Mr. Wachacha joined the U. S. Marine Corps after graduation and now works for the North Carolina State Highway Department. Both he and his wife, Yvonne, attend college part-time.

REUBEN TEESATUSKIE

Reuben Teesatuskie was educated in Cherokee schools and also attended the Institute of American Indian Arts in Santa Fe, New Mexico, as well as Southwestern Community College. He has held a number of Tribal positions including editor of the Tribal newspaper (*One Feather*), Tribal Councilman and Cherokee police officer. Mr. Teesatuskie also served as a member of the North Carolina Arts Council. He lives in the Big Cove community where he enjoys fishing and hunting and silversmithing.

KAREN FRENCH OWL

Karen Owl was reared in the Big Cove community and is the daughter of Roy French, a prominent Cherokee preacher. She lives on the reservation with her husband, George, and their two children. Mrs. Owl teaches at the Cherokee Elementary school while her husband works for the Cherokee Agency (BIA). A graduate of Western Carolina University, Karen is currently working on her Masters degree in education.

LORETTA HORNBUCKLE

Loretta Hornbuckle is a young Indian woman who grew up in the Cherokee Children's Home with Jim and Suzanne Hornbuckle. She has a beautiful voice and has subsequently been elected both "Miss Fall Festival" (1976-77) and "Miss Cherokee" (1978-79), the highest Tribal honors bestowed upon its young women. A recent graduate of the Cherokee High School, Miss Hornbuckle plans to attend college in the future and to continue her singing career.